PATH THROUGH
SCRIPTURE

From Genesis to Revelation

by Mark Link, S.J.

TABOR
PUBLISHING

Valencia, CA   Allen, TX

W9-APC-849

About the Book

This book grew out of three challenges.

The first came from a friend who said, "Tell the story of the Bible in a single book. There's no book like this available for the average person."

The second challenge came from a teacher who said, "Include in that book the best activities, discussion topics, and prayer exercises you've gleaned in twenty years of teaching."

The third challenge came from a businessman who said, "Write that book in nontechnical language. Use lots of examples and stories."

This is how *Path through Scripture* came about. May it lead young people and adults to a deeper love of the Hebrew and the Christian Scriptures.

A detailed Resource Manual, including chapter-by-chapter reproducible handouts and quizzes, is available for teachers and study group moderators.

Easter 1987

Mark Link, S.J.

Cover design: Art Associates

Imprimi Potest
   Robert A. Wild, S.J.
Nihil Obstat
   Rev. Msgr. Joseph K. Pollard, S.T.D.
Imprimatur
   †Roger Mahony
   Archbishop of Los Angeles
   January 29, 1987

Copyright © 1987 by Mark Link

All rights reserved. No part of this book shall be reproduced or transmitted in any form or by any means, electronic or mechanical, including photocopying, recording, or by any information or retrieval system, without written permission from the Publisher.

Send all inquiries to:
Tabor Publishing
25115 Avenue Stanford, Suite 130
Valencia, California 91355

Printed in the United States of America

ISBN 0-89505-402-7 (Student Text)
ISBN 0-89505-403-5 (Teacher Resource Manual)

 2 3 4 5   91 90 89 88 87

Contents

Contents

Contents

Old Testament Time Chart

B.C.

1800	Abraham leaves Ur
1600	Israelites in Egypt
1280	Israelites leave Egypt
1260	Israelites enter land
1000	David rules
922	Israel (North) revolts
722	Israel destroyed
587	Judah (South) exiled
539	Judah returns
168	Maccabees revolt
142	Judah wins freedom
63	Romans occupy Judah
37	Herod rules Judah

Part One

Hebrew Scriptures

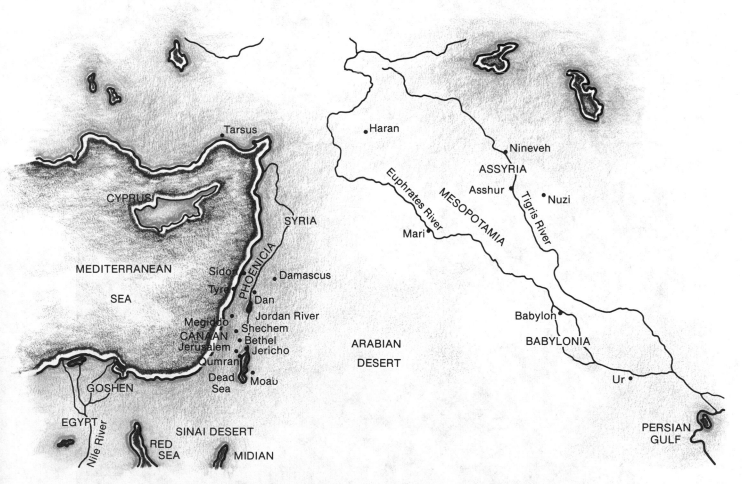

Old Testament World

1 Creation

On March 21, 1925, the Tennessee legislature passed a law forbidding public schools to teach the theory of evolution. Within days, the American Civil Liberties Union voted to test the legality of the law. John Scopes, a biology teacher who taught evolution, agreed to submit to arrest. Clarence Darrow, the famous criminal lawyer from Chicago, agreed to defend Scopes without fee.

Meanwhile, to offset the fame and reputation of Darrow, the World's Fundamentalist Association hired former presidential candidate William Jennings Bryan to assist the prosecution.

On July 10, 1925, the trial began at Dayton, Tennessee. To everyone's surprise, one of Darrow's first moves was to call Bryan to the witness stand. Darrow opened the Bible and read from the Book of Genesis.

Evening passed and morning followed—that was the first day.

Turning to Bryan, he said, "Do you believe the sun was created on the fourth day?" Bryan said he did. Darrow replied, "Can you tell me how it was possible to have morning and evening on the first day if the sun wasn't created until the fourth day?" A few snickers rippled across the courtroom.

Then Darrow asked Bryan a second question. "Do you believe God punished the serpent by condemning snakes forever after to crawl on their bellies?" Bryan said he did. Darrow replied, "Can you tell me how snakes moved about before God condemned them to crawl?" A wave of laughter swept across the courtroom.

Then Bryan exploded. "Your honor," he shouted, "I'll answer all Mr. Darrow's questions at once. This man who doesn't believe in God is using a Tennessee court to ridicule him."

"I object to that statement," Darrow shouted. "I'm questioning you on your fool ideas that no thinking Christian believes."

What Do We Believe?

Christians split into two main groups when it comes to reading the Bible. For the sake of clarity, we may call them *literal readers* and *contextual readers*.

Literal readers (also called fundamentalists) take the Bible at face value. They say it means exactly what it says. To understand the Bible, all we need do is read the *text*.

Contextual readers take a less simplistic view. They say that the text is not always enough. Sometimes we must consider its *context*. In other words, we need to know something about the times in which the biblical authors wrote. An example will illustrate what the contextual readers are getting at.

Truck drivers with CB radios have a language all their own. For instance, they say, "There's a bear in the air." They do not mean this *literally*. It is merely their way of saying that a police helicopter is clocking traffic and motorists should beware. Thus, the *context* of an expression is sometimes crucial to understanding its meaning.

The same is true with certain biblical stories. Sometimes we need to consider the *context* in which the story was written if we are to understand its meaning.

This is especially true of the early chapters of the Book of Genesis, where stories deal with *prehistory:* that foggy era between the appearance of people on earth and their first attempt to tell their story.

For example, the third chapter of Genesis portrays a snake as talking to Eve. Did the biblical writer intend to teach that snakes once talked with humans? Or when the first chapter of Genesis says that man was created last, and the next chapter says he was created first, wasn't the biblical writer aware that these remarks are contradictory, if taken literally?

In brief, then, Bible readers fall into two main groups: literal readers and contextual readers. Literal readers hold that the Bible text is sufficient to understand its meaning. Contextual readers hold that, sometimes, the text is not enough. The context in which a story was written must also be kept in mind. This book adopts the contextual position.

This brings us to the biblical story of creation.

How Do We Understand Creation?

Four days before Christmas 1968, *Apollo 8* lifted off from Cape Kennedy. On board the spaceship were astronauts Frank Borman, Bill Anders, and Jim Lovell.

Three days later, on Christmas Eve, *Apollo 8* lost all contact with earth as it disappeared behind the moon. Millions of people on earth sat glued to their TV sets, waiting and praying for the spaceship to emerge safely. Then came a spectacular moment.

As *Apollo 8* rounded the moon and came into view, the crew took turns reading this biblical Christmas greeting to the people on earth:

In the beginning,
when God created the universe,
the earth was formless and desolate.
The raging ocean that covered everything
was engulfed in total darkness,
and the power of God
was moving over the water.

Then God commanded,
"Let there be light"—
and light appeared. . . .
Then he separated the light from
the darkness, and he named the light "Day"
and the darkness "Night."
Evening passed and morning came—
that was the first day.

Then God commanded,
"Let there be a dome to divide the water
and to keep it in two separate places"—
and it was done.
So God made a dome,
and it separated the water under it
from the water above it.
He named the dome "Sky."
Evening passed and morning came—
that was the second day.

Then God commanded,
"Let the water below the sky come together
in one place,
so that the land will appear"—
and it was done.
He named the land "Earth,"
and the water . . . "Sea."
And God was pleased with what he saw.
Then he commanded,
"Let the earth produce all kinds
of plants . . ."—and it was done. . . .
God was pleased with what he saw.
Evening passed and morning came—
that was the third day.

Then God commanded,
"Let lights appear in the sky
to separate day from night . . . ;
they will shine in the sky
to give light to the earth"—
and it was done.
So God made the two larger lights,
the sun to rule over the day
and the moon to rule over the night;
he also made the stars. . . .
And God was pleased with what he saw.
Evening passed and morning came—
that was the fourth day.

Then God commanded,
"Let the waters be filled
with many kinds of living beings,
and let the air be filled with birds.". . .
And God was pleased with what he saw.
He blessed them all. . . .
Evening passed and morning came—
that was the fifth day.

Then God commanded,
"Let the earth produce all kinds of animal life:
domestic and wild, large and small"—
and it was done.
So God made them all,
and he was pleased with what he saw.
Then God said,
"And now we will make human beings;
they will be like us and resemble us.
They will have power over the fish,
the birds, and all animals. . . ."
So God created human beings . . .
blessed them, and said,
"Have many children, so that your descendants
will live all over the earth
and bring it under their control. . . ."
God looked at everything he had made,
and he was very pleased.
Evening passed and morning came—
that was the sixth day.

And so the whole universe was completed.
By the seventh day
God finished what he had been doing
and stopped working.
He blessed the seventh day
and set it apart as a special day.

GENESIS 1:1–2:3

Four Truths

The biblical writer's description of creation reads like a poem. He describes each day according to a definite pattern. In general, that pattern has five parts:

1. Introducing the day: *"God commanded"*
2. Expressing a command: *"Let the water . . ."*
3. Obeying the command: *"It was done"*
4. Rejoicing at the result: *"God was pleased"*
5. Identifying the day: *"The third day"*

What is true of the days of creation is true, also, of the week of creation. It, too, follows a definite pattern:

Day 1: God creates light and *separates* it from the darkness.
Day 2: God *separates* the water above (rain) from the water below (sea).
Day 3: God *separates* the water below (sea) from the dry land.
Day 4: God *populates* the sky with sun, moon, and stars.
Day 5: God *populates* the air with birds and the sea with fish.
Day 6: God *populates* the land with animals and with people.
Day 7: God *celebrates*. He blesses the day and rests on it.

Thus, the week of creation follows this three-fold pattern: (1) three days of separation, (2) three days of population, and (3) one day of celebration.

This suggests that we are dealing with a special kind of writing. It is not the kind of writing that is found in eyewitness accounts or in science books. Rather, it is the kind of writing found in children's books.

The authors of children's books use simple, poetic stories to teach children about life. Such stories are fun to read and easy to remember.

The biblical authors chose a similar approach to teach the people of their times about God. Here we must remember that most people in ancient times could not read or write. They learned everything by word of mouth.

What the Story Teaches

To understand what the biblical writer intended to teach by his creation story, we must keep in mind the time in which he wrote. In his day people worshiped every kind of god imaginable. The writer refers to this when he warned the people:

This four-faced god is one of many gods worshiped by ancient Babylonians. Archaeologists retrieved it from a sandy grave, where it lay buried for nearly four thousand years.

Do not sin by making for yourselves an idol in any form at all—whether man or woman, animal or bird, reptile or fish. Do not be tempted to worship and serve what you see in the sky— the sun, the moon, and the stars.
DEUTERONOMY 4:16–19

This brings us to the first truth the biblical writer intended to teach through the creation story: *There is only one God.*

The writer makes this point by having one God create all the other gods that people worship: humans, animals, heavenly bodies. If humans, animals, and heavenly bodies were created, they cannot be gods. There is only one God, the one who made everything.

This brings us to the second point the biblical writer intended to teach: *God planned creation.*

Many ancient peoples believed (as do some modern ones) that the world came into being by chance. An ancient Babylonian story, called *Enuma Elish,* teaches this.

Contrary to the Babylonian story, the biblical writer portrays God as creating the world in an orderly way, the way a builder or a carpenter works. His point is that God planned creation; it did not happen by chance or by accident.

This brings us to the biblical writer's third teaching: *God created everything good.*

Ancient peoples believed that parts of creation were evil. For example, many believed the human

body was evil. They came to this conclusion because the body seemed to war against the spirit. They believed, therefore, that God created the human spirit, while the devil created the human body.

Against this belief, the biblical writer describes God as being "pleased" with every part of creation, including the human body.

This leads to the biblical writer's final teaching about creation: *The Sabbath is holy.*

In ancient times, the seventh day of the week, the Sabbath, was like any other day. The biblical writer, however, portrays God as blessing the seventh day and setting it apart as a special day. It is to be a day of rest and of prayer.

In summary, the creation story teaches these four truths:

1. There is only one God,
2. God planned everything,
3. God created everything good,
4. God made the Sabbath holy.

These seventh-century B.C. clay tablets contain the ancient Babylonian story of creation.

Second Creation Story

Some Bible readers are surprised to discover that the Book of Genesis contains two creation stories. The second story begins in chapter 2.

> *When the LORD God made the universe,*
> *there were no plants on the earth*
> *and no seeds had sprouted,*
> *because he had not sent any rain,*
> *and there was no one to cultivate the land;*
> *but water would come up from beneath*
> *the surface and water the ground.*
>
> *Then the LORD God*
> *took some soil from the ground*
> *and formed a man out of it;*
> *he breathed life-giving breath*
> *into his nostrils*
> *and the man began to live.*
>
> *Then the LORD God*
> *planted a garden in Eden, in the East,*
> *and there he put the man he had formed.*
> *He made all kinds of beautiful trees*
> *grow there and produce good fruit.*
> GENESIS 2:4–9

To understand why this second story was added to the first, we must keep in mind that the first five books of the Bible, called the *Torah* ("Instruction"), were passed on orally for centuries. Only later were they written down.

Apparently, there were two oral traditions of the creation story. When the biblical writer was inspired to put the Torah in writing, he was also inspired to include both versions. They complemented one another.

A closer look at the second story will show how it complements the first one.

Creation of Man

God is pictured as working patiently over the body of man, much as a potter works patiently over a vase. When God got the body just right, he bent over it and breathed into it "life-giving breath." At that moment, the first human being began to live.

This moving scene makes an important point. It shows the close relationship between the first human being and God. It does this in two ways. First, it shows God creating the first human being before he created any other being. Second, it shows God sharing with the first human being a part of himself: his own "life-giving breath."

In ancient times, this was a revolutionary idea. Other religions stressed the distance between gods and human beings. The Bible stresses the closeness between them. God and the first human are as closely related as a mother and her baby.

The second creation story continues with another delightful scene. After God created animals and birds, he brought them "to the man to see what he would name them" (*Genesis 2:19*).

In ancient times, the power to name meant the power to control what was named. Having the man name the birds and the animals shows that God gave human beings control over them. God shared with them his own power. Thus the second creation story underscores what was stated in the first story, when God said:

> *"And now we will make human beings;*
> *they will be like us and resemble us.*
> *They will have power over the fish,*
> *the birds, and all animals."*
> GENESIS 1:26

Biblical Scrolls

An Arab teenager was tending his goats on the shore of the Dead Sea. Suddenly he noticed one goat was missing. He went off to search for it.

In the course of his search, he came upon a cave. Thinking the goat might be inside, he threw a stone through the entrance and heard something break. It turned out to be a jar containing a two-thousand-year-old biblical scroll.

The boy's discovery touched off a massive search of other caves in the area. Between 1947 and 1956, nearly two hundred caves were searched. Eleven yielded up six hundred ancient scrolls and fragments of scrolls, like the one shown here. About one-fourth of these were biblical scrolls. The rest were scrolls containing other ancient writings.

Some of the biblical scrolls found in the caves date back two hundred years before Jesus. Practically every book of the Old Testament is represented. Known as the Dead Sea Scrolls, these books are one thousand years older than any other copies of Old Testament books in existence.

How did the scrolls get into the caves? They were hidden there by Essenes (Jewish "monks") living in a "monastery" at Qumran. The scrolls were apparently put in the caves to protect them from invading Roman armies around A.D. 70.

Creation of Woman

The second creation story ends with God making a "suitable companion" for the man.

GOD   *It is not good*
for the man to live alone.
I will make a suitable companion
to help him.

NARRATOR   *. . . Then the LORD God*
made the man fall into a deep sleep,
and while he was sleeping,
he took out one of the man's ribs
and closed up the flesh.
He formed a woman out of the rib
and brought her to him.

MAN   *. . . Here is one of my own kind—*
Bone taken from my bone,
and flesh from my flesh.
"Woman" is her name
because she was taken out of man.

NARRATOR   *That is why*
a man leaves his father and mother
and is united with his wife,
and they become one.
The man and the woman were both
naked, but they were not embarrassed.
GENESIS 2:18–25

The biblical author lived in a society controlled by men. That society considered women to be second-class citizens. They were valued primarily as bearers of children—especially male children: warriors and workers. Many Bible readers interpret the story of woman's origin to be the Bible's way of rejecting that prejudiced social situation. By portraying woman as coming from the same material as man, the biblical writer teaches that men and women are equal in dignity.

The second creation story also teaches about the intimacy of marriage. God instructed the couple to be "united" and to "become one." God called them to a close relationship, like the one he enjoyed with them. By doing this, God indicates that the purpose of marriage includes more than having children. It also includes an intimate relationship of love and support between husband and wife.

In summary, the second creation story complements the first one in three ways. The second story underscores—

1. the intimacy between God and humans,
2. the power God shares with humans,
3. the intimacy and equality of the sexes.

Understanding Creation

Review

1. Identify: Scopes, Darrow, Bryan, Torah, *Enuma Elish,* prehistory.

2. List and explain the two main groups into which modern Bible readers divide.

3. List and explain the general fivefold pattern the biblical author uses to describe each day of creation.

4. List and explain the threefold pattern used to describe the week of creation.

5. What do these patterns suggest concerning the kind of writing the author uses to teach about creation? Why this kind of writing?

6. List and explain the four truths the biblical author teaches through the first creation story.

7. Why are there two creation stories in the Book of Genesis?

8. List and explain three ways the second story complements the first story.

9. When, why, and by whom were the Dead Sea Scrolls hidden? When, where, and by whom was the first of these scrolls found? About how many of these scrolls contain biblical writings?

Discuss

1. An unusual meeting takes place on Tuesday mornings in the seventh-floor private dining room of the New York Stock Exchange. Businessmen read and discuss the Bible together. Commenting on this and other Bible meetings like it, a former Conoco executive said, "It's a growing movement. But its growth has purposely been kept quiet."

Why are executives suddenly turning to the Bible for guidance? Why keep the growth quiet?

2. Some people think God dictated to the biblical writers as a boss dictates to his secretary. Others think the writers were inspired religiously, much as a songwriter is inspired musically. Still others think God enlightened the writers in a special way so that they wrote all and only what God wanted them to write.

Which group of people do you agree with? Why?

3. A clone is a child created from a single body cell. The child is a carbon copy of the person from whom it was taken. By scraping your arm, you can get enough cells for a thousand clones. Nobel Prize winner Joshua Lederberg suggests that clones from the same person could communicate almost with the ease of reading the other's mind. Some scientists think human clones will someday be possible.

Do you think God intended this kind of scientific experimentation with his creation; or is it like murder, something we can do but shouldn't? Explain.

Activities

1. Hebrews viewed the universe as having three worlds: God's world, their world, and the nether world, or world of the dead. God's world was above the dome of the sky (Psalm 104:3). Their world was below the dome, and the nether world was below their world (Psalm 139:8). Draw a sketch of this universe.

2. Not all evolutionists are atheists. For example, Saint Augustine suggested that God could have created a "seed" from which the universe evolved. Modern "Big Bang" scientists agree. They believe the matter of the universe was once concentrated in a fireball. It exploded (bang!). Then, all the matter expanded outward, forming stars, planets, and galaxies.

Interview three adults. Ask them if they believe humans could have evolved from lower life forms. If so, how do they square this with the biblical story of creation? Record your findings and share them with the group.

3. CB talk illustrates that certain expressions cannot be taken literally. Match the CB talk on the left with its correct meaning on the right.

_____ nap trap	**a.** police radar unit
_____ seat covers	**b.** passengers
_____ Willy Weaver	**c.** rainstorm
_____ window washer	**d.** motel
_____ camera	**e.** drunk driver

4. Pair up with a partner and prepare a skit on what you think might have been said in the first conversation between Adam and Eve.

Bible Reading

Pick a passage. After reading it, (1) summarize its main point, (2) tell how it relates to the chapter, and (3) list one or two thoughts that entered your mind as you read it.

1. Fantastic job   Psalm 104:1–9
2. Voice in the storm   Job 38:1–24
3. God's commercial   Psalm 19:1–6
4. In a class by himself   Isaiah 40:12–31
5. New creation   Revelation 21:1–8

Prayer Journal

Find a magazine photograph of some part of creation: a beach, a lake, a mountain, a river, a flower, a cloud.

Write a prayer about it. The prayer should have three paragraphs: (1) thanking God for it, (2) telling God why you like it, (3) telling God why it reminds you of him. Mount the photograph and the prayer on an 8½″ by 11″ sheet.

Here is a sample prayer. You may use it as a model.

Lord, thank you for creating trees, especially apple trees.

In spring they bloom and make the air smell good. In summer they become a motel for birds and offer shade to everybody. In fall they give away free fruit and shed their leaves to fertilize the soil. In winter they go to sleep and store up energy for spring.

Lord, trees remind me of you. They serve others and make our world a better place to live in.

2 De-creation

Some years ago, Dr. Norman McDonald addressed a group of anthropologists from around the globe. Talking about violence in our world, he said:

> Man is a killer, the greatest predator
> the world has ever known. . . .
> From the time he fashioned a club
> as his first weapon, man has insisted
> on developing more powerful weapons
> so that now, instead of killing individuals
> or groups, he can annihilate a planet.

Dr. McDonald's remarks are sobering. They make us ask ourselves, "If God created us good, what caused us to go bad? What caused evil to enter our hearts? Where did pain and death come from?"

The First Couple Sins

These questions cried out for an answer in biblical times. They still cry out for an answer today. The biblical writer faces these questions right after he describes creation.

NARRATOR	*The snake was the most cunning animal that the LORD God had made. The snake asked the woman,*
SNAKE	*Did God really tell you not to eat fruit from any tree in the garden?*
WOMAN	*We may eat the fruit of any tree . . . except the tree in the middle. . . . God told us not to eat the fruit of that tree or even touch it; if we do, we will die.*
SNAKE	*That's not true; you will not die. God said that because he knows that when you eat it, you will be like God and know what is good and what is bad. . . .*
NARRATOR	*So she took some of the fruit. . . . Then she gave some to her husband. . . .*
	As soon as they had eaten it, they were given understanding and realized that they were naked.

GENESIS 3:1–7

Contextual readers view this story as they do the creation narrative. It is a *poetic* story, designed to answer the question, "If God made everything good, how did evil enter the world?"

The key to understanding the story lies in its two symbols: the *snake* and the *eating* of the fruit.

The *snake* symbolizes the devil, the evil one. Even today, people find snakes distasteful. Ancient Hebrews found them even more distasteful. This is because their enemy, the Canaanites, used snakes in their pagan worship. Thus, the snake made a perfect symbol for the devil.

The second symbol is *eating the fruit.* The biblical writer did not intend this expression to be taken literally. He intended it to be taken symbolically. Recall that the snake promised that if the woman *ate* from the tree, she would "be like God and *know* what is good and what is evil."

Eating is connected with *knowing.* To know for ancient peoples was to learn from experience, not from books. *To eat* is a symbolic way of saying that the first couple learned evil by the *experience* of becoming evil. They sinned. Because they were good and became evil, they now "*know* what is good and what is evil."

What sin did they commit? Some think it was disobedience (doing what God said not to do). Others think it was pride (wanting to be "like God").

Contextual readers hold that the biblical writer never intended to reveal what sin was committed. He was only interested in answering the question, "How did evil enter the world?" His answer is, *"Evil entered the world when the first couple sinned."*

Understanding Sin

After the first couple sinned, the Bible says they "realized that they were naked" (*Genesis 3:7*). Why this strange statement?

To understand it, we must go back to the end of the second creation story. There we read, "The man and the woman were both naked, but they were not embarrassed" (*Genesis 2:25*). The couple's awareness of their nakedness *after* they sinned suggests that a change took place in their consciousness *as a result of sin.* They were no longer at ease with themselves. Sin had worked a profound change in them. Thus, the first effect of sin is this: *It alienates or divides people from themselves.*

But the effects of sin did not stop here. The biblical writer goes on to say of the first couple:

NARRATOR	*That evening* *they heard the* LORD *God* *walking in the garden,* *and they hid from him* *among the trees.*
GOD	*Where are you?*
MAN	*I heard you in the garden;* *I was afraid and hid from you,* *because I was naked.*
GOD	*Who told you that you were naked?* *Did you eat the fruit* *that I told you not to eat?*
MAN	*The woman you put here with me* *gave me the fruit,* *and I ate it.*
GOD	*[to woman]* *Why did you do this?*
WOMAN	*The snake tricked me* *into eating it.* GENESIS 3:8–13

The second effect of sin is this: *It alienates people from God.* After the first couple sinned, they no longer were at ease in God's presence. Before sinning, they felt comfortable with God: they walked in the garden with God. Now they feel uncomfortable in God's presence: they hide.

This brings us to the third effect of sin. We learn about it right after the first couple explains to God what happened. God addresses the snake, the woman, and the man in turn.

TO SNAKE	*From now on* *you will crawl on your belly. . . .* *I will make you and the woman* *hate each other; her offspring* *and yours will always be enemies.* *Her offspring will crush your head,* *and you will bite their heel.*
TO WOMAN	*I will increase* *your trouble in pregnancy* *and your pain in giving birth. . . .*
TO MAN	*The ground* *will be under a curse. . . .* *It will produce weeds and thorns,* *and you will have to eat wild plants.*

*You will have to work hard
and sweat
to make the soil produce anything,
until you go back to the soil
from which you were formed.
You were made from soil,
and you will become soil again.*
GENESIS 3:14–19

The third effect of sin is this: *It alienates people from nature.* We see this in two ways.

First, as a result of the first couple's sin, nature is pictured as being at war with them. The soil brings forth weeds and thorns. It causes them to labor and to sweat.

Second, as a result of sin, the first couple's bodies also war against them. Their bodies are no longer under their control; they are controlled by pain and death.

Bible readers view God's remark to the snake ("I will make you and the woman hate each other; her offspring . . . will crush your head") as a ray of hope. To understand their reasoning, recall that Jesus said of the devil, "From the very beginning he . . . [was] a liar" (*John 8:44*). "The Son of God appeared for this very reason, to destroy what the Devil had done" (*1 John 3:8*).

In other words, hostility between the devil and people has existed from the beginning. But people (in the offspring of Jesus) will destroy the devil. It is in this sense that God's remark to the snake is a ray of hope: *Jesus will eventually crush the devil and his power.*

The first sin story ends with God expelling the first couple from the Garden of Eden.

After Adam and Eve were expelled, they began to till the soil as God had commanded them. In time, Eve gave birth to two sons: Cain and Abel. As the boys grew up, Cain became jealous of Abel and plotted to kill him.

CAIN   *Let's go out in the fields.*

NARRATOR   *When they were out in the fields,
            Cain turned on his brother
            and killed him.*

LORD   *Where is your brother Abel?*

CAIN   *I don't know. Am I supposed
            to take care of my brother?*

LORD   *. . . Your brother's blood
            is crying out to me from the ground. . . .*

NARRATOR   *Cain went away from the LORD's
            presence and lived in a land . . .
            east of Eden.*
            GENESIS 4:8–10, 16

Again, this is a symbol story. Its main purpose is to teach that when people break faith with God, they soon break faith with one another, as well.

Thus, the story reveals yet a fourth effect of sin. Besides alienating people from themselves (nakedness), God (hiding), and nature (curse), it also *alienates people from each other.*

Sin Spreads

Cain's sin sets in motion a tidal wave of sin. The writer teaches this symbolically. He lists two family trees (genealogies). The first one begins with Adam and ends with Noah (Genesis 5:1–32). Fantastic ages are given to the people:

Adam lived 930 years,
Seth lived 912 years,
Lamech lived 777 years.

The second family tree begins with Shem, Noah's son, and ends with Terah, Abraham's father (Genesis 11:10–32):

Shem lived 600 years,
Eber lived 464 years,
Terah lived 205 years.

The biblical writer uses the family trees to do two things.

First, they further the sin theme of the Book of Genesis. They do this by showing a steady decline in human life spans. (Recall that one effect of sin was sickness and death. Thus a decrease in life suggests an increase in sin.)

Second, the family trees build a literary bridge between Adam, the father of all people, and Abraham, the father of the Hebrew people. They provide an easy way to move rapidly through thousands and thousands of years of human history.

Legendary Watchdog

After God expelled the first couple from the garden, he put "the cherubim and the fiery revolving sword" at the entrance to the garden "to guard the way to the tree of life" (*Genesis 3:24, NAB*).

Archaeologists have clarified this passage. The *cherubim* is a winged animal with a human head. Found at entrances to ancient buildings and cities, it served as a legendary watchdog to keep away evil or unworthy intruders. The one shown here stands sixteen feet tall and came from the eighth-century B.C. palace of Sargon II. The animal's fifth leg was added by the ancient artist for visual purposes. When viewed from the front, the creature appeared in perfect symmetry. When viewed from the side, it gave the impression of balance and motion.

Scholars say the *fiery sword* refers to lightning. Ancients viewed lightning as a weapon which God flashed about in the sky when he grew angry.

Finally, the *tree of life* refers to a legendary plant which ancients thought gave immortality (freedom from death) to those who ate its fruit.

And so the cherubim keeps the first couple from entering the garden and eating from the tree of life, which would give them immortality. The biblical writer's point is this: *Sin had made the first couple evil intruders, unworthy to walk with God and live with him forever.*

In brief, the biblical writer's family trees serve two purposes:

1. they show sin increasing from generation to generation,
2. they act as a literary bridge (rapid passage of time) between Adam and Abraham.

Sin Destroys

The famous preacher James Weldon Johnson wrote a delightful book of sermons. One is called "Noah Built the Ark." It begins by describing a small storm cloud forming in the sky. Slowly it spreads, like a "bottle of ink" that has spilled. Next, thunder begins to roll, like a "rumbling drum." Then, lightning begins to "jump from pole to pole."

And it rained down rain, rain, rain,
Great God, but didn't it rain! . . .
And the old ark-a she begun to ride;
The old ark-a she begun to rock;
Sinners came a-running down to the ark;
Sinners came a-swimming all round the ark;
Sinners pleaded and sinners prayed—
Sinners wept and sinners wailed—
But Noah'd done barred the door.

Even people who know little about the Bible are familiar with the story of Noah and the ark. The biblical writer describes it this way:

NARRATOR   *God looked at the world*
            and saw that it was evil . . .
            people were all living evil lives.

GOD   *[to Noah]*
            I have decided to put an end
            to all mankind. . . .
            Build a boat. . . . Go into the boat
            with your wife, your sons,
            and their wives.
            Take into the boat with you
            a male and a female
            of every kind of animal
            and of every kind of bird. . . .

NARRATOR   *Seven days later*
            the flood came. . . .
            The flood continued
            for forty days, and . . .
            covered the highest mountains.
            GENESIS 6:12–14, 18–20; 7:10, 17, 19

Literal readers believe this story describes a real flood. They say it destroyed everything on earth that was not in the ark.

Contextual readers believe the flood narrative is a symbol story. Some think it may be *based* on a real flood, but the biblical writer did not intend his readers to take it literally.

Regardless of how we interpret the flood story, its main point remains the same: *Sin leads to the destruction of ourselves and our world.*

Sign of hope.

Sign of Hope

God left the people with hope after the first sin story (Genesis 3:15). He did the same after the flood story.

> *God said to Noah and his sons,*
> *"I am now making my covenant*
> *with you and with your descendants,*
> *and with all living beings. . . . I promise*
> *that never again will all living beings*
> *be destroyed by a flood. . . .*
>
> *"As a sign of this everlasting covenant*
> *which I am making with you . . .*
> *I am putting my bow in the clouds. . . .*
> *When the rainbow appears in the clouds,*
> *I will see it*
> *and remember the everlasting covenant*
> *between me and all living beings on earth."*
> GENESIS 9:8–13, 16

This passage makes the first reference to a covenant (holy agreement) between God and human beings. God promises that *he will never again permit a flood to devastate the earth.* The rainbow is the sign of that promise.

Tower of Babylon

The chain of symbolic sin stories ends with the Tower of Babylon story. It takes place after Noah's descendants had grown numerous. One day they said, "Now let's build a city with a tower that reaches the sky, so that we may make a name for ourselves" (*Genesis 11:4*). But God confused the speech of the people, and they were forced to quit work on the tower. The story ends with the people scattering and splitting up into nations.

Archaeologists think the biblical writer had in mind a ziggurat (pyramidlike structure) when he wrote about the tower. Ancient peoples believed that the top of a ziggurat was a place for people to meet with gods. The writer uses the ziggurat as a pride-symbol of people's desire to "make a name" for themselves and become "like God."

Ruins of a ziggurat.

Some scholars think the original purpose of the story was to explain the origins of nations and languages. But since the biblical writer situates it within the context of a series of symbolic sin stories, he gives it a deeper meaning. He uses it to teach us the fifth and final effect of sin: *It alienates nation from nation.*

The chain of sin stories (Genesis 3–11) leaves us with two important conclusions.

1. Sin has five effects on people. It alienates them from—
   God (couple's hiding),
   self (couple's nakedness),
   nature (curse),
   other people (Cain's violence),
   other nations (Babylon story).
2. Sin is destroying people. It is spreading across the world like a forest fire. Only God can save the human race.

It is on this bleak note that the chain of symbolic sin stories comes to an end.

Understanding De-creation

Review

1. Identify: cherubim, fiery sword, tree of life, Cain, Abel, ziggurat.

2. What question does the biblical writer seek to answer by the first sin story? What do the "snake" and "eating the fruit" symbolize?

3. Explain how the biblical writer teaches that sin alienated the first couple from (a) themselves, (b) God, (c) nature.

4. Explain how God's remarks to the snake are a "ray of hope."

5. How does the biblical writer teach that sin alienates people from one another?

6. List and explain the twofold purpose for which the biblical writer uses family trees.

7. What is the main point of the flood story? What is the rainbow a sign of?

8. How does the biblical writer teach that sin alienates nations from one another?

9. What two important conclusions do we draw from the chain of sin stories in Genesis 3–11?

Discuss

1. A factory worker holds a pair of tongs in his hand. Gripped between its jaws is a small chunk of metal. If you wanted to learn if the metal were hot or not, what are three ways you could use to find out?

By which of these three ways did the first couple learn about sin? Explain.

2. Journalist Dorothy Thompson says what frightens her about the Nazi death camps is that "good" prisoners helped commit the crimes in those camps. She writes: "The physicians who inoculated concentration camp victims with malaria . . . were prisoners of the Nazis themselves." By assisting in the extermination of their fellow prisoners, they won prolongation of their own lives.

How does this fact confirm the conclusion we draw from the sin stories in Genesis 3–11?

3. In Avery Corman's book *Oh, God!* someone rebukes God for not lifting a finger to help destroy the suffering in the world. When God doesn't defend himself, the person says, "So you've decided to just let us stumble along and never do a thing to help?"

God looks at the person and says, "Such a smart fella and you missed the point. . . . I set all this up for you and made it so it can work. Only the deal is *you* have to work at it and you shouldn't look to me to do it for you."

What is God's point, and do you agree or disagree with it?

4. The film *Lord of the Flies* is about a group of fourteen-year-old boys who get marooned on a deserted island when a plane goes down at sea. The pilot is killed, but the boys survive. Eventually, all but one boy turn into savages. The film's point is that people are basically evil. When you leave them on their own without law or order, they turn into animals.

The book *Catcher in the Rye* is about an innocent youth, Holden Caulfield. His contact with adult society eventually destroys his innocence. Things he never dreamed of doing before, he now does. The story's point is that people are basically good, but society corrupts them.

Which view do you hold? Imagine that your group got marooned on an island that had enough food and water for survival *if* you used both sparingly. Do you think you would survive long on the island without violence? Explain.

Activities

1. A TV commercial shows an Indian looking sadly at the rape of nature: litter on roadsides, sewage flowing into lakes, exhaust streaming from trucks, noise drowning out the song of birds.

List five things you could do to combat this rape of nature.

2. Psychiatrist Dr. Karl Menninger is frightened by the growing number of people who refuse to admit they sin. He is even more frightened by groups of nations who deny *collective* sinning: terrorism, apartheid, pornography.

What Bible story does this refusal to admit sin recall? Why do people deny sinning? What is a *collective* sin? How can individuals combat collective sins?

Prayer Journal

Find a newspaper headline and paragraph that deal with de-creation: environmental pollution, crime, violence, destruction of life or property.

Write a prayer about it. The prayer should have three paragraphs: (1) speaking to God about it, (2) praying for those responsible for it, (3) praying for those hurt by it. Here is a sample headline, paragraph, and prayer.

Blacks Gather to Mourn Dead in South Africa

JOHANNESBURG, SOUTH AFRICA—*Blacks gathered by the tens of thousands Friday to mourn their dead. . . . Witnesses said police broke up one ceremony with rubber whips and birdshot.*

Lord, why must blacks suffer so much in South Africa? Why do your children treat each other so badly? What can I do about this situation?

Lord, move the hearts of officials in South Africa to help them seek a peaceful resolution to their problems.

Above all, Lord, give blacks a spirit of forgiveness and the courage to keep seeking their rights.

3. Interview three adults over sixty. Ask them why they think evil is or is not more widespread today than formerly.

Write out their responses and report back to the group.

4. Construct a family tree of either your mother's or your father's side of the family. Go back as far as you can.

5. Get the book *Prayers from the Ark* by Carmen B. DeGasztold.

Select one or two prayers to read to the group. Write one of your own and share it with the group.

6. Look up these passages: Isaiah 54:9, Wisdom 10:4, Wisdom 14:6, Matthew 24:37–39, Luke 17:26–27, Hebrews 11:7, 1 Peter 3:20.

Tell how each speaks about the flood.

Bible Reading

Pick a passage. After reading it, (1) summarize its main point, (2) tell how it relates to the chapter, and (3) list one or two thoughts that entered your mind as you read it.

1. Homeless wanderer	Genesis 4
2. Riding out the flood	Genesis 7
3. The dove test	Genesis 8
4. No excuse	Romans 1:18–32
5. Wash me, Lord	Psalm 51:1–15

3 Re-creation

Mark Twain wrote a story called "The Terrible Catastrophe." The story is about a group of people who get trapped in a hopeless situation. They are doomed to die. They have no way to escape. They are, indeed, on the verge of a terrible catastrophe.

Mark Twain did not want the story to end sadly, but he could not think of a way to save the people. It was like having them trapped in a plane that was ten feet away from crashing into a mountain.

And so Mark Twain ended his story with this remark: "I have these people in such a fix that I cannot get them out of it. Anyone who thinks he can is welcome to try."

In one sense that is an unfair ending. But in another sense it is a good ending. It makes us think. It gets us involved.

Thousands of years ago the human race found itself in a similar situation. Sin had entered the world and was spreading out of control, like a forest fire. The human race was trapped. There was no way it could save itself.

God the Father saw the situation and did not want the story to end sadly. He loved the human race too much for that. So he decided to do something about it. What God did is what the rest of the Bible is all about. We might call it the *re-creation* of the world. The story begins with Abram in chapter 12 of the Book of Genesis.

God Intervenes

Genesis contains fifty chapters. The first two, as we saw, deal with *creation.* The next nine deal with *de-creation,* people's misuse of creation. Chapter 12 begins the *re-creation* part of the Bible.

Creation and de-creation both deal with *pre-historical* times, that is, times before history was recorded. The biblical writer, therefore, talks about them in *symbol* stories.

Re-creation, on the other hand, deals with *historical* times. Thus, beginning with Abram in chapter 12, the biblical writer makes use of *folk* stories and *eyewitness* stories.

Folk stories are stories that were passed on by word of mouth. They are expressed in anecdotes that were often simplified and exaggerated in order to make a point.

Eyewitness stories, on the other hand, are stories that were reported or recorded by someone who actually witnessed the event. Thus the prophet Isaiah writes:

> God told me to write down in a book
> what the people are like,
> so that there would be a permanent record.
> ISAIAH 30:8

Let us now turn to chapter 12 and Abram.

God Calls Abraham

Abram grew up in the city of Ur, near the Persian Gulf. All that is left of Ur and its surroundings today is a giant, crumbling ziggurat. On top of this man-made mountain of bricks once stood a temple to the moon god, whom the people of Ur worshiped.

When Abram reached adulthood, his family moved north to Haran. There something happened to Abram that changed his life. He encountered (met in a personal way) the mysterious reality we call God.

> The LORD said to Abram,
> "Leave your country, your relatives,
> and your father's home, and go
> to a land that I am going to show you. . . ."
>
> Abram took his wife Sarai, his nephew Lot,
> and all the wealth and all the slaves
> they had acquired in Haran,
> and they started out for the land of Canaan.
>
> When they arrived at Canaan,
> Abram traveled through the land
> until he came to . . .
> the holy place at Shechem.
> GENESIS 12:1, 5–6

This first encounter with God is referred to as Abram's *call*. It begins a pattern that repeats itself over and over again in biblical history. Certain people experience an inner invitation or call to leave all and embark upon a mission that God reveals to them only gradually. Abram was the first of this long line of people.

Once in Canaan, Abram settled down to his new life. At this point in time, his wife, Sarai, was childless. Sarai, however, had a maid servant called Hagar. One day Sarai approached Abram.

SARAI
> The LORD has kept me
> from having children.
> Why don't you sleep with my slave girl?
> Perhaps she can have a child for me.

NARRATOR
> Abram agreed. . . .
> Hagar bore Abram a son,
> and he named him Ishmael.
> GENESIS 16:2, 15

Ancient clay tablets found in the Near East help clarify this puzzling passage. Among the tablets was an old marriage contract. It stated that a sterile wife had to provide her husband with a substitute wife for childbearing. This explains Sarai's action. She appeared to be sterile, and was merely carrying out the requirements of the marriage contract.

God Covenants Abraham

Sometime after Ishmael's birth Abram encountered God a second time. It happened one night when Abram was standing alone under the starry sky.

GOD
> Look at the sky
> and try to count the stars;
> you will have
> as many descendants as that. . . .
>
> Bring me a cow, a goat, and a ram,
> each of them three years old,
> and a dove and a pigeon.

NARRATOR
> Abram brought the animals . . .
> cut them in half,
> and placed the halves
> opposite each other. . . .
>
> A flaming torch suddenly appeared
> and passed between the pieces. . . .
> Then and there the LORD
> made a covenant with Abram.

GOD
> I promise to give your descendants
> all this land.
> GENESIS 15:5, 9–10, 17–18

The unusual ceremony described here is known as "cutting a covenant." Unlike modern peoples, ancients rarely signed treaties or contracts. Rather, they made oral agreements and confirmed them with a ceremony.

One such ceremony was for the two parties to split an animal in half, lay the sides opposite each other, and walk between them. The ritual signified that they would rather be killed and split in half than break their agreement (Jeremiah 34:18–19).

The "flaming torch" passing between the cut-up animals was a sign that God was entering into such a covenant with Abram. Through this covenant God promised Abram two things: descendants and land.

But even greater things were in store for Abram. Sometime after his second meeting with God, Abram met God again.

GOD   *I am the Almighty God. . . .*
Your name will no longer be Abram,
but Abraham. . . .

You and your descendants
must all agree to circumcise
every male among you . . .
a physical sign to show
that my covenant with you
is everlasting.

You must no longer call your wife Sarai;
from now on her name is Sarah.
I will bless her,
and I will give you a son by her. . . .
You will name him Isaac. . . .

NARRATOR   *When God finished*
speaking to Abraham, he left him.
GENESIS 17:1, 5, 10, 13, 15–16, 19, 22

Abram's final meeting with God results in a new name and a special mark.

The new name is a sign of Abram's new vocation. *Abram* means "exalted father." *Abraham* means "father of many." Abraham's new name fits his new calling or vocation.

The special mark is a sign of God's covenant with Abraham and his descendants. Like a brand or a tattoo, it identifies the bearer of it as belonging to a special group, God's chosen people.

Clay Tablets

The oldest writing on earth is found on clay tablets. The one shown here was made before Abram was born. The "picture writing" on it reads from top to bottom and right to left.

Picture writing eventually gave way to wedge-shaped (cuneiform) writing. At first each wedge-shaped symbol stood for an abstract idea. For example, the symbol for "foot" stood for "walking." Later, the symbol stood for a human sound. Thus, the symbol for "foot" stood for the sound "foot" as in "football."

While picture writing was done on soft clay with a pointed pen, wedge-shaped writing was done with a triangular pen, as shown here. Once the writing was complete, the clay hardened like a brick.

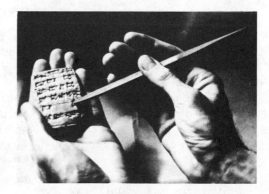

When scholars learned to read these tablets, a library of information about ancient times opened up. Suddenly, cities like Ur, Abram's birthplace, burst into "living color." A whole new world came alive—a world that has helped people read the Bible with greater accuracy and better understanding.

Thus, by a series of meetings, God revealed himself to Abraham and set in motion the *re-creation* of the world.

God Tests Abraham

God's promise that Sarah would bear Abraham a son, Isaac, came to pass. Isaac grew rapidly into boyhood. Then one day, Abraham experienced a strange command from God.

GOD   *Take your son, your only son, Isaac,*
              whom you love so much. . . .
              Offer him as a sacrifice to me. . . .

NARRATOR   *Abraham cut some wood. . . .*
              Abraham made Isaac
              carry the wood for the sacrifice,
              and he himself carried a knife. . . .

              When they came to the place
              which God had told him about,
              Abraham build an altar. . . .

ANGEL   *Abraham, Abraham! . . .*
              Don't hurt the boy. . . .
              Now I know that you
              have obedient reverence for God,
              because you have not kept back
              your only son from me.
              GENESIS 22:2–3, 6, 9, 11–12

Two points need to be stressed in this unusual episode from Abraham's life.

First, modern readers find it hard to realize that human sacrifice was not unusual in Abraham's time. James Michener discussed the practice in his novel *The Source.* In one episode of the story, he describes how the people of ancient Makor adopted a new god, named Melak, who demanded human sacrifice of them. Michener says they adopted Melak

partly because his demands upon them
were severe, as if this proved his power,
and partly because they had grown
somewhat contemptuous of their local gods
precisely because they were not demanding.

What did God want to teach Abraham through this episode? Bible readers interpret it as God's way of teaching him that he did not want human sacrifice. God dramatizes this teaching in such a way that Abraham would never forget it.

This leads us to the second point. The Isaac episode also taught Abraham about faith in God.

First, faith involves *loving trust.*

When God asked Abraham to sacrifice Isaac, Abraham's reason told him that this was illogical. It meant destroying the person through whom God promised him descendants. Yet, Abraham trusted God rather than his reason.

Second, faith involves *a constant struggle.*

When God promised Abraham land and descendants, Abraham believed. He never doubted. The Isaac episode gave Abraham his first good reason to doubt. It taught him that faith involves more than a one-time decision to believe. Rather, it involves a series of decisions to continue believing. There is no such thing as "getting the faith" and never having to struggle with it again.

Finally, faith involves *times of darkness.*

There are times when our faith seems to go behind a cloud—and even seem lost. In other words, there are times when God seems to "test" our faith, as he did Abraham's faith. When these "times of darkness" come, we should recall the words that a fugitive from the Nazis wrote on a wall of a basement in which he was hiding:

I believe in the sun even when it is not shining.
I believe in love even when I do not feel it.
I believe in God even when he is silent.

In conclusion, the Isaac episode taught Abraham two important things:

1. that God did not want human sacrifice, and
2. that faith in God involves loving trust, an unending series of decisions, and times of darkness.

God's Intervention Continues

In 1977, Egyptian President Anwar Sadat did something no previous Muslim leader dared to do. He risked the anger of the Arab world by going to Israel and addressing the Knesset, the Israeli parliament.

In his address on November 27, Sadat pointed out that the day was an Islamic holy day. It celebrated Abraham's willingness to sacrifice his son Isaac. Sadat chose this day to show his willingness to sacrifice his life for the sake of peace between Arabs and Jews.

Sadat's reference to Abraham surprised many people. For the first time they discovered that Muslims, like Jews and Christians, look upon Abraham as their father in the faith.

Muslims trace their descendancy to Abraham through Ishmael, Abraham's son by Hagar, the maidservant of Sarah. Jews and Christians trace their descendancy through Isaac, Abraham's son by Sarah, his true wife.

Keeping this in mind, let us now turn to Isaac to see how God continues his work of re-creation though him.

Isaac

Abraham and Sarah both died in old age. Isaac and Ishmael buried them in Canaan. "After the death of Abraham, God blessed his son Isaac" (*Genesis 25:11*).

Isaac married Rebecca when he was forty years old. Rebecca bore him two healthy sons, named Esau and Jacob.

Esau became a skilled hunter . . .
but Jacob was a quiet man who stayed at home.
Isaac preferred Esau, because he enjoyed
eating the animals Esau killed,
but Rebecca preferred Jacob.

One day
while Jacob was cooking some bean soup,

Esau came in from hunting.
He was hungry and said to Jacob,
"I'm starving;
give me some of that red stuff.". . .

Jacob answered,
"I will give it to you if you give me
your rights as the first-born son."
Esau said, "All right! . . ."
Esau made the vow
and gave his rights to Jacob.
GENESIS 25:27–33

The day eventually came when Isaac's health failed badly and he became blind. It was time for him to bless his elder son and give him the special rights that went to the firstborn sons.

Ignorant of Esau's vow, Isaac told Esau to kill an animal and prepare a meal. He would eat it and then give Esau his blessing. Rebecca overheard the conversation. When Esau departed, she ran to Jacob and told him to prepare the meal, pretend he was Esau, and receive the blessing. He did.

When Esau learned what had happened, he was furious and plotted to kill Jacob. But Jacob learned of his plan and fled from home.

The story of Esau and Jacob highlights an important point. It shows how God dealt with people in biblical times. He did not program them to be saints. Nor did God dangle them at the ends of his fingers, like puppets, making them do only what he wanted.

On the contrary, God gave them the same kind of freedom that he gives us. He worked through their actions, even when these were sinful.

Jacob

After Jacob fled from Esau, he went in the direction of Haran. One night he came to a holy place and decided to pitch camp there. He built a campfire and lay down to sleep.

NARRATOR   *He dreamed that he saw a stairway*
reaching from earth to heaven,
with angels going up
and coming down on it.

This modern nomad sets up camp much as Jacob did two thousand years ago.

*And there was the LORD
standing beside him.*

GOD   *I am the LORD,
the God of Abraham and Isaac.
I will give to you
and to your descendants
this land on which you are lying.
They will be as numerous
as the specks of dust on the earth.
They will extend their territory
in all directions,
and through you and your descendants
I will bless all the nations.*
GENESIS 28:12–14

Jacob settled in Haran. Later he returned to the site of his dream. Again, he experienced God's presence.

GOD   *Your name is Jacob,
but from now on it will be Israel. . . .
Nations will be descended from you
and you will be the ancestor of kings. . . .*

NARRATOR   *Then God left him.
There, where God had spoken to him,
Jacob set up a memorial stone
and consecrated it
by pouring wine and olive oil on it.
He named the place Bethel.*
GENESIS 35:10–11, 13–15

Jacob's name change confirms that he is the official bearer of God's covenant promise. Like Isaac before him, he is the successor to Abraham.

Joseph

Jacob (Israel) settled in Canaan and fathered twelve sons. Of these sons, Jacob loved Joseph best. This caused the other brothers to grow jealous.

One day Joseph had a dream, which he shared with his brothers.

*"Listen to the dream I had.
We were all in the field
tying up sheaves of wheat,
when my sheaf got up and stood up straight.
Yours formed a circle around mine
and bowed down to it.". . .
So they hated him even more.*
GENESIS 37:6–8

Eventually, the brothers grew so jealous that they secretly sold Joseph into slavery. The slave traders took him to Egypt and sold him to Potiphar, one of the king's officers. Joseph prospered in Potiphar's household and won fame as an interpreter of dreams.

One night the king of Egypt had two disturbing dreams. He sent for Joseph and asked him to interpret his dreams. Joseph told the king:

"The two dreams mean the same thing. . . .
There will be seven years of great plenty
in all the land of Egypt.
After that,
there will be seven years of famine."
GENESIS 41:25, 29–30

Medieval Christians called the pyramids
"Joseph barns," thinking Joseph stored his
grain in them. The pyramids were also over
a thousand years old in Joseph's time.

The king immediately put Joseph in charge of storing up grain during the years of plenty, to be rationed out during the years of famine.

When the famine struck, people came from all over to buy grain. One group that came was Joseph's own brothers. Joseph recognized them immediately. After putting them to a test, to see if they had changed, he revealed himself to them.

"I am your brother Joseph,
whom you sold into Egypt.
Now do not be upset or blame yourselves. . . .
It was really God who sent me ahead of you
to save people's lives. . . .

"Now hurry back to my father and tell him . . .
[to] come to me without delay.
You can live in the region of Goshen."
GENESIS 45:4–5, 9–10

When Joseph's father heard this, he was overjoyed. He took all his descendants and went to Egypt. They settled in Goshen, where they grew in numbers and wealth.

The head of this Sphinx is as tall as a seven-story building; its body is as long as a football field. The Sphinx was over a thousand years old when Joseph looked upon it 3,500 years ago.

New Understanding

Joseph's rise to power in Egypt was once surrounded by a fairy-tale glamor. How could a Hebrew slave rise so quickly to a position of power in a foreign country? We now learn from ancient Egyptian records that in Joseph's time Egypt was overrun by Hyksos invaders. This makes Joseph's rise to power more understandable. He moved up the ladder in a time of political upheaval.

Similarly, other details of the Joseph story are clarified by ancient Egyptian records. A papyrus, dating from 1300 B.C., contains detailed instructions for interpreting dreams. Dream interpretation was a highly respected art in Joseph's time.

Finally, ancient Egyptian records tell of severe famines. One record quotes a high official as saying:

My heart is heavy
over the failure of the Nile floods
for the past seven years.
There is little fruit;
vegetables are in short supply;
there is a shortage of food in general. . . .
The storehouses have been opened,
but everything in them has been consumed.

When we look back over the stories of Abraham, Isaac, and Joseph, we are struck by one big fact: *God did not always choose holy people to become involved in his work of re-creating the world.* The biblical writer made this painfully clear. He did not gloss over Jacob's lie to Isaac. He did not excuse the jealous behavior of Joseph's brothers. He simply told it like it was. If God used sinful people to do his work then, he can use sinful people, *like us,* to continue it now.

Understanding Re-creation

Review

1. Identify: Haran, Hagar, Ishmael, Esau, Rebecca, Potiphar, Goshen.

2. What is meant by de-creation? Re-creation?

3. Which chapters of the Book of Genesis deal with creation? With de-creation? With re-creation? Which deal with prehistory? With folk history? With eyewitness history?

4. Explain how ancient peoples made and sealed important contracts and treaties.

5. For what purpose did God call Abraham? What twofold promise did God make to him?

6. Explain the purpose of the new sign and the special mark that God gave Abraham.

7. How did God test Abraham, and what two points does God teach us through this test? Explain the second point in detail.

8. Why did Esau hate his brother Jacob? When and how did Jacob become the bearer of God's covenant promise?

9. Why did Joseph's brothers hate him? How did Joseph end up in Egypt? How did Jacob and his descendants (Hebrews) end up in Egypt?

10. How are Joseph's rise to power, his interpretation of dreams, and the famine supported by ancient Egyptian records outside the Bible?

11. In what sense does God further his work of re-creation through people just like us?

Discuss

1. James Michener says in *The Source* that the people of Makor started worshiping a new god, called Melak, "partly because his demands upon them were severe, as if this proved his power, and partly because they had grown somewhat contemptuous of their local gods precisely because they were not demanding."

Do you think modern religions are too demanding or not demanding enough? How demanding is Jesus' teaching: slightly, fairly, extremely? Explain.

2. Alert Bible readers note that Isaac resembles Jesus. He is the father's only son. He carried on his shoulder the wood on which he would be sacrificed. His sacrifice was to take place on a hill. Death did not destroy him. There are other parallels between Old Testament events and New Testament events (John 3:14–15, 1 Corinthians 15:45–49).

Why do/don't you think these are coincidental?

3. A high school boy wrote: "One day, I decided to make God the center of my life. This decision gave me great peace and joy. But two days later I did something no Christian would ever do. I was totally discouraged and concluded I had not really committed myself to God at all. I had only psyched myself into believing I had."

Why do you agree/disagree with the boy's conclusion about his commitment to God?

4. God was active in surprising ways in the everyday lives of Abraham, Isaac, Jacob, and Joseph.

Discuss ways in which God is active in your life today.

Activities

1. God often enlightened people in biblical times through dreams. Dreams have also been an occasion for enlightenment outside the Bible. Physicist Niels Bohr (1885–1962) got his idea for his atom model from a dream. Mozart, Einstein, and Poe also got ideas from dreams.

List two dreams that are discussed in this chapter. Why did God speak to people in dreams, rather than when they were awake? Did you ever have a dream that affected you deeply? Explain.

2. Imagine you are Abraham. Your father, Terah, expects you to take over the family business in a few years. He knows nothing of God's call to you.

Write a letter to your father, explaining why you must leave home and follow God's call.

3. In *The Power Within You,* Pat Williams says Joseph was the butt of the first good news/bad news jokes in history. Here is a paraphrase of what he says.

> *Joseph, the good news is that you're your father's favorite son; the bad news is that your brothers are going to sell you into slavery.*
>
> *Joseph, the good news is that you'll be bought and befriended by a powerful man in Egypt; the bad news is that his wife will frame you and jail you. The good news is that while you're in jail, Pharaoh's servant promises to free you; the bad news is that he'll forget about it for two years.*

Write a similar good news/bad news joke about Abraham.

4. In *The Devil's Advocate,* Morris West describes a person whose faith in God suddenly seemed to die. The person says:

> *I groped for him and could not find him. I prayed to him unknown and he did not answer. I wept at night for the loss of him. . . . Then, one day, he was there again. . . . I had a Father and he knew me and the world was the house he had built for me. . . . I had never understood till this moment the meaning of the words "gift of faith."*

Did your faith ever seem to die for a while? Explain. On a scale of 1 (weak) to 10 (strong), grade your faith in (a) God, (b) Jesus, (c) the Church. Explain your grades.

Bible Reading

Pick a passage. After reading it (1) summarize its main point, (2) tell how it relates to the chapter, and (3) list one or two thoughts that entered your mind as you read it.

1. Abraham pleads for Sodom   Genesis 18:16–13
2. Joseph is framed   Genesis 39
3. Joseph's brothers in Egypt   Genesis 42–43
4. Joseph tests his brothers   Genesis 44
5. Joseph reveals himself   Genesis 45

Prayer Journal

Find a newspaper or magazine headline, paragraph, and photo that deal with re-creation: saving a life, helping someone in need, making the world better in some way.

Compose a prayer about it. It should have two paragraphs: (1) speaking to God about it and (2) asking God to inspire similar efforts by others. Here is a sample headline, paragraph, and prayer.

Soviet Girl Brings Message of Peace

CHICAGO—*Katerina Lycheva . . . brought messages of peace from her Soviet friends to American school children Friday as she began a two-week peace mission to the United States. "Even if I accomplish a little thing, it will be a tiny contribution toward peace," the blue-eyed 11-year-old said.*

> *God our Father, you created both Russians and Americans alike. You intended them to live together in peace. Thank you for Katerina's visit. It shows the world that young people want peace and are doing something creative about it.*
>
> *Inspire more people like Katerina to do creative things for peace. Give me the light to see what creative thing I can do in my situation.*

4 Covenant

Famous people have a way of staying in the headlines. An example is Rameses II, Egypt's greatest pharaoh. His mummified head is still a popular exhibit in a Cairo museum. And as late as 1965, he was still grabbing newspaper headlines.

The new Aswan Dam had doomed to a watery grave the three-thousand-year-old temple that he had built on the Nile River at Abu Simbel. But United Nations engineers came to the rescue. They took apart the temple (with its six-story-high statues) and lifted it up two hundred feet to dry ground. It was this same Rameses who played a key role in biblical history.

God's People Are Enslaved

The Book of Genesis ends with the deaths of Israel (Jacob) and Joseph. Before Israel dies, he blesses each of his twelve sons. Their descendants will become the "twelve tribes" of Israel.

The deaths of Jacob and Joseph signal the end of prosperity for the Hebrews ("Israelites") in Egypt. The Book of Exodus begins by picking up the story a number of years later.

> *Then, a new king,*
> *who knew nothing about Joseph,*
> *came to power in Egypt.*
> *He said to his people,*
> *"These Israelites are so numerous and strong*
> *that they are a threat to us. . . ."*
> *So the Egyptians put slave drivers over them*
> *to crush their spirits with hard labor.*
> *The Israelites built the cities of Pithom*
> *and Rameses to serve as supply centers*
> *for the king.*
> EXODUS 1:8–9, 11

The plight of the Hebrew slaves has been vividly re-created by novelist Sholem Asch in his book *Moses.* He writes of them:

> *Their bodies*
> *showed the ribs and backbone starkly.*
> *In the blazing sunlight the black-scorched skin,*
> *wetted by the sweat of anguish and labor,*
> *glistened like copper.*
>
> *Their faces were dumb and careworn,*
> *the lips thin, close-locked, parched. . . .*
> *They did their work in dull silence;*
> *their motions and footsteps maintained*
> *a heavy rhythm under the threat of whips.*

Into this tragic situation came one of the greatest figures of the Bible.

God Calls Moses

Moses was born at a time when the Egyptian authorities had ordered the death of all Hebrew male babies. The Egyptians wanted to control the number of Israelites so that they would be easier to keep in check. Moses, however, was saved by the cleverness of his mother. She hid him in a watertight basket and put it among the reeds at the river's edge. Pharaoh's daughter found the basket while she was bathing in the river. Even though she knew the child was a Hebrew, she treated Moses like her own son.

So, Moses grew up in the household of Pharaoh. He was given good schooling and he enjoyed a comfortable life. He almost forgot about the rest of the Hebrew people.

When Moses was in his twenties, he got into serious trouble. He saw an Egyptian foreman beating a Hebrew slave. All at once, Moses remembered his roots. He struck the Egyptian and killed him. Even though Moses had spent his whole life in Pharaoh's family, killing an Egyptian was a great crime for a Hebrew. In fear of Pharaoh's anger, Moses ran away to Midian. There he became a shepherd.

One day while watching his sheep, Moses noticed a nearby bush on fire. There was nothing alarming about that. Often, a dried bush would burst into flame in the hot desert sun. Then the flame would quickly die. This flame did not go out. Moses decided to go nearer and find out why.

GOD

> *Do not come any closer.*
> *Take off your sandals,*
> *because you are standing*
> *on holy ground.*
> *I am the God of your ancestors,*
> *the God of Abraham,*
> *Isaac, and Jacob. . . .*
>
> *I have seen how cruelly*
> *my people are being treated*
> *in Egypt. . . .*
> *I am sending you to the king*
> *of Egypt so that you can lead*
> *my people out of his country.*

MOSES

> *I am nobody.*
> *How can I go to the king*
> *and bring the Israelites*
> *out of Egypt?*

GOD	*I will be with you. . . .*
MOSES	*When I go to the Israelites and say to them, "The God of your ancestors sent me to you," they will ask me, "What is his name?" So what can I tell them?*
GOD	*I am who I am. You must tell them: "The one who is called I AM has sent me to you.". . . This is my name forever.*

EXODUS 3:5–7, 10–15

By telling Moses his name—"I AM"—God entered into a personal relationship with him. The Hebrews believed that to tell another person your name was to give that person your trust and friendship.

The Hebrew spelling of God's name is YHWH (Hebrew has no vowels). We translate YHWH as LORD in English Bibles.

Latter-day Jews never pronounced God's name. Thus its pronunciation became lost. Medieval scholars decided YHWH should be pronounced "Y-*a*-H-*o*-W-*a*-H," or Jehovah in English. Scholars no longer accept this pronunciation, even though some religious groups still use it. Modern scholars, with better resources at their disposal, say YHWH is pronounced Yahweh.

These hieroglyphic symbols date back to the time of Rameses II, the Pharaoh in Moses' day.

Moses Confronts Pharaoh

After Moses met God in the burning bush, his life as a simple shepherd was over. Returning to Egypt, he told his story to the Israelites. They believed and accepted him as a prophet, someone who spoke for God. Then Moses went to Pharaoh.

MOSES	*The LORD, the God of Israel, says, "Let my people go. . . ."*
PHARAOH	*Who is the LORD? Why should I listen to him and let Israel go? I do not know the LORD; and I will not let Israel go.*

EXODUS 5:1–2

Nine different times Moses presented his demands to Pharaoh. Nine times Pharaoh refused. After each refusal, something terrible happened to the Egyptian people. These happenings have come to be known as the plagues:

1. the Nile changed to blood,
2. frogs carpeted the land,
3. gnats swarmed as thick as dust,
4. flies buzzed everywhere,
5. boils infected the people and the animals,
6. animals toppled over sick,
7. hail splintered trees and plants,
8. locusts devoured what the hail had missed,
9. darkness blanketed the land.

Even after the nine plagues, Pharaoh still remained stubborn.

> Then the LORD said to Moses,
> "I will send only one more punishment
> on the king of Egypt and his people.
> After that he will let you leave.
> In fact, he will drive all of you out. . . ."
> Moses then said to the king,
> "The LORD says, 'At about midnight
> I will go through Egypt,
> and every first-born son in Egypt will die.' "
> EXODUS 11:1, 4–5

God then instructed Moses to prepare the Israelites for the tenth and final plague.

The Passover

God told the Israelites to sacrifice a lamb and smear its blood on the outer door frame of their houses. Once this was done, they were to remain indoors.

> When the LORD goes through Egypt
> to kill the Egyptians, he will see the blood
> on the beams and the doorposts
> and will not let the Angel of Death
> enter your houses and kill you.
> EXODUS 12:23

To celebrate the angel's "passing over" their houses, God told the Israelites to eat the sacrificed lamb whose blood will save them. This celebration, called the *Passover,* was to become a regular part of their religious worship. It was to be celebrated each year.

> "When your children ask you,
> 'What does this ritual mean?' you will answer,
> 'It is the sacrifice of Passover
> to honor the LORD, because he passed over
> the houses of the Israelites in Egypt.
> He killed the Egyptians, but spared us.' "
> EXODUS 12:26–27

The final plague struck in the middle of the night. The Bible describes it this way:

> At midnight
> the LORD killed all the first-born sons
> in Egypt. . . .
> There was loud crying throughout Egypt,
> because there was not one home
> in which there was not a dead son.
> EXODUS 12:29–30

God Frees His People

The same night that the final plague struck, Pharaoh called Moses and his brother Aaron and said, "Get out, you and your Israelites! . . . Take your sheep, goats, and cattle, and leave" (*Exodus 12:31–32*). With shouts of joy, the Israelites began their great "exodus" from Egypt. It was a moment they would never forget.

In the days that followed, the Lord led his people with a "pillar of cloud" by day and a "pillar of fire" by night (*Exodus 13:21*). Bible readers ask, "Could these pillars have been caused by an active, fiery volcano sending up a column of smoke that glowed like a pillar of fire at night?"

There are volcanoes in the Sinai mountains, but scholars have found no evidence that they were active at this time. They prefer to interpret the "pillars" as an expression of Israel's experience of God's guiding hand during their flight from Egypt.

Meanwhile, Pharaoh regretted letting the Israelites go. So he sent his army after them and caught up with them at the Red Sea.

> Moses held out his hand over the sea,
> and the LORD drove the sea back
> with a strong east wind.
> It blew all night
> and turned the sea into dry land.
> The water was divided, and the Israelites
> went through the sea on dry ground,
> with walls of water on both sides.

The Egyptians pursued them. . . .
The LORD . . . made the wheels
of their chariots get stuck,
so that they moved with great difficulty. . . .

The LORD said to Moses,
"Hold out your hand over the sea. . . ."
So Moses held out his hand over the sea,
and at daybreak the water returned
to its normal level . . .
and covered the chariots, the drivers,
and all the Egyptian army. . . .

On that day
the LORD saved the people of Israel . . .
and they had faith in the LORD
and in his servant Moses.
EXODUS 14:21–28, 30–31

The Bible calls the crossing place *yam suph.* While this is usually translated as "Red Sea," it can also be translated "Reed Sea." This latter translation suggests that the area was a marshland, typical of lake regions. The biblical account seems to support this when it says of the Egyptians, "The LORD . . . made the wheels of their chariots get stuck."

Again, it is not important whether the Egyptians got stuck and were drowned by an incoming tide from the sea. What is important is that God rescued the Israelites in their hour of need.

God Covenants His People

It doesn't make sense! Historians shake their heads. How did it happen? How did a band of ex-slaves, with no organization, no education, and no apparent way to survive, change the tide of history? This is just what Moses and the Israelites eventually did.

The only explanation that makes sense is Israel's own explanation. At the foot of Mount Sinai the Israelites met God. In the course of that meeting, God made a covenant (sacred agreement) with them. That covenant changed them in a remarkable way. It gave them a new identity and a new destiny.

Their new identity was to be God's chosen people. They were called to be a holy nation, a people set apart and loved by God in a special way.

Their new destiny was to be God's chosen instrument. They were called to be the special means by which God would reveal himself to all people of all times.

Here is how the Bible describes what happened at Mount Sinai:

NARRATOR *The people of Israel . . .*
on the first day of the third month
after they had left Egypt . . .
set up camp
at the foot of Mount Sinai,
and Moses went up the mountain
to meet with God. . . .

GOD *You saw . . .*
how I carried you
as an eagle carries her young
on her wings,
and brought you here to me.
Now, if you will obey me
and keep my covenant . . .
you will be my chosen people,
a people dedicated to me alone,
and you will serve me as priests.

NARRATOR *So Moses went down*
and called the leaders
of the people together
and told them everything
that the LORD had commanded him.

PEOPLE *We will do everything*
that the LORD has said. . . .

NARRATOR *On the morning of the third day*
there was thunder and lightning,
a thick cloud
appeared on the mountain,
and a very loud trumpet blast
was heard.
All the people in the camp
trembled with fear. . . .
The LORD came down
on the top of Mount Sinai
and called Moses
to the top of the mountain.
EXODUS 19:1–8, 16, 20

What Happened?

The ancient Egyptian stone carving shown here pictures slaves carrying a boat. Israelite slaves, like these, were saved by the plagues.

Few biblical events have caused more discussion than the plagues. Were they natural events or not? Some say yes. Others say no. Some hold that only the timing was miraculous.

Typical of the discussion is this excerpt from *Everyday Life in Bible Times* by the National Geographic Society.

> *Extraordinary as they seem,*
> *these plagues have natural counterparts today.*
> *Silt and microbes*
> *sometimes pollute and redden the Nile in flood.*
> *"The River,"*
> *laments a text ancient in Moses' day, "is blood.*
> *If one drinks of it,*
> *one rejects it as human and thirsts for water."*
>
> *Floodlands breed gnats and mosquitoes;*
> *even ancients took refuge under netting.*
>
> *Frogs breed when the river peaks;*
> *hordes hop ashore from freak floods. . . .*
>
> *As frog swarms die,*
> *vermin breed on the carcasses.*
> *Pests such as the screwworm fly*
> *inflame skin of man and beast,*
> *sometimes killing animals.*
>
> *Though hailstorms rarely hit Egypt,*
> *locusts menace it still.*
> *Some African swarms blanket 2,000 square miles,*
> *stripping the land,*
> *fouling the air with excrement,*
> *triggering epidemics as locust bodies rot.*

> *Modern Egypt has tried traps, poison,*
> *even flamethrowers, but swarms still threaten*
> *devastation about once a decade.*
> *And the khamsin still howls—*
> *the hot desert sandstorm*
> *that darkens spring days.*

Similarly, the remarkable events that accompanied the Israelites' journey into the desert have caused much discussion.

For example, Moses is described as getting water from a rock by striking it with a rod (Exodus 17). Some people read this episode with disbelief. But in the 1930s Major C. S. Jarvis, the British governor of the Sinai, reported seeing water gush from a pocket in a limestone rock when a workman accidentally cracked through the rock's outer crust with a shovel.

Likewise, the "rain" of manna and quail upon the Israelite camp (Exodus 16) is often questioned. But history and a knowledge of the desert are shedding new light on these episodes.

The manna may have been related to the sap that flows from certain desert shrubs and trees when their bark is punctured by insects. The sap dries into a sweet flaky substance and can be eaten.

Finally, "falling quail" are still reported today. Every year, quail migrate between Europe and Africa. After their long flight across the Mediterranean they drop to the ground, exhausted, and can be easily caught.

Were the desert episodes miracles? Were they natural happenings? One thing is clear. As the Israelites remembered the chain of events that marked their difficult days in the desert, they were convinced beyond a shadow of doubt that the guiding hand of God was at work in their lives.

Then God handed over to Moses his Law—the Law that is now commonly called the Ten Commandments:

1. I am the LORD your God who brought you out of Egypt where you were slaves. Worship no god but me.
2. Do not use my name for evil purposes.
3. Observe the Sabbath and keep it holy.
4. Respect your father and your mother.
5. Do not commit murder.
6. Do not commit adultery.
7. Do not steal.
8. Do not accuse anyone falsely.
9. Do not desire another man's . . . wife.
10. Do not desire anything else that [another person] owns. (*Exodus 20:2–3, 7–8, 12–17*)

Moses wrote down everything the Lord commanded. Early the next morning, he built an altar at the foot of the mountain. After sacrificing some cattle, he read from the covenant tablets to the people. Then, to seal the covenant, he poured half of the animal blood on the altar and half on the people. As he sprinkled the blood on the people, Moses said:

> *"This is the blood that sealed the covenant which the LORD made with you when he gave all these commands."*
> EXODUS 24:8

After this, Moses took the seventy leaders of Israel and went up the mountain. There they "saw God" and shared a sacred meal together (Exodus 24:11).

The mountains of the Sinai speak of danger, challenge, and mystery.

New Life-style

Israel's meeting with God at the foot of Mount Sinai changed the people's vision of themselves and their lives. They had promised to do everything that the Lord had said. And so they took on a whole new life-style.

Their guide was the Ten Commandments. The people cherished the commandments as a special sign of God's love for them. They saw them as something precious. The commandments were God's own guidelines for freeing them from selfishness and setting them on the road to love and service. The Israelites summed up their feelings about the commandments in this prayer to God:

> *How I love your law! . . .*
> *How sweet is the taste of your instructions—*
> *sweeter even than honey! . . .*
> *Your word is a lamp to guide me*
> *and a light for my path.*
> PSALM 119:97, 103, 105

Modern Jews celebrate the feast of Simchat Torah ("Rejoicing in the Law").

New Worship Style

Israel's covenant experience also introduced the people to a new worship style.

While the Israelites were encamped at the foot of Mount Sinai, God instructed Moses to take the stone tablets on which the Ten Commandments were written and place them in a special container called the ark of the covenant. The ark was placed behind a curtain in a specially designed tent, or tabernacle.

When the tent was complete, and the ark was placed in it behind the curtain, "the dazzling light of the LORD's presence filled" the tent (*Exodus 40:34*). *Thus, besides serving as a house of the ark, the tent also served as the house of God's presence among his chosen people.* Because Moses used to go into the tent to "meet" God and talk to him, the structure was also known as the "meeting tent."

Typical of Israel's new worship style is the Day of Atonement, Yom Kippur. This day was set aside each year to ask God's forgiveness for the sins of the past year. It was the only day of the year when the high priest, who was in charge of the meeting tent and the worship services held there, would go behind the curtain into what was called the holy of holies.

The high priest sprinkled sacrificial goat's blood on the ark to seek forgiveness for the sins of the community. After that came the "scapegoat" ceremony.

Leaving the holy of holies, the high priest took a goat, placed his hands on its head, and confessed over it the sins of the community. This symbolized transferring the community's sins to the goat's head. The ceremony ended with the goat being driven off, carrying the sins away into the desert (Leviticus 16:20–22).

Although the ceremony was dramatic, the important thing was not just the ceremony, but the community's spirit of sorrow that gave it meaning.

God Tests His People

Moses and the people stayed at Mount Sinai for about a year. Then, they broke camp and set out into the desert in search of a land that God had promised them.

The desert into which the Israelite caravans went was made up of three regions: stretches of sand where nothing grew; expanses of rock, with an occasional spring; and patches of semiarid land, with just enough growth to nourish sheep and goats. This vast wilderness of sand and rock became the stage for a forty-year-long drama of Israelite history. The fourth book of the Bible—the Book of Numbers—narrates it with disarming candor.

Once the Israelites penetrated the desert, discouragement set in. The honeymoon days of Mount Sinai quickly faded. Any desert traveler who has experienced the blazing heat of the Sinai can understand the Israelites' reaction.

This does not excuse the years of grumbling and complaining on the part of the Israelites. It does, however, explain why the people began to long for the green fields of the Nile delta. Soon, discouragement gave way to outright protest.

> *"In Egypt*
> *we used to eat all the fish we wanted,*
> *and it cost us nothing. . . .*
> *But now our strength is gone.*
> *There is nothing at all to eat—nothing*
> *but this manna day after day!"*
> NUMBERS 11:5–6

The situation went from bad to worse, and the people singled out Moses as their target.

> *"Why have you*
> *brought us out into this wilderness?*
> *Just so that we can die here*
> *with our animals?. . .*
> *There is not even any water to drink!"*
> NUMBERS 20:4–5

Death of Moses

Eventually, after forty years of wandering, the Israelites emerged from the desert. They camped on the high plateaus of Moab. Stretching out below them lay a green and fertile valley—as far as the eye could see. This was the Promised Land.

Moses called the people together for instruction before entering the land. The Book of Deuteronomy records the spirit of this series of instructions. Moses explained how Israel's desert experience was a way of testing its loyalty to God.

> *"Remember how the LORD your God led you . . .*
> *through the desert these past forty years,*
> *sending hardships to test you,*
> *so that he might know*
> *what you intended to do*
> *and whether you would obey his commands."*
> DEUTERONOMY 8:2

But Moses, the hero of the covenant, never left the plains of Moab. He died before entering the land which God had promised.

> *So Moses, the LORD's servant,*
> *died there in the land of Moab. . . .*
> *The LORD buried him in a valley in Moab,*
> *opposite the town of Bethpeor,*
> *but to this day no one knows*
> *the exact place of his burial. . . .*
>
> *The people of Israel*
> *mourned for him for thirty days*
> *in the plains of Moab.*
> DEUTERONOMY 34:5–6, 8

It is one of the ironies of history that great leaders who fight valiantly for causes often die without enjoying the results of their struggles.

The death of Moses is the final entry in the Jewish Torah, which is the name given to the first five books of the Bible. These books are Genesis, Exodus, Leviticus, Numbers, and Deuteronomy. The Torah is the foundation upon which the rest of the Old Testament is built.

Understanding Covenant

Review

1. How was Moses saved from death as a baby? Why did he flee Egypt as a young man?

2. How did Moses meet God in the desert? What did God say his name was? How is it spelled in Hebrew, pronounced, and translated into English?

3. Give one example to show how some people think the plagues may have a natural explanation. What is the point of the plagues?

4. How did the Israelites protect their firstborn from the tenth plague? What meal was instituted to commemorate this event?

5. How did God guide the Israelites in the desert? Provide them with food and drink?

6. What is a covenant, and what new identity and destiny did it give the Israelites? How was it sealed?

7. List the Ten Commandments. How did the Israelites look upon the Ten Commandments? What name did they give to the container in which the tablets of the commandments were kept? Why was the tent in which the container was housed called the "meeting tent"? What else (special presence) did the meeting tent house?

8. What is the purpose of Yom Kippur? Explain the symbolism behind the ancient scapegoat ceremony.

9. What book of the Bible describes what happened to the Israelites between the time they left Mount Sinai and their arrival at the Promised Land? What purpose did this period serve?

10. What five books make up the Torah? With what event does the Torah end?

Discuss

1. A newspaper reporter asked Cecil B. DeMille, producer of *The Ten Commandments,* what commandment people today break most often. DeMille answered, "The first commandment. It's the one Israel broke first, and it's the one we break most. Oh, we don't worship idols, but we do worship a lot of other gods."

What is DeMille's point? Name some of the "other gods" people worship today.

2. A man said, "When I misuse God's name, I don't mean anything by it. It's just a bad habit I've gotten into."

What would happen if you used that excuse with a police officer who caught you speeding, or with a boss the next time you are late for work? Why do some of your friends misuse God's name?

3. A Jewish rabbi said, "The Sabbath kept Israel more than Israel kept the Sabbath."

What is the rabbi's point? Why does/doesn't it apply also to Christians and Sundays? Why do some of your friends fail to worship on Sunday?

4. The British writer George Bernard Shaw said, "The liar's punishment is not that he is not believed, but that he can't believe anyone else."

What is Shaw's point? Why is lying so widespread today?

Activities

1. *Newsweek* magazine for October 11, 1976, contains a story with photos of the mummified remains of Rameses II.

Find the magazine in a library. Prepare a brief report on it, and make a photocopy of the photographs to pass around to the group.

2. Check back issues of the daily newspaper for an article that reminds you of the Hebrews' struggle for freedom.

Clip the article and do a brief report, explaining why it reminds you of their struggle.

3. Judge William Campbell gives this description of an unborn baby in a court decision on abortion:

Seven weeks after conception the fertilized egg develops into a well-proportioned small-scale baby. . . . It has muscles, hands with fingers and thumbs; legs have recognizable knees, ankles and toes. . . . The brain is operative. . . . The heart beats; the stomach produces digestive juices; the liver manufactures blood cells.

What is Judge Campbell's point. Against what commandment is the taking of human life? Check the yellow pages for abortion services. What did you find? Describe any pro-life activity you have been involved in.

4. Exodus 25:10–22 describes the ark of the covenant.

Make a model or drawing of the ark. For additional help on how the ark looked, ask the librarian where you might find drawings or pictures of it.

Bible Reading

Pick a passage. After reading it, (1) summarize its main point, (2) tell how it relates to the chapter, and (3) list one or two thoughts that entered your mind as you read it.

1. Tired arms Exodus 17:6–16
2. Hurray for God! Psalm 136
3. Unfriendly neighbors Numbers 20:14–20
4. Moses gets angry Deuteronomy 9:15–10:5
5. Unusual laws Deuteronomy 24:5–12

Prayer Journal

Moses' first experience of God occurred at the burning bush. A symbol for his experience might be fire.

Describe a time when you seemed to experience God's presence in a special way. Choose a symbol for it. Mount it on a sheet along with a description of your experience. Here is one student's description and symbol.

> My first big experience of God occurred in my sophomore year.
>
> One night, I was ice skating with some friends in a lagoon off a big lake. We had a fire burning and everyone was laughing and talking. For some strange reason, I felt moved to leave my friends and skate out alone into the dark on the lake. It was like I was being called. The moon was bright and there was about a half inch of snow on the ice. All of a sudden, I got this really great feeling. I loved everything and everybody. I remember thinking to myself: "This must be what heaven is like." I talked to God as I stood all alone in the center of the lake. Then I returned to my friends. I didn't tell them what happened.
>
> If I had to choose a symbol for my God experience, I'd choose a pair of ice skates.

5 Nationhood

"Moses is dead!" When the reality of these words sank in, some Israelites had second thoughts about entering the Promised Land. They feared its Canaanite inhabitants. But their fears were ill founded. Archaeological records show the Canaanite fortifications were weak at this time.

The land itself was a spectacular sight. A ten-mile-wide valley cut through the center of it. At the northern end was the Sea of Galilee; at the southern end, the Dead Sea. The two seas were linked by the Jordan River.

The People Enter the Land

Before Moses died, he put Joshua in command of the people. When Joshua had completed all preparation, he led the Israelites to the bank of the Jordan. Horns sounded, and the crossing began. The first to cross were the priests carrying the ark of the covenant.

As soon as the priests stepped into the river,
the water stopped flowing and piled up. . . .
The flow downstream to the Dead Sea
was completely cut off.
JOSHUA 3:15–16

The stoppage of the Jordan has led some people to ask if it could have been related to an earthquake. The question is not out of line because the Jordan lies along an earth fault that has produced several earthquakes in history. One occurred in 1927, killing five hundred people. A landslide from this quake blocked the Jordan for twenty-four hours.

Whether an earthquake dammed the Jordan or not is incidental. The point of the biblical story is that God was with his people, just as he was when they crossed the Red (Reed) Sea. The two crossings are opposite sides of the same coin. The first marks the Israelites' *exit* from the land of slavery. The second marks their *entry* into the land of freedom.

Once the Israelites had crossed, Joshua pitched camp and prepared to attack the city of Jericho. God promised Joshua:

"I am putting into your hands Jericho. . . .
March around the city seven times
while the priests blow the trumpets.
Then they are to sound one long note.

53

As soon as you hear it,
all the men are to give a loud shout,
and the city walls will collapse."
JOSHUA 6:2, 4–5

Joshua did as the Lord commanded, and the walls came tumbling down. Once again, people ask if an earthquake could have been involved. And once again, the question is not a bad one. Archaeological excavations show that earlier in Jericho's history an earthquake had destroyed its walls. But there is no clear evidence that such was the case in Joshua's time. Maybe time has erased the evidence.

After Jericho fell, Joshua quickly captured other strategic cities in the land.

Clay tablets found in Egypt testify to a
weakened Canaan prior to Joshua's invasion.

Book of Joshua

Israel's entry into the Promised Land is described in the Book of Joshua. Although some Bibles list it as a "historical" book, it is not historical in our modern sense of the word.

First, much of the book was handed down orally for generations before being written down.

Second, the victories of Joshua's armies were simplified, and the time between them has been telescoped. This is typical of oral communication.

But there is another reason for the simplification. The editor of the book wants to make sure that its point is not lost: God, and not Joshua's armies, is responsible for the takeover of the land.

Ancient Graveyards

Archaeologists have excavated many of the sites referred to in the Book of Joshua. The location of such sites is rather easy to spot. They assume the appearance of a lone hill standing on a plain.

Called "tells," these hills contain the remains of long-destroyed cities. Wind, sand, and centuries have buried them, giving them the appearance of a hill or mound.

Excavated tell at Beer-Sheva.

To understand how tells developed, we must realize that when an ancient city was destroyed by fire or war, the debris of the old city was not carted away. The inhabitants merely built on top of the debris. The walls of the destroyed city were simply built higher. Thus, they contained the tell as it grew.

Some tells have ten to twelve layers, meaning that the debris from ten or twelve cities is piled up in pancake fashion. The University of Chicago uncovered twenty strata in the thirteen-acre tell at Megiddo (1 Kings 9:15). The site has witnessed so many historic battles that the author of the Book of Revelation made it the symbolic site for the final battle on earth between the forces of good and evil. The book refers to the site as Armageddon, that is, *har* ("Mount") Megiddo (Revelation 16:16).

Close-up of tell.

Death of Joshua

Eventually, Joshua secured the land for his people. He divided it into twelve parts, one for each of the twelve tribes of Israel (descendants of Jacob's twelve sons).

When Joshua reached old age, he ordered the tribes to gather at Shechem, the site where God told Abraham, "This is the country that I am going to give to your descendants" (*Genesis 12:7*).

Joshua began by reviewing what God had done for the Israelites over the centuries: rescued them from Egypt, guided them across the trackless desert, given them the Promised Land.

Joshua ended his "farewell address" by having the people renew the Sinai covenant.

> *Then Joshua sent the people away,*
> *and everyone returned*
> *to his own part of the land. After that,*
> *the LORD's servant Joshua son of Nun died.*
> JOSHUA 24:28–29

Book of Judges

What happens when a leader dies and there is no one to take his place? This problem faced the twelve tribes after Joshua died. Without a leader, they were without direction. As a result they drifted further and further from the covenant. Soon they even began to worship other gods.

When this happened, something else occurred. God left the people on their own, and enemy armies began to conquer them tribe by tribe. In their fear and panic the people turned back to God. And God rescued them.

This pattern repeats itself over and over in the Book of Judges. We might compare it to a play with four acts.

Act I	The people sin.
Act II	God punishes them.
Act III	The people repent.
Act IV	God forgives them.

Typical of this pattern was Israel's struggle against the Canaanite king, named Jabin.

Act I
. . . the people of Israel
sinned against the LORD again.

Act II
So the LORD let them be conquered by Jabin,
a Canaanite king.

Act III
Then the people of Israel
cried out to the LORD for help.

Act IV
Deborah . . . was serving as a judge
for the Israelites. She sent for Barak. . . .
Deborah said to Barak,
"Go! The LORD is leading you!
Today he has given you victory!"
JUDGES 4:1–4, 6, 14

The name *Deborah* introduces us to that colorful line of leaders called judges. Giving their name to the Book of Judges, they provided leadership from Joshua's death (ca. 1220 B.C.) to the coming of the kings (ca. 1020 B.C.). Besides Deborah, there were also men like Gideon, Jephthah, and Samson (Judges 6–8; 11; 13–16).

These judges were not black-robed figures who sat in courtrooms and decided cases. They were leaders or champions who surfaced at key times to defend Israel, uphold her honor, and lead her back to God.

The judges were not always holy people. On the contrary, they were products of their time. God acted through them, in spite of their personal shortcomings. Such a person was Samson.

Belonging to the tribe of Dan, Samson is said to have owed his legendary strength to his uncut hair. A mistress, Delilah, learned his secret, cut his hair while he slept, and betrayed him to the Philistines. They imprisoned him, blinded him, and condemned him to work like an animal.

Eventually, Samson's hair grew back and so did his strength. He restored Israel's honor by toppling the center columns of a Philistine temple, killing five of their leaders, who were worshiping their pagan god.

Once again, in Samson's case, the fourfold theme of the Book of Judges is dramatized; sin, punishment, repentance, and forgiveness.

Book of Ruth

The brief Book of Ruth brings to a close the two-hundred-year Era of the Judges. It tells the story of a non-Jewish woman (Ruth) and her kindness toward her Jewish mother-in-law (Naomi).

The book serves as a bridge between the Era of the Judges and the Era of the Kings. It does this by presenting a family tree that leads to David, Israel's greatest king.

> *Ruth . . . became pregnant and had a son. . . .*
> *The women . . . named the boy Obed. . . .*
> *Obed became the father of Jesse,*
> *who was the father of David.*
> RUTH 4:13, 17

Bowl with unique Philistine design.

The People Become a Nation

When the Era of the Judges ended, Israel was like a ship without a captain. It had no leader. Into this gap stepped Samuel. Although details of his life are sketchy, his role in Israel's history is clear and powerful. For this reason alone, he deserves to have two books of the Bible bear his name.

Perhaps the best way to describe Samuel's role is to say that he was a "bridge man" between the Era of the Judges and the Era of the Kings, just as the Book of Ruth was a "bridge book."

When Samuel took the helm, Israel was in danger from within and from without. From within, the people were drifting from the covenant. They were mixing worship of Baal, the Canaanite god, with worship of Yahweh. From without, they were being threatened by hostile neighbors.

The biggest threat came from the Philistines. Modern archaeologists trace their expansion along the borders of Israel through the unique design of their pottery. The reason the Philistines were such a threat was that they had learned to process iron ore and use it for military weapons. Thus, the Israelites found themselves on the losing end of an arms race.

In brief, the ship of state was in danger of sinking. Samuel had to do something drastic to save it. Samuel anointed a king to lead the nation.

King Saul

The man God inspired Samuel to anoint was Saul. Like the judges, Saul was a military hero.

> *After Saul became king of Israel,*
> *he fought all his enemies everywhere.*
> *Wherever he fought he was victorious.*
> 1 SAMUEL 14:47

But success has a way of turning a person's head. Soon Saul began to follow his own will instead of God's.

> *The LORD said to Samuel, "I am sorry*
> *that I made Saul king; he has turned away*
> *from me and disobeyed my commands."*
> 1 SAMUEL 15:10-11

As the star of Saul began to set, the star of another young man began to rise. That man was a young shepherd named David.

Michelangelo's David.

King David

While David tended his flocks on the hillside, he practiced the shepherd's best defense against wild animals: the slingshot. Little did he realize that his mastery of the slingshot would catapult him into the limelight of Israelite history.

David's unexpected moment came when Philistine armies crossed the borders of Israel and set up camp. A giant Philistine, named Goliath, dared any Israelite to fight him. When no one would, David (too young to be in the army) heard about the challenge and accepted it.

The slow-moving Goliath was no match for the quick-footed youth and his sling. David's shepherding days were over, and his career as a warrior was launched.

With natural battle instincts and with a flashing personality to match, David captured the imagination of everyone. Even Saul was eclipsed in the public eye by David.

> *Women from every town in Israel*
> *came out to meet King Saul. . . .*
> *In their celebration the women sang,*
> *"Saul has killed thousands,*
> *but David tens of thousands."*
> *Saul did not like this,*
> *and he became very angry.*
> *He said,*

> *"For David they claim tens of thousands,*
> *but only thousands for me.*
> *They will be making him king next!"*
> *And so he was jealous*
> *and suspicious of David from that day on.*
> 1 SAMUEL 18:6–9

Saul's resentment of David ended only with his own death. It happened during a battle on Mount Gilboa. Seeing his own three sons killed before his eyes, Saul fell on his own sword in anguish.

David became king after Saul's death. Under David's leadership, Israel began its "years of lightning." David quickly made Jerusalem the capital city and the center of religious worship. Eventually, he ordered the ark of the covenant to be brought into the city.

A stone portrayal of the ark of the covenant and the cart used to transport it.

Amid shouts of joy, the ark was carried into Jerusalem (2 Samuel 6:1–16). Once inside the city, it was placed in the "meeting tent."

Then one day David began feeling guilty about living in a house of cedar, while the ark (symbol of God's presence) dwelt in a tent. He decided to build a beautiful temple for the ark. But that night God appeared to the prophet Nathan and gave him this message for David:

> " 'You are not the one
> to build a temple for me. . . .
> I will make one of your sons king. . . .

He will be the one to build a temple for me,
and I will make sure
that his dynasty continues forever.
I will be his father, and he will be my son.' "
2 SAMUEL 7:5, 12–14

After David heard this glorious promise from Nathan, he went into the tent of the ark and gave thanks to God.

"LORD, I am not worthy
of what you have already done for me. . . .
How great you are. . . .
You have made Israel
your own people forever. . . .
And now, LORD God, fulfill for all time
the promise you made about me
and my descendants."
2 SAMUEL 7:18, 22, 24–25

God's promise that David's line will last forever is one of the most important in the Bible. It is the first of a series of promises that point to a person who, in time, will come to be known as the Messiah. The word *Messiah* means "anointed one" or "king." The series of "messianic" promises were eventually fulfilled in Jesus.

David and the Psalms

David is often credited with writing the Book of Psalms. Actually, he probably wrote only a few psalms. Ancient peoples frequently credited authorship to a great person who began or gave support to an important writing project.

Begun in David's time, the Book of Psalms was not completed until 400 B.C. Thus, over six hundred years elapsed before all 150 psalms were collected and edited into the form they now have.

The psalms may be divided into these five types: praise, wisdom, royal, thanksgiving, and lament.

Praise psalms concern God's glory and frequently begin "Praise the Lord."

Praise the LORD! . . .
Praise him with drums and dancing.
Praise him with harps and flutes.
PSALM 150:1, 4

Wisdom psalms concern human conduct and frequently begin "Happy are those."

Happy are those
who are concerned for the poor;
the LORD will help them
when they are in trouble.
The LORD will protect them.
PSALM 41:1–2

Royal psalms concern the king. Beginning with God's promise to David, the king became more than a political figure. He became a religious symbol as well. Each new king was one step closer to the coming of the "king of kings," the promised Messiah.

Long live the king! . . .
May prayers be said for him at all times;
may God's blessings be on him always!
PSALM 72:15

Thanksgiving psalms express gratitude to God for some benefit or blessing.

You have changed my sadness
into a joyful dance;
you have taken away my sorrow. . . .
I will give you thanks forever.
PSALM 30:11–12

Lament psalms are "songs of woe" in which the psalmist pours out his heart to God about some situation. They often deal with defeat at the hands of an enemy or injury at the hands of a wicked man.

I am like a wild bird in the desert. . . .
I am like a lonely bird on a housetop.
All day long my enemies insult me.
PSALM 102:6–8

Soul Book

Three teens climbing Mount Hood got trapped in a blizzard. They holed up in a snow cave. Sixteen days later, when they were down to a daily ration of two spoonfuls of pancake batter, the blizzard broke. How did they survive the long hours? "We read the Bible," they said, "especially the Book of Psalms."

The Book of Psalms was an excellent choice. More than any other biblical book, it puts readers in touch with the soul of Israel. It shows how the people prayed to God in times of danger, doubt, and joy.

Called Israel's prayerbook, the 150 psalms were not only prayed but sung. Thus they were Israel's hymnbook, as well. To catch the spirit of how they were sung, let us imagine two settings, especially.

The first is under the open stars at night. Gathered around a campfire are Israelites, relaxing after a day's work. Suddenly a man begins strumming a musical instrument. The crowd hushes, and he begins to sing:

> *Listen, my people,*
> *to my teaching, and pay attention to . . .*
> *things that our fathers told us.*
> *We will not keep them from our children;*
> *we will tell the next generation about*
> *the LORD's power and his great deeds.*
>
> PSALM 78:1, 3-4

Children learned the psalms by heart from their parents and sang them at play and at worship.

This blind harpist dates back to Hebrew slave days in Egypt.

A second setting in which the psalms were sung was in the Temple on holidays and on the Sabbath. At these times, they were not merely sung but performed.

Psalm 150 provides an insight into how elaborate these performances were. The psalm can be read in twenty seconds. Actually, it probably took closer to twenty minutes—perhaps even two hours—to perform.

Apparently written as a grand finale to worship, Psalm 150 was intended to be sung, played, and danced. Thus it involved a leader of song, a chorus, musicians, dancers, and the entire congregation.

> *Praise the LORD!*
>
> *Praise God in his Temple!*
> *Praise his strength in heaven!*
> *Praise him for the mighty things he has done.*
> *Praise his supreme greatness.*
>
> *Praise him with trumpets.*
> *Praise him with harps and lyres.*
> *Praise him with drums and dancing.*
> *Praise him with harps and flutes.*
> *Praise him with cymbals.*
> *Praise him with loud cymbals.*
> *Praise the LORD, all living creatures!*
>
> *Praise the LORD!*
>
> PSALM 150

David the Person

David was unmatched as a warrior and king. But when it came to being a human person, he was just like everyone else. He was weak. This weakness resulted in a great tragedy in his life. It led him to desire and steal the wife of a lowly soldier named Uriah.

The great King David, who had everything, robbed lowly Uriah of his only possession—his wife, Bathsheba, whom he loved dearly. Then to get rid of Uriah, David had him sent into battle on a suicide mission.

When Nathan, the prophet, learned about this, he was horrified. He knew he must confront David. But he wanted to do it in a way that would make David see how terrible his crime was. So he presented David with this imaginary case:

NATHAN   *There were two men*
who lived in the same town;
one was rich and the other poor.
The rich man had many cattle . . .
while the poor man
had only one lamb. . . .
He took care of it, and it grew up
in his home with his children. . . .
One day a visitor arrived
at the rich man's home.
The rich man didn't want to kill
one of his own animals
to fix a meal for him;
instead, he took the poor man's lamb
and prepared a meal for his guest. . . .

DAVID   *The man who did this ought to die! . . .*

NATHAN   *You are that man. . . .*
You had Uriah killed . . .
and then you took his wife! . . .

DAVID   *I have sinned against the LORD.*
2 SAMUEL 12:1–5, 7, 9, 13

Tragedy soon descended upon David. He and Bathsheba had a son, but the child died. Next, Absalom, David's son by a prior wife, revolted against his father and was killed by one of David's officers. Finally, death came for David himself.

Copper-bearing rocks still stand in the vicinity of Solomon's copper mines.

King Solomon

Solomon, another son of David and Bathsheba, succeeded his father to the throne. If David united Israel, Solomon made it strong. Clever in politics and shrewd in finance, Solomon entered the arena of international trade. Money poured in and the economy ballooned.

With the increase in income, Solomon stockpiled Israel's arsenal, purchasing an army of war horses and chariots. 1 Kings 10:26 says that Solomon built up a force of "fourteen hundred chariots and twelve thousand cavalry horses."

Solomon's greatest fame, however, lay in his gift of wisdom. It is this side of Solomon's portrait that the Bible paints most vividly.

God gave Solomon
unusual wisdom and insight. . . .
Solomon was wiser
than the wise men of the East. . . .
Kings all over the world . . .
sent people to listen to him.
1 KINGS 4:29–30, 34

But Solomon's greatest achievement was to fulfill his father's wish and build a temple. Taking more than seven years to build, the Temple was glorious. When it was finished, the priests placed the ark of the covenant in the Temple's special room, the holy of holies.

> *Solomon went and stood in front of the altar,*
> *where he raised his arms and prayed,*
> *"Lord God of Israel . . .*
> *not even all of heaven*
> *is large enough to hold you,*
> *so how can this Temple that I have built*
> *be large enough? . . .*
> *Hear my prayers and the prayers of your people*
> *when they face this place and pray."*
> 1 KINGS 8:22–23, 27, 30

It is hard to believe that the young Solomon who prayed that prayer ended up so tragically. But that is what happened. Prosperity took its toll, and Solomon's palace gradually took on all the glitter of a typical oriental court. Solomon began his career wisely but ended it foolishly.

> *So the Lord was angry with Solomon*
> *and said to him,*
> *"Because you have deliberately broken*
> *your covenant with me . . .*
> *I will take the kingdom away from you*
> *and give it to one of your officials. . . .*
> *I will leave him one tribe*
> *for the sake of my servant David*
> *and for the sake of Jerusalem,*
> *the city I have made my own."*
> 1 KINGS 11:10–13

Three Wisdom Books

Because of his great wisdom, Solomon is frequently credited with writing three "wisdom" books: Proverbs, Song of Songs, and Ecclesiastes. The first two books mention him by name; the third alludes to him.

Actually, Solomon probably did not write these books. As we saw earlier, ancient peoples frequently credited authorship to a great person who encouraged a writing project. Still, a brief word about these books is fitting here. Let's begin with the Book of Proverbs.

Every nation has its proverbs. For example, Russians have a proverb that says, "Pray to God but continue to row to the shore." Similarly, Italians say, "The same fire that burns the straw purifies the gold."

Cervantes described a proverb as "a short sentence based on long experience." Lord Russell described it as "the wisdom of many and the wit of one."

Israel had a great deal of proverbs. Many of them are recorded in the Book of Proverbs. The purpose of this book is to help everyone, especially the young, learn what is right. Typical of its sayings are these two:

> *If you repay good with evil,*
> *you will never get evil out of your house.*
> PROVERBS 17:13

> *If you refuse to listen to the cry of the poor,*
> *your own cry for help will not be heard.*
> PROVERBS 21:13

This brings us to the second book attributed to Solomon: the Song of Songs. It takes the form of a love poem. Consider this sample:

> *Come then, my love;*
> *my darling, come with me.*
> *The winter is over; the rains have stopped;*
> *in the countryside the flowers are in bloom.*
> *This is the time for singing;*
> *the song of doves is heard in the fields.*
> *Figs are beginning to ripen. . . .*
> *Come then, my love;*
> *my darling, come with me.*
> SONG OF SONGS 2:10–13

Some biblical scholars think the poem was used as part of the Israelite marriage ceremony. The groom's love for his bride is a symbol of God's love for Israel.

Thus the poem has two levels of meaning. On the surface it is a description of a love of two people. At a deeper level, it is an expression of God's love for his people.

The final book attributed to Solomon is Ecclesiastes, which is discussed in chapter 8.

Understanding Nationhood

Review

1. How are the crossing of the Reed Sea and the crossing of the Jordan River related?

2. Why isn't the Book of Joshua *historical* in the modern sense of the word?

3. Why did Joshua gather the twelve tribes at Shechem before he died?

4. What are tells, and how did they grow?

5. Explain the fourfold pattern that repeats itself in the Book of Judges. Who were the judges?

6. How does the Book of Ruth act as a bridge between the Era of the Judges and the Era of the Kings?

7. How does the person Samuel act as a bridge between these same two eras?

8. How did David first enter the limelight in Israel?

9. What two important moves did David make after becoming king?

10. What promise did God make to David through Nathan? Why is it such an important promise?

11. What role did the Book of Psalms play in Israel? How many psalms are there? List and briefly describe the five groups into which they are often divided.

12. What serious sin did David commit before he died?

13. Who succeeded David, and what was his greatest achievement? Explain how the reign of David's successor ended.

Discuss

1. A movie opens with a gunman stalking Hitler. When he gets him squarely within the crosshairs of his rifle, he pulls the trigger. "Click!" The gun is empty. The gunman smiles to himself and walks away unnoticed by police.

The rest of the movie is a flashback, giving the story behind the episode. The gunman never planned to kill Hitler. He merely wanted to prove to himself that he could if he wished. Read 1 Samuel 26 where David does almost the identical thing to Saul.

Do you think David did it for a similar reason? Explain.

2. David spared Saul's life because he respected the office of kingship, even though he disliked the person who occupied the office.

Explain the important distinction David makes between office and person. Give one or two examples to show how this distinction should also be kept in mind today.

3. David's decision to build a beautiful temple comes when he reflects, "Here I am living in a house built of cedar, while God's Covenant Box [symbol of God] is kept in a tent!" (*2 Samuel 7:2*). David concludes that God's house should be the most beautiful house in the world. Some people today take the opposite view. They complain about beautiful churches and say God would prefer us to spend all this money on the poor.

How do you feel about this issue?

4. What do the following proverbs mean?
  a. Whoever falls in love with himself will have no rivals.
  b. Strike now, while the iron is hot.
  c. Whoever is his own doctor has a fool for a patient.
  d. A stitch in time saves nine.
  e. Whoever makes no mistakes makes nothing.
  f. In the land of the blind, the one-eyed man is king.

5. Read what Proverbs 23:29-30 says about drinking. It is one of the most entertaining and colorful paragraphs in the book.

Explain why drinking is/isn't a problem among your friends.

Activities

1. Some people think there is a similarity between the psalms and certain modern songs.

Write out the lyrics to a song that you like. Explain why you like the song. Why do/don't you think its lyrics qualify as a modern psalm?

2. Psalm 29 is sometimes called the "Psalm of the Seven Thunders." Copy the psalm on a sheet of paper. Illustrate it with a photograph. Underline the "seven thunders" in the psalm.

3. Copy the following psalm excerpts on a sheet of paper: 30:11-12, 32:1-2, 38:9-11, 45:1-3, 103:1-2.

Under each excerpt, list whether it is from a praise, a royal, a wisdom, a lament, or a thanksgiving psalm. Underline the word or words that give the clue to the psalm's identity.

4. In spite of Saul's jealousy of David, a deep friendship developed between Jonathan and David. "Jonathan swore eternal friendship with David because of his deep affection for him" (*1 Samuel 18:3*). When Jonathan was killed in battle, David wept over his fallen body, saying, "'I grieve for you, my brother Jonathan; how dear you were to me! How wonderful was your love for me, better even than the love of women'" (*2 Samuel 1:26*).

List eight love relationships that are possible: for example, man for a man, brother for a sister. Which of these relationships is strongest in your own life? Explain.

Bible Reading

Pick a passage. After reading it, (1) summarize its main point, (2) tell how it relates to the chapter, and (3) list one or two thoughts that entered your mind as you read it.

1. Battle of wits   Joshua 9:3–27
2. The spies   Joshua 2
3. Voice in the dark   1 Samuel 3
4. Choice nobody expected   1 Samuel 16
5. Two prostitutes   1 Kings 3:16–28

Prayer Journal

Read Psalm 1. Using it as a model, compose your own psalm. Illustrate it with a photograph or a drawing. Here is how one person used the psalm as a model and rewrote it.

*Happy are those who don't copy their homework,
     but do it themselves.*
They are like an athlete who stays in condition.
*But the person who copies his work isn't like that
     at all.*
He is like an athlete who is out of shape.
He isn't ready when the time of testing comes.
Those who do their own homework will be happy.
Those who copy it from others will be sorry.

If you need a start on your psalm, here are some suggestions for an opening line:

*Happy are those who don't goof off during
     practice.*
Happy are those who don't make fun of others.
*Happy are those who don't pretend to be more than
     they are.*

6 Division

Years ago, someone did a study of Native Americans living on Pine Ridge Reservation in South Dakota. They found that 88 percent of Pine Ridge's ten thousand Native Americans lived in slums. Half were unemployed, largely because the nearest public transportation was thirty miles away. The life expectancy of the Pine Ridge red man was twenty-five years below that of the white man.

Fifty percent of the population was under twenty-one. Yet there were no movie theaters, drive-ins, or bowling alleys. Only one house in ten had electricity. And of the five hundred telephones on the reservation, most were in government offices and stores.

This study helps to explain why minority groups sometimes turn to violence to call attention to their plight.

Ignoring the plight of people also stirred up violence in ancient Israel when Solomon died.

Israel Revolts

During his reign, Solomon had taxed the people heavily in money and manpower for his national building projects. The people did not mind being taxed, but they did mind Solomon's tax system. There had always been a whispered suspicion that he overtaxed the ten northern tribes and undertaxed the two southern tribes.

When Solomon died and his son Rehoboam became king, the whispers became shouts. The ten northern tribes went to the king and demanded reform.

NARRATOR *King Rehoboam consulted the older men who had served as his father Solomon's advisers.*

KING *What answer do you advise me to give these people?*

OLD MEN *If you want to serve this people well, give a favorable answer to their request. . . .*

NARRATOR *But he ignored the advice . . . and went instead*

	to the young men who had *grown up with him. . . .*
KING	*What do you advise me to do?. . .*
YOUNG MEN	*Tell them, "My father* *placed heavy burdens on you;* *I will make them even heavier.* *He beat you with whips;* *I'll flog you with bullwhips!"* 1 KINGS 12:6–11

The king followed the advice of the young men. The ten northern tribes reacted swiftly. Uniting under a leader named Jeroboam, they revolted and broke with the southern tribes.

David's work of unification went down the drain. In 922 B.C. the kingdom split into two nations: Judah in the south and Israel in the north.

The leaders of Israel immediately set up religious centers at Bethel and Dan, in opposition to Jerusalem. These centers not only crippled religious unity but set the stage for religious idolatry.

Israel Declines

When Jeroboam died, political problems arose. As yet, the North had no clear line of kingship. The throne fell to whomever was strong enough to seize it. This created political trouble for about twenty-five years.

Eventually, a strong leader named Omri seized the kingship and stabilized the nation. He made Samaria the capital city of Israel and married off his son, Ahab, to a Phoenician princess named Jezebel. Thus Israel and Phoenicia became political friends. Next, Omri expanded Israel by defeating Mesha, king of Moab.

After Omri's death, Ahab succeeded him. He was a weak man and a weak king. New problems arose immediately. Ahab's wife, Jezebel, worshiped the pagan god Baal. With Omri dead, she persuaded Ahab to permit altars and priests of Baal to be located in Israel. That opened the door to religious idolatry.

Into the midst of this tragic situation stepped one of the great figures of Jewish history, Elijah.

The Prophet Elijah

No informed tourist to the Holy Land can enter the port of Haifa without thinking of Elijah. Incoming ships offer a breathtaking view of Mount Carmel.

At that site, twenty-five centuries ago, Elijah challenged the pagan god of Baal. He took on 450 prophets of Baal all by himself. A vast crowd of worshipers of Baal and of Yahweh gathered on the mountain to decide whether Baal or Yahweh was the true God. When all was ready, Elijah cried out:

ELIJAH	*Bring two bulls;* *let the prophets of Baal* *take one . . .* *and put it on the wood—* *but don't light the fire.* *I will do the same* *with the other bull.* *Then let the prophets of Baal* *pray to their god,* *and I will pray to the LORD,* *and the god who answers* *by sending fire—he is God.*
NARRATOR	*The people* *shouted their approval. . . .* *[The prophets began.]* *They shouted,* *"Answer us, Baal!"* *and kept dancing around* *the altar they had built.* *But no answer came.* *At noon,* *Elijah started making fun of them.*
ELIJAH	*Pray louder! He is a god!* *Maybe he is day-dreaming. . . .* *Or maybe he's sleeping,* *and you've got to wake him up!*
NARRATOR	*So the prophets prayed louder* *and cut themselves* *with knives and daggers,* *according to their ritual . . .* *but no answer came,* *not a sound was heard.* *Then Elijah . . .* *approached the altar and prayed.*
ELIJAH	*O LORD, the God of Abraham,* *Isaac, and Jacob . . . answer me,* *so that this people will know*

that you, the LORD, are God
and that you are bringing them
back to yourself.

NARRATOR   *The LORD sent fire down,*
and it burned up the sacrifice,
the wood, and the stones. . . .
When the people saw this,
they threw themselves on the ground.

PEOPLE   *The LORD is God;*
the LORD alone is God!
1 KINGS 18:23–30, 36–39

Few stories in the Hebrew Scriptures match this one for dramatic power. It has all the ingredients of good drama: hero, villain, suspense, and humor. Like the other stories about Elijah, it was passed on orally for centuries before being recorded. Storytellers recited it around campfires and in worship situations to teach the people that Yahweh alone is God and that Elijah's faith and courage should be a model for their own faith and courage.

Today, Elijah ranks with Moses as one of Judaism's greatest heroes. Christians also hold Elijah in the highest regard. Recall that during Jesus' transfiguration on Mount Tabor, Elijah (symbol of the prophets) and Moses (symbol of the Law) "appeared in heavenly glory and talked with Jesus" (*Luke 9:31*).

Eventually, Elijah's ministry came to an end. He was taken to heaven in "a chariot of fire pulled by horses of fire" (*2 Kings 2:11*). Symbolic or not, this description serves as a fitting climax to Elijah's glorious ministry.

Before Elijah left this earth, he communicated his prophetic gifts to Elisha, his disciple.

The Prophet Elisha

Elisha's ministry spanned fifty stormy years of history. He saw six kings come and go. Like Elijah, he won fame as a wonder-worker, healing the sick and even raising the dead (2 Kings 4:32–37). He also rerouted the line of northern kings. It happened this way.

After Ahab died, his two irresponsible sons followed him to the throne. If Ahab was bad, his sons were worse. Enough was enough! Elisha directed a military leader, Jehu, to be anointed king.

Jehu and his successors reigned nearly seventy-five years. They guided Israel through a dangerous era, managing to keep peace with the fierce Assyrians to the northeast.

Eventually, Jeroboam II ascended to the throne. Under his leadership, Israel enjoyed forty years of prosperity, but that prosperity was deceiving. The nation was shot through with decay. Baalism was ever-present. So was the scandalous gap between the rich and the poor.

Archaeological excavations at Samaria testify to this gap. There excavators found palaces and hovels side by side. They also found luxurious ivory carvings, confirming biblical reports of "houses decorated with ivory" (*Amos 3:15*). While the rich decorated their houses with ivory, the poor could hardly keep a roof over their heads.

Ivory comb, similar to ivory carvings and decorations found at Samaria.

The Assyrians

Their young men and their maidens
I burned in fire.
The heads of their warriors I cut off
and formed into a pillar over against
their city.

Archaeologists found this grotesque inscription while excavating the palace of an ancient Assyrian king. It paints a grim picture of Assyrian battle practices.

A stone panel from the palace confirms the Assyrian king's boast. It shows Assyrian warriors stacking up human heads against a city wall.

Archaeologists also found another panel showing how Assyrian soldiers had stripped and impaled captured enemy soldiers on spikelike poles on a hillside. The same panel shows Assyrian archers behind wicker shields, sending a shower of arrows toward their enemy.

Besides using brutal battle tactics, the Assyrians also used psychological warfare. They sent out paid agents ahead of their armies to frighten their enemy with false tales about their army's size and strength.

Terrified of the Assyrians' reputation, King Jehu of Israel struck up an uneasy truce with them. By a series of deals and lucky breaks, he and his successors reigned seventy-five years without engaging the Assyrians in battle.

The Writing Prophets Begin

Without the prophets, we would have no apostles. Without the prophets, Jesus would have remained a carpenter, unknown and unsung. Without the prophets, Muhammad would have stayed an obscure camel driver. This is another way of saying that the prophets kept faith alive in Israel when it flickered and almost went out.

Foremost among these "spiritual giants" were the "writing" prophets, those individuals whose words are recorded in books. They are sometimes divided into the four major prophets (long writings) and the twelve minor prophets (short writings). The major prophets are:

Isaiah	Ezekiel
Jeremiah	Daniel

The twelve minor prophets are:

Hosea	Jonah	Zephaniah
Joel	Micah	Haggai
Amos	Nahum	Zechariah
Obadiah	Habbakuk	Malachi

Also included among the prophetic books are two other works (associated with Jeremiah): the Book of Lamentations and the Book of Baruch.

For the most part, prophets and kings walk along together in the Bible. They are like the two rails of a train track. Wherever you find one, you usually find the other. This is because part of the prophet's job was to advise and correct the king. We see this in the case of Nathan and David. Nathan was both a *foreteller* (he communicated God's promise to David) and a *forthteller* (he confronted David for his crime against Uriah).

The Prophet Amos

The first writing prophet to speak out against Israel's treatment of the poor was Amos. Born near Bethlehem, he was a southerner, not a northerner. Strangely enough, he does not seem to have been especially prepared to prophesy to Israel. First, he was a citizen of Judah. Second, he was a simple farmer (Amos 7:14–15). Pointing his finger at the rich, who took advantage of the poor, Amos said:

> The LORD says . . . "They sell into slavery
> honest men who cannot pay their debts. . . .
> They trample down the weak and helpless
> and push the poor out of the way."
> AMOS 2:6–7

Besides speaking out against the rich, Amos spoke out against religious formalism. That is, he condemned the hypocritical way the people lived their religion. Failing to serve God in their daily lives, they eased their conscience by multiplying altars and sacrifices. Religion became an empty shell—all show and no soul. Speaking in God's name, Amos said:

> "I hate your religious festivals;
> I cannot stand them! . . .
> Stop your noisy songs;
> I do not want to listen to your harps.
> Instead, let justice flow like a stream,
> and righteousness like a river
> that never goes dry."
> AMOS 5:21, 23–24

Amos has been called the prophet of social justice. Indeed, he was. He stressed that social justice and religious worship are two sides of the same coin. Helping the poor and worshiping God go hand in hand. You cannot worship God and ignore your brothers and sisters.

As you would expect, Amos was unpopular with civil and religious authorities. He was a thorn in their side. There was only one thing to do: banish Amos, get rid of him! The priest of Bethel gave the order.

> "That's enough, prophet!
> Go on back to Judah
> and do your preaching there."
> AMOS 7:12

And so Amos shook the dust from his shoes and went back to his herds and fig trees. But his words continued to echo in Israel long after he left.

The Prophet Hosea

A prophet's shoes never remained empty long in Israel. After Amos left, a northern prophet took his place. That prophet was Hosea.

Hosea, too, was shocked at the evil in Israel and spoke out against it. His words, however, had a more compassionate ring than did the words of Amos. Perhaps this was due to the tragedy he suffered in his own personal life. He married an adultress, whom he loved deeply in spite of her sinful ways.

Conditioned by this painful experience, Hosea tried to draw Israel back to God's covenant by love, rather than by threat. He compared God's love for Israel to that of a loyal husband for his disloyal wife.

> She will run after her lovers
> but will not catch them. . . .
> Then she will say,
> "I am going back to my first husband—
> I was better off then than I am now."
> HOSEA 2:7

Later, Hosea compared God's love for Israel to that of a caring parent.

> "When Israel was a child, I loved him
> and called him out of Egypt as my son.
> But the more I called to him,
> the more he turned away from me. . . .
> How can I give you up, Israel?
> How can I abandon you? . . .
> My heart will not let me do it!
> My love for you is too strong."
> HOSEA 11:1–2, 8

The prophets disturbed the comfortable, but they also comforted the disturbed. Hosea did both with delicate balance. Sadly, however, neither Amos' loud shouts nor Hosea's gentle whispers could persuade Israel to turn back to God and the covenant.

Understanding Division

Review

1. What were the northern tribes' grievances against Solomon?

2. What happened when Rehoboam refused to redress their grievances?

3. What situation in the northern kingdom initiated the Era of the Prophets?

4. What two important points are made by the story of Elijah's encounter with the prophets of Baal?

5. What prophet succeeded Elijah?

6. Name one contribution Elisha made to Israel's history.

7. What situation in Israel sparked the "writing" prophets into action?

8. How many writing prophets are there? How many are known as major prophets? Why?

9. Why are prophets and kings often found paired up in the Old Testament?

10. What do we mean when we say prophets were "foretellers" and "forthtellers"?

11. Give two reasons why Amos seems to have been unprepared to be a prophet, especially to Israel.

12. What two evils, especially, did Amos preach against?

13. What brought an end to Amos' ministry in Israel, and who succeeded him?

14. How was his successor's approach to Israel different from Amos', and what influenced it?

Discuss

1. If we would shrink the earth's population to 1,000 people, only 60 of these people would be Americans. Yet, these 60 Americans would control half of the world's income and would own 15 times more material possessions than the average citizen on earth. Of the remaining 940 people, 60 people would be starving. Half of the babies born to these 60 starving people would die in infancy. The other half would be crippled mentally or physically for life.

   Why does this situation exist? How do you feel about it?

2. "Give a person a fish and you feed that person for a day. Teach a person to fish and you feed that person for a lifetime."

   How does this principle apply to helping the poor? What about those poor who are too old, sick, retarded, or handicapped to learn "to fish"?

3. A high school student council hosted an "Insight Day." It began with a film on world injustice. After the film, the students broke into discussion groups of six:

two students holding red tickets, two holding white tickets, and two holding blue tickets. The discussions were lifeless.

At noon, two dollars were collected from each student for lunch. When they got to the cafeteria, the red tickets got pizza, a burger, fries, and a shake. The white tickets got a burger and a soft drink. The blue tickets got a small bag of popcorn and a paper cup of lukewarm water.

After the meal, the students returned to their discussion groups to reflect on the experiment. This time the discussions were charged with emotion.

Why the difference in the discussions? Why call the day an "Insight Day"? What is your personal reaction to such a day?

4. In the light of social injustice, what point is being made by the following statements?

a. "Come, Debbie," coaxed her mother, "thousands of children in Ethiopia would give anything to eat potatoes like those on your plate." Debbie replied, "Name one!"

b. Under *Dog* in the yellow pages of the Evanston, Illinois, telephone directory is an ad for a "Pet Motel." Here are some of the services it provides for pets while their owners are vacationing:

Deluxe and imperial suites   Daily cookie breaks
FM music in every room   Beauty salon
Senior citizens' care plan   Tender loving care

c. "If a free society can't help the many who are poor, it cannot save the few who are rich" (John F. Kennedy).

d. A Christian looked up to heaven and shouted, "Lord, why don't you do something about poverty in the world?" A short pause ensued. Then a voice from heaven said, "I did do something. I made you."

Activities

1. Dramatize the encounter between Elijah and the prophets of Baal.

2. In the spirit of Amos, write a paragraph concerning social injustices that exist in your neighborhood, town, or city (for example, poor people are ignored or treated badly).

3. List some "prophets" who speak to us today. Why do you regard them as prophets? How are they like/different from Amos and Hosea?

4. Imagine you have just been appointed prophet to your city's mayor or to the president. What three injustices would you confront him with?

Bible Reading

Pick a passage. After reading it, (1) summarize its main point, (2) tell how it relates to the chapter, and (3) list one or two thoughts that entered your mind as you read it.

1. A dead boy lives   1 Kings 17:8–23
2. A terrible deed   1 Kings 21:1–19
3. Violent death   1 Kings 22:29–40
4. Day of doom   Amos 2:6–16
5. Where's your love?   Hosea 6

Prayer Journal

Prayer is speaking to God from the heart. It is being honest to God and not holding back on our feelings. It is telling it like it is.

Here is an excerpt from such a prayer by the prophet Jeremiah.

LORD . . .
Everyone makes fun of me;
they laugh at me all day long. . . .
I am ridiculed and scorned all the time
because I proclaim your message. . . .
I hear everybody whispering. . . .
Even my close friends wait for my downfall. . . .
Why was I born?
Was it only to have trouble and sorrow,
to end my life in disgrace?
JEREMIAH 20:7–8, 10, 18

Pick out some problem from your life or the world. Compose a prayer to God about it. Speak from the heart. You may wish to illustrate your prayer with a photograph from a magazine or newspaper.

If you need a start on your prayer, here are some suggestions for opening lines:

Lord, life is grossly unfair!
Lord, why did you make growing up such a hassle?
Lord, I don't understand why you created drugs
    like heroine and cocaine.

7 Exile

In *The Power and the Glory,* novelist Graham Greene describes a priest who lived in Mexico during a time of religious persecution. The danger of being caught and the work of serving his people finally got the best of him. The priest turned to drink and became an alcoholic. Eventually, he was caught and sentenced to death.

The morning of his execution, he awoke with an empty brandy flask in his hand. He tried to recite an act of contrition (prayer asking God to forgive him), but he was too confused to remember the words.

Suddenly, he caught sight of his shadow on the whitewashed wall. He stared at it for a minute. Then, tears rolled down his cheeks. He was not crying because he was afraid to die. He was crying because he had to go to God so empty-handed. At that moment, he would have given anything to be able to relive his life.

Israel Falls

A moment like this came for the northern tribes. In spite of Elijah and Elisha, in spite of Amos and Hosea, they did not change their ways. And so dawned the "Day of the Lord," the day of gloom without brightness (Amos 5:20).

The powerful Assyrians decided to invade Israel. The outcome was a foregone conclusion. In 722 B.C., the North fell to King Sargon II. What the prophets had tried to avoid was now written into the pages of history.

Most of the northern Jews were led away and never heard from again. Historians sometimes refer to them as the "lost tribes" of Israel. A few inhabitants, however, were allowed to remain behind. But their fate soon fell under a shadow. They intermarried with the occupation forces. This drew down upon them the hatred of all other Jews. The Samaritans, as they later became known, were never again held in respect.

Judah Drifts

Shock waves rumbled through the South when news arrived of Israel's fall. But the people of Judah did not panic. They naively believed that no such tragedy could strike them. Wasn't Judah ruled by David's successors? Weren't they heirs to God's promise of an unending kingship?

Perhaps this attitude explains why the southern kingdom started to drift into the same evils that destroyed the North: idolatry, religious formalism (going through the motions of worship), and mistreatment of the poor.

And so two prophets, Micah and Isaiah, began to step up their preaching in the South. Both had been calling for change before the fall. In fact, many of their warnings were aimed at the North.

The Prophet Micah

Micah is the lesser known of the two prophets. His unpolished style suggests that he was of humble origin, like Amos. Yet Micah could be forceful when he had to be. Speaking in God's name, he said:

> *"You attack my people like enemies.*
> *Men return from battle,*
> *thinking they are safe at home,*
> *but there you are, waiting*
> *to steal the coats off their backs.*
> *You drive the women of my people*
> *out of the homes they love,*
> *and you have robbed their children*
> *of my blessings forever. Get up and go;*
> *there is no safety here any more.*
> *Your sins have doomed this place*
> *to destruction."*
> MICAH 2:8–10

Although filled with warnings, Micah's prophecies are also laced with hope.

> *The LORD says, "Bethlehem Ephrathah,*
> *you are one of the smallest towns in Judah,*

> *but out of you I will bring a ruler*
> *for Israel. . . ." His people will live*
> *in safety . . . and he will bring peace.*
> MICAH 5:2, 4–5

New Testament writers recalled this prophecy shortly after Jesus' birth.

The Prophet Isaiah

No prophet, apart from Elijah, is more highly thought of than Isaiah. His ministry arched like a great umbrella over forty years of Judah's history. Born in Jerusalem, he was qualified by birth and education to walk with kings. In contrast to the rough manners of Micah, Isaiah was elegant and had class.

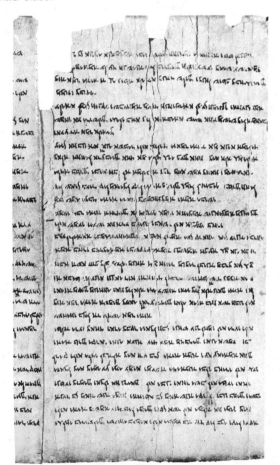

A portion of the "Isaiah Scroll" found in a cave near Qumran on the shore of the Dead Sea.

Scholars call him the prophet of God's holiness. This is because his writings show a deep appreciation of the holiness ("otherness") of God. This appreciation grew out of Isaiah's first encounter with God, an experience that frightened and fascinated him.

ISAIAH   *I saw the Lord.*
            He was sitting on his throne,
            high and exalted,
            and his robe filled the whole Temple.
            Around him flaming creatures
            were standing. . . .

CREATURES   *Holy, holy, holy!*
            The LORD Almighty is holy!
            His glory fills the world.

ISAIAH   *The sound of their voices*
            made the foundation of the Temple
            shake. . . .

            Then one of the creatures
            flew down to me,
            carrying a burning coal. . . .
            He touched my lips
            with the burning coal.

CREATURE   *This has touched your lips,*
            and now your guilt is gone,
            and your sins are forgiven.

ISAIAH   *Then I heard the Lord . . .*

LORD   *Whom shall I send?*
            Who will be our messenger?

ISAIAH   *I answered,*
            "I will go! Send me!"
            So he told me to go.
            ISAIAH 6:1–4, 6–9

Because of his keen sense of holiness, Isaiah spoke out wherever he found evil. Condemning religious formalism, he speaks for God, saying:

   "I am tired of the blood
   of bulls and sheep and goats. . . .
   It's useless to bring your offerings.
   I am disgusted
   with the smell of the incense you burn."
   ISAIAH 1:11, 13

Isaiah's purpose, however, was not to condemn the people, but to call them to conversion. God says through him:

"Stop all this evil that I see you doing. . . .
Help those who are oppressed, give orphans
their rights, and defend widows. . . .
Although your stains are deep red,
you will be as white as wool."
ISAIAH 1:16–18

Isaiah warned the people, however, that if they did not change their ways, they were "doomed to die" (*Isaiah 1:20*). One of his warnings is a moving parable, expressed in song.

Listen while I sing you this song,
a song of my friend and his vineyard:
My friend had a vineyard on a very fertile hill.
He dug the soil and cleared it of stones. . . .
He waited for the grapes to ripen,
but every grape was sour.

So now my friend says, "You people
who live in Jerusalem and Judah. . . .
Here is what I am going to do to my vineyard:
I will take away the hedge around it . . .
and let wild animals eat it and trample it. . . .
I will let briers and thorns cover it.
I will even forbid the clouds
to let rain fall on it."

Israel is the vineyard of the LORD Almighty;
the people of Judah are the vines he planted.
ISAIAH 5:1–3, 5–7

Isaiah's song began on a pleasant note, but ended with the bitter truth. Like an arrow, it pierced the hearer's heart.

Sadly, Isaiah's warnings fell on deaf ears. It soon became clear that only a shock would get the people to change their ways.

Judah Declines

The shock came in 705 B.C., during the reign of Hezekiah, one of Judah's few good kings during this period. Sargon II, who had just crushed the northern kingdom, was assassinated and replaced by the colorful Sennacherib. Hezekiah began to fear for his people. He knew that the new Assyrian king was a warrior at heart. Hezekiah's fears were well founded.

Prism of Sennacherib. A portion of this ancient record reads: "As for Hezekiah of Judah, he did not submit to me, so I laid siege to forty-six of his strong cities . . . and captured them. . . . I shut him up in Jerusalem . . . like a bird in a cage."

In 701 B.C., Sennecherib's armies marched toward Jerusalem. As they approached the city, warning horns sounded. Farmers fled their fields and raced to the city. The great bronze gates were slammed and bolted. Hezekiah and his generals waited nervously.

When the Assyrians came within striking range of the city walls, they pitched camp and prepared for battle. The people of Jerusalem were filled with terror. Then came a surprise. Isaiah sent this message to Hezekiah:

> *"This is what the LORD has said*
> *about the Assyrian emperor:*
> *'He will not enter this city*
> *or shoot a single arrow against it. . . .*
> *I will defend this city and protect it,*
> *for the sake of my own honor and because of*
> *the promise I made to my servant David.' "*
> 2 KINGS 19:32, 34

Night fell. A jittery Jerusalem lay awake in fear of the dawn. When the sun rose, the people could scarcely believe what they saw. The Assyrians were breaking camp and leaving.

When the Assyrian armies had gone, Hebrew patrols went out to the campsite and found it littered with dead.

Two books of the Bible report the event. The Second Book of Kings says, "an angel of the LORD went to the Assyrian camp and killed 185,000 soldiers" (*2 Kings 19:35*). The Book of Sirach says that God struck the Assyrian camp "with a plague" (*Sirach 48:21, NAB*).

Ancient historians, taking their cue from the Book of Sirach, suggest that a sudden outbreak of the bubonic plague triggered the disaster. (It was truly an "angel" from heaven in Judah's eyes.)

After the Assyrian pullout, Jerusalem breathed a sigh of relief. But it was to be short-lived. For, as Assyria's power faded, the power of Babylon began to grow. Babylon would soon play a major role in Judah's fate.

One would think the Assyrian scare would put the fear of God into the southern kingdom, but it did not. Things got worse. When Isaiah and Hezekiah died, Hezekiah's son, Manasseh, took the throne. Historians consider him Judah's worst king.

He sacrificed his son as a burnt offering.
He practiced divination and magic
and consulted fortunetellers and mediums.
He sinned greatly against the LORD
and stirred up his anger.

2 KINGS 21:6

No wonder there were few tears shed when Manasseh died in 638 B.C.

Eventually, the throne of Judah passed to an eight-year-old boy-king, Josiah. The youth turned out to be a remarkable ruler. In his twenties, he ordered the Temple remodeled. During the work, someone found an old book of the Law. When the book was read to Josiah, "he tore his clothes in dismay" (*2 Kings 22:11*). He saw how far Judah had wandered from the Law.

Josiah ordered a reform to take place in accord with the Law set down in the book. The reform was backed by an impressive group of prophets: Nahum, Zephaniah, Habakkuk, and Jeremiah.

Of these, Jeremiah towered above the rest like a giant.

The Prophet Jeremiah

The Book of Jeremiah blends prophecy, history, and biography. It portrays the failures of a nation and the feelings of a prophet who had to confront that nation.

Jeremiah appears to have been a deeply sensitive man. Like Josiah, he was called by God at a young age. Describing his response to the call, Jeremiah writes:

I answered, "Sovereign LORD,
I don't know how to speak; I am too young."...
Then the LORD reached out,
touched my lips, and said to me ...
"Today I give you authority over nations ...
to uproot and to pull down ...
to build and to plant."

JEREMIAH 1:6, 9–10

At first, Jeremiah enjoyed Josiah's support in calling the people to reform. But then came tragedy. Josiah was killed. This left Jeremiah standing by himself like a lone tree in a great field. But Jeremiah did not flinch. He stationed himself outside the Temple and, speaking for God, told the people:

Hezekiah's Tunnel

One hot day, a schoolboy was exploring an old section of Jerusalem. He stumbled upon the ancient tunnel shown here. At one spot on the wall of the tunnel was some strange-looking writing. It turned out to be an ancient inscription, telling how King Hezekiah built the tunnel to bring water into the walled city. Part of the inscription reads:

Quarry men cut through the rock,
each man working toward his fellow,
axe against axe.

In other words, two groups of men started at opposite ends (1,800 feet apart) and worked toward each other. The place where they met is clearly observable in the tunnel.

The importance of the tunnel is underscored by the fact that the Bible mentions it in three different places: 2 Kings 20:20, 2 Chronicles 32:30, Sirach 48:17.

*"Change the way you are living
and stop doing the things you are doing.
Be fair in your treatment of one another. . . .
Stop killing innocent people in this land.
Stop worshiping other gods."*
JEREMIAH 7:5–6

Over and over, Jeremiah tried to warn the people, but they refused to listen. Then one day, pointing his finger in the direction of Babylon, he shouted, "Your enemies are coming" (*Jeremiah 13:20*).

Finally, the day came when Jeremiah had to pass sentence on the nation he loved. The people were enraged. They threw Jeremiah into a pit (Jeremiah 38:1–6).

Brutal treatment like this wounded Jeremiah's sensitive nature. In one section of his book, Jeremiah gives us an insight into the turmoil that raged inside his soul at times. He cries out in agony to God:

*LORD, you have deceived me. . . .
You have overpowered me. . . .
I am ridiculed and scorned all the time
because I proclaim your message. . . .*

*Curse the day I was born!
Forget the day my mother gave me birth!
Curse the man who made my father glad
when he brought him the news,
"It's a boy! You have a son!"*
JEREMIAH 20:7–8, 14–15

This clay tablet, found in an excavated Assyrian palace, confirms the biblical report in 2 Kings 24:10–17. The tablet reads:

"In his seventh year in the month of Kislev, the king of Babylon mustered his army and marched to Palestine, where he besieged Judah. On the second day of Adar [March 16, 597 B.C.], he captured the city and seized the king. He appointed there a king of his own choice, received heavy tribute, and brought it back to Babylon."

Judah Is Exiled

Eventually, Jeremiah's warning became a reality. Babylonian armies invaded Judah. The battle for Jerusalem took place in 597 B.C., and the city fell quickly. The Babylonian king personally directed operations, deporting "all the important men to Babylonia, seven thousand in all, and one thousand skilled workers" (*2 Kings 24:16*).

Again, one would think that Babylon's action would strike fear into the hearts of the people. But it did not. Some even rejoiced, saying, "God is protecting us; our city and our Temple are still standing."

Jeremiah saw things differently. He saw the invasion as the first rumble of thunder of a bigger storm to come. Speaking in God's name, he warned Zedekiah, Judah's new king:

*"I, the LORD,
command you to do what is just and right.
Protect the person who is being cheated. . . .
Do not mistreat or oppress
aliens, orphans, or widows. . . .*

*But if you do not obey my commands . . .
this palace will fall into ruins."*
JEREMIAH 22:3, 5

The king would not change. Instead, he turned to Egypt for military support. It was too little and too late.

The storm broke in 587 B.C. That date is branded on the heart of every Jew. It marks the date of the fall of Judah and the destruction of Jerusalem and the Temple. It designates the year when the people of Judah were led away in chains to Babylon. Pondering the catastrophe, the Book of Lamentations says:

*How lonely lies Jerusalem,
once so full of people! . . .*

Assyrian soldiers lead away prisoners to labor camps.

*All night long she cries;
tears run down her cheeks. . . .
The LORD has made her suffer
for all her many sins;
Her children have been captured
and taken away.
The splendor of Jerusalem
is a thing of the past.*
LAMENTATIONS 1:1–2, 5–6

It is impossible for us to imagine what the fall of Jerusalem meant to Jews. The three great pillars that joined them to God's covenant now lay in ruins: the king was dethroned, the Temple was in ashes, and the nation was in chains. No wonder the psalmist cried out as he sat weeping in a foreign land, far away from the Temple on Mount Zion.

*By the river of Babylon we sat down;
there we wept when we remembered Zion.
On the willows near by we hung up our harps.
Those who captured us told us to sing;
they told us to entertain them:
"Sing us a song about Zion."*

*How can we sing a song to the LORD
in a foreign land?*
PSALM 137:1–4

Life in Babylon

With Jerusalem in ruins, Jewish history shifted to Babylon.

After the shock wore off, the Jews adjusted to their new situation. In time, many were given considerable freedom; some even established themselves in trades and took on Babylonian ways.

Another group of Jews, however, began to reflect on their past. This group experienced a deep religious conversion. With the Temple a heap of rubble hundreds of miles away, they turned to God's Word to keep their faith alive. They gathered regularly on the Sabbath to hear the Word recited from memory or read from scrolls.

Two important developments grew out of these weekly meetings.

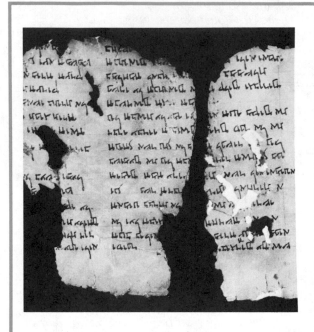

Bible Translations

This fragment of the Book of Habakkuk was found in a cave on the shore of the Dead Sea. It was once part of the library of Qumran, a "monastery" belonging to a community of Essene "monks." The writing on the fragment is Hebrew.

The Hebrew version of the Old Testament was translated into Greek about two hundred years before Jesus. It was known as the *Septuagint,* meaning "seventy," after the number of scholars reportedly involved in the translation.

When Matthew, Mark, Luke, and John quoted from the Old Testament, they usually quoted from the Septuagint.

The Septuagint contains writings that Jews do not have in their modern Bible. These include Baruch, Daniel 3:24-90 and 13-14, Esther (long version), Judith, 1 and 2 Maccabees, Sirach, Tobit, and Wisdom.

Unlike modern Jews and most Protestants, Catholics include these books in their official Bible.

The Old Testament was translated into Latin by Saint Jerome around A.D. 400. The first complete English translation was made in the fourteenth century.

First, a new worship place emerged. Known as the *synagogue,* it was primarily a place of instruction: reading, studying, and praying over God's Word. Thus it stood in contrast to the Temple, which was primarily a place of sacrifice.

Second, scribes began to record God's Word. Prior to the exile, much of it was passed on orally. Now, it was written down on papyrus sheets. Later, scribes would edit these sheets into books.

As the Jews turned toward God, so God turned toward them. He sent them two new prophets: Ezekiel and Second Isaiah.

The Prophet Ezekiel

Ezekiel grew up in Jerusalem. After the first invasion, he was deported to Babylon. There he received his prophetic call. Ezekiel's ministry divides into two periods: *before* and *after* the fall of Jerusalem.

During the first period, Ezekiel was the *disturber.* He warned the exiles of the first invasion against their unfounded belief that Jerusalem and the Temple would never fall.

During the second period, he was the *comforter.* Following the fall of Jerusalem and the Temple, Ezekiel lifted the sagging spirits of the exiles by prophesying a threefold message of hope.

First, he prophesied the restoration of the people. This word came to him in his famous vision of the "valley of the dry bones." God said:

> *"I will put my breath in them [my people],*
> *bring them back to life,*
> *and let them live in their own land."*
> EZEKIEL 37:14

Second, he prophesied the restoration of the king. God said:

> *"I will give them a king like my servant David*
> *to be their one shepherd,*
> *and he will take care of them."*
> EZEKIEL 34:23

Finally, Ezekiel prophesied the restoration of the Temple. He said:

*I saw that the Temple was filled
with the glory of the LORD. . . .
I heard the LORD speak to me out of the Temple:
"Mortal man, here is my throne.
I will live here among the people of Israel
and rule them forever."*
EZEKIEL 43:5–7

The New Testament describes how Jesus fulfilled all three of these prophesies, in a final way.

First, Jesus sent the breath of the Holy Spirit into the "dry bones" of his followers on Pentecost and made them a holy people (Acts 2).

Second, Jesus was the Shepherd, the restored king of Israel (John 10:11, 16).

Finally, Jesus fashioned his followers into the new, living temple of God (1 Corinthians 3:16–17).

Second Isaiah

A second prophet of the exile is called "Second Isaiah," because he spoke in the spirit of the great Isaiah. His writings were added to those of the earlier prophet. They form chapters 40 to 55 of the Book of Isaiah, and are often referred to as the Book of Consolation.

With words like the following, the prophet encouraged the exiles:

*The LORD is the everlasting God;
he created all the world. . . .
Those who trust in the LORD for help
will find their strength renewed.
They will rise on wings like eagles;
they will run and not get weary;
they will walk and not grow weak.*
ISAIAH 40:28, 31

The Exiles Return

Then one day, news of the military victories of King Cyrus of Persia spread throughout Babylon. The Jews got excited. Was it possible? Would Cyrus invade Babylon? Would he be the instrument by which God would free them? Second Isaiah answered these questions with an unforgettable prophecy.

*To Cyrus the LORD says . . .
"I appoint you to help my servant Israel."*
ISAIAH 45:1, 4

The Jews could not believe their ears. God had heard their prayers.

Finally, the happy day came. Cyrus invaded Babylon, and the city fell quickly. One ancient record, called the Cyrus Cylinder, says he entered the city as a friend. Immediately, Cyrus told the Jews to go to Jerusalem and rebuild the Temple (Ezra 1:3).

It was too good to be true. The joy of the Jews was beyond description. The psalmist recalled the moment this way: "It was like a dream! How we laughed, how we sang for joy!" (*Psalm 126:1–2*).

Cylinder of Cyrus. A portion of this ancient Persian record reads: "I am Cyrus, king of the world, great king, mighty king."

Understanding Exile

Review

1. When and by whom was the northern kingdom conquered?

2. What name is sometimes given to the northern citizens who were led away into captivity?

3. What name is given to the northern citizens who intermarried with the occupying forces? Why did later Jews disdain them?

4. What was the southern kingdom's response to the news that the northern kingdom had fallen?

5. What two prophets warned the southern kingdom that the same fate may await them?

6. Who is called the prophet of God's holiness, and why?

7. When and how was Judah saved from Sennacherib's army?

8. How did the people of Judah respond to Jeremiah's preaching?

9. How did the people respond to Babylon's first invasion of Judah? What was Jeremiah's response?

10. When did Judah fall, and what three great pillars of Jewish life lay in ruins after the fall?

11. What two important developments of Jewish religious life took place in Babylon? What is the Septuagint? What does the word *Septuagint* mean?

12. Into what two periods was Ezekiel's ministry divided?

13. What threefold message of hope did Ezekiel prophesy? Explain how New Testament writers saw Ezekiel's threefold prophecy reach "final" fulfillment in Jesus.

14. Who was Second Isaiah, and why did he get this name? What is the Book of Consolation?

15. Who freed the Jews from Babylon?

Discuss

1. Jews disdained Samaritans. They would not even accept their testimony in a court of law.

Can you recall anything that reflects Jesus' attitude toward Samaritans? (See Luke 10:25–27, 17:11–19; John 4:1–42.)

2. Jeremiah was a poor speaker and felt unqualified to be a prophet. Similarly, Amos was a herder and a vine dresser, and felt unqualified to be a prophet. Gideon was also surprised when God called him to rescue Israel, saying, "My clan is the weakest in the tribe . . . and I am the least important member of my family" (*Judges 6:15*).

Why do you think God picks unlikely people to do some of his biggest jobs?

3. Lord Byron wrote a poem about an event described in this chapter. Here is an excerpt from it.

The Assyrian came down like a wolf on the fold,
And his cohorts were gleaming in purple and
  gold. . . .
Like the leaves of the forest when Summer is
  green,
That host with their banners at sunset was seen;
Like the leaves of the forest when Autumn hath
  blown,
That host on the morrow lay withered and
  strown. . . .
And the might of the Gentile, unsmote by the
  sword,
Hath melted like snow in the glance of the Lord!

What event does Byron describe? What progressive imagery does Byron employ in the four stanzas? Why this imagery?

Activities

1. A cartoon shows a modern "sidewalk prophet" in tattered clothes carrying a sign reading, "Repent, the end is near!" The cartoon caption reads, "Have you noticed? No one's laughing at him anymore."

What point is the cartoon making? How is the sidewalk prophet like biblical prophets? Unlike them? What makes you think/doubt that "the end is near"?

2. Reread the story from *The Power and the Glory* that introduces this chapter.

If you died tonight, what two things would you be most proud of in your life? Most sorry about? Explain. Ask your father or mother the same question. Why were/weren't you surprised at their response?

3. Team up with three or four friends. Have one friend read Isaiah 53:4–9 out loud. Then have another friend read 1 Peter 2:22–25 out loud. Next, have the group reflect silently and prayerfully on the two passages for a few minutes. Conclude by sharing your reflections. Write out a brief report of your experience.

4. The textbook says, "Like Josiah, Jeremiah was called by God at a young age."

Interview a priest, deacon, or religious. How old was the person when he or she felt called? What form did the call take? Did he or she resist it at first, as did Jeremiah? Why would/wouldn't the person recommend the religious life to a young person today?

Bible Reading

Pick a passage. After reading it, (1) summarize its main point, (2) tell how it relates to the chapter, and (3) list one or two thoughts that entered your mind as you read it.

1. Blood-covered hands!   Isaiah 1:10–20
2. Get ready to die   Isaiah 38
3. How stupid can you get?   Isaiah 44:9–20
4. The smashed jar   Jeremiah 19
5. Valley of the dry bones   Ezekiel 37

Prayer Journal

Prayer is not only speaking to God from the heart, but also *listening* to God speak to us from his heart. For example, page 78 contains an excerpt from a "complaint" prayer by Jeremiah: "LORD, you have deceived me . . ."

Write an answer God might give to Jeremiah. Or, if you wish, compose an answer God might give to the "complaint" prayer you wrote for chapter 6. An example of such a prayer is this actual answer God gave to a complaint by Israel.

> *Israel, why then do you complain*
> *that the LORD doesn't know your troubles*
> *or care if you suffer injustice?*
> *Don't you know? Haven't you heard?. . .*
> *Those who trust in the LORD . . .*
> *will find their strength renewed.*
> *They will rise on wings like eagles;*
> *they will run and not get weary;*
> *they will walk and not grow weak.*
> ISAIAH 40:27–28, 31

Here is another answer from God:

> *Israel . . . "Do not be afraid—I will save you.*
> *I have called you by name—you are mine.*
> *When you pass through deep waters,*
> *I will be with you. . . .*
> *When you pass through fire,*
> *you will not be burned. . . .*
> *You are precious to me. . . .*
> *Do not be afraid—I am with you!"*
> ISAIAH 43:1–2, 4–5

8 Rebirth

A huge airliner was making its final approach for a landing. On the ground a large crowd watched excitedly, pointing to the plane. When the plane touched down, a cheer burst forth from the people.

As the plane taxied to a stop, the gangway was moved to the cabin door. The crowd surged forth, chanting "Welcome home! Welcome home!"

Inside the plane, the passengers also began to cheer and shout. They were American prisoners of war, returning from Vietnam.

No such homecoming greeted the Hebrew prisoners of war as they returned to Jerusalem from Babylon. They were met only by a desolate city and a destroyed temple.

The Nation Rebuilds

In the months ahead, the people cleared the rubble and began to rebuild their homes. But it was not an easy task. Surrounding neighbors tried to block their efforts. At times, the people found themselves building with one hand and fighting with the other.

Even the land seemed to be against them. The first crop failed. The people's initial joy at their freedom soured. Bickering broke out, and the rebuilding of the Temple was postponed. The people felt abandoned and forgotten.

Into this critical situation stepped two prophets: Haggai and Zechariah.

Haggai rebuked the people. Speaking in God's name, he said of their plight:

> "Can't you see why this has happened? . . .
> Because my Temple lies in ruins
> while every one of you is busy working
> on his own house."
> HAGGAI 1:7, 9

Zechariah encouraged the people and reminded them of the promise of a messiah.

> Rejoice, rejoice, people of Zion!
> Shout for joy, you people of Jerusalem!
> Look, your king is coming to you!
> He comes triumphant and victorious,
> but humble and riding on a donkey—
> on a colt, the foal of a donkey. . . .
> The LORD says,
> "He will rule . . . to the ends of the earth."
> ZECHARIAH 9:9–10

The gospel writers quoted these exact words of Zechariah when Jesus rode into Jerusalem on Palm Sunday (John 12:12–16).

A big boost came when a second wave of exiles returned to Jerusalem from Babylon. The people joined together and rebuilt the Temple and the city walls. Under the leadership of Nehemiah, the job was finally completed.

At last, the day for celebration came. Another leader, Ezra, gathered the people to renew the covenant with God. "The people . . . were so moved that they began to cry" (*Nehemiah 8:9*). They were home, at last.

In the years that followed, the Jews isolated themselves from the world. And, once again, they isolated themselves from God. They made him over into their own image and likeness. The Creator of the Universe became a one-nation God who was concerned only about Jews, not the rest of the world.

Two prophets emerged to challenge this warped view of God. Their words are recorded in the Book of Malachi and in the Book of Jonah.

Book of Malachi

Far from being concerned only about the Jews, the God of Malachi praises the other nations of the world.

> *People from one end of the world*
> *to the other honor me.*
> *Everywhere they burn incense to me*
> *and offer acceptable sacrifices. . . .*
> *But you dishonor me.*
> MALACHI 1:11–12

Book of Jonah

The most forceful challenge to Jewish nationalism, however, comes in the Book of Jonah. This book takes the form of an instructional short story. It opens with God telling Jonah to go to Nineveh, the capital of Assyria, to tell the people to change their ways. Jonah cannot believe his ears, because Assyria is the Jews' biggest enemy. Why should God be concerned about them? They are sinners who should be destroyed, not saved.

Jonah decides he will not go. So he flees from God, goes to Joppa, and boards a ship headed for Spain. During the trip a storm arises. Jonah ends up overboard. He is swallowed by a giant fish and spit out on a beach.

Again, God appears to Jonah and tells him to go to Nineveh. This time Jonah obeys. To his surprise the people heed his message and change their ways.

The point of the Book of Jonah is clear: God is concerned not just about Jews, but about all people.

The Nation Is Threatened

Jewish isolation ended when the Greek armies of Alexander the Great invaded the Near East. At the age of thirty-two, Alexander headed the largest empire ever ruled by one man. The First Book of Maccabees says of Alexander:

> *He fought many battles,*
> *captured fortified cities, and put*
> *the kings of the region to death. . . .*
> *When he had conquered the world,*
> *he became proud and arrogant.*
> 1 MACCABEES 1:2–3

After Alexander's early death, two great kingdoms emerged from his empire: the Syrian (Seleucid) and the Egyptian (Ptolemy).

The Jews found themselves controlled first by one kingdom, then by the other. This pawnlike existence hurt Jewish pride and shattered their dreams of independence. A deep sense of incompleteness and confusion came over them.

Nowhere are their feelings better expressed than in the Book of Ecclesiastes.

Portrait of Alexander the Great, part of a larger mosaic unearthed at Pompeii.

Book of Ecclesiastes

The word *ecclesiastes* is sometimes translated as "the Philosopher." The book begins, "These are the words of the Philosopher." What follows is a series of reflections that are often pessimistic. Here is an example:

> *Everything leads to weariness. . . .*
> *I have seen everything done in this world,*
> *and I tell you, it is all useless.*
> *It is like chasing the wind.*
> ECCLESIASTES 1:8, 14

Another passage reads:

> *Fast runners do not always win the races,*
> *and the brave do not always win the battles.*
> *Wise men do not always earn a living.*
> ECCLESIASTES 9:11

All of this puzzles the Philosopher. He scratches his head and wonders why this is the case. But he never comes up with a satisfactory answer.

The Book of Ecclesiastes reminds us of someone trying to put a puzzle together with half the pieces missing. But this is precisely where its value lies. It allows us to enter the heart of a Jew who is waiting for further revelation from God.

To appreciate the book fully, we must remember that the Jews of this period had little or no idea of reward and punishment in an afterlife. Rather, they assumed that God rewards and punishes people in *this* life. And this is what troubled them. They asked themselves, "If God rewards and punishes in this life, why are so many evil people prospering, and why are so many good people suffering?"

It is to this question that the Book of Job addresses itself.

Book of Job

The Book of Job is one of the most beautifully written books of the Old Testament or Hebrew Scriptures. It deals with a man named Job, who has spent his whole life doing good. He is a real saint.

Then one day a series of terrible tragedies comes crashing down on him: rustlers steal his cattle, enemies kill his servants, a storm destroys his home and kills his family. Finally, a disease afflicts his body.

Job cannot understand why these things are happening to him, because he has led a good life. His friends tell him he must have sinned, if God is punishing him. But Job insists that he is innocent. He has done no wrong.

In the end, Job is left by himself to try to search for an answer. At one point he becomes so confused that he toys with the idea that God is out to get him.

> *"He has set a trap to catch me. . . .*
> *God has blocked the way,*
> *and I can't get through;*
> *he has hidden my path in darkness. . . .*
> *He uproots my hope*
> *and leaves me to wither and die."*
> JOB 19:6, 8, 10

But the more Job thinks about this idea, the more he rejects it. God isn't like that. He doesn't destroy people. At this point a great storm blows up. God speaks to Job out of the storm. He asks Job a series of questions.

> *"Have you been to the springs*
> *in the depths of the sea?*
> *Have you walked on the floor of the ocean?*
> *Has anyone ever shown you the gates*
> *that guard the dark world of the dead? . . .*
> *Does a hawk learn from you how to fly*
> *when it spreads its wings toward the south?*
> *Does an eagle wait for your command*
> *to build its nest high in the mountains?"*
> JOB 38:16–17; 39:26–27

What is God's point in asking Job these questions?

God's point is this: If Job admits that God's wisdom greatly surpasses his, why does he question God's fairness to him? In other words, God's wisdom is so much greater than Job's that it is folly for Job to challenge God. Job had forgotten what God had taught years before through the prophet Isaiah.

> *"My thoughts . . . are not like yours,*
> *and my ways are different from yours.*
> *As high as the heavens are above the earth,*
> *so high are my ways and thoughts above yours."*
> ISAIAH 55:8–9

In the end, Job's experience of God changes him from a sage (someone who seeks an answer for everything) into a saint (someone who is willing to trust God).

The teaching of the Book of Job is this: God wants us to walk by the light of faith as well as by the light of reason. We are called to be saints as well as sages.

Book of Daniel

The turmoil in Jewish hearts eventually exploded into agony. Around 200 B.C., Syrian armies conquered Egypt. Judah passed from Egyptian hands to Syrian hands. The ruler of Syria was a Greek-minded tyrant, Antiochus IV. He decided to make

Who taught the birds to fly? .

Greeks out of his Jewish subjects. And so he commanded them to build pagan altars and shrines.

This decree created an impossible situation for the Jews. Those who obeyed it broke the covenant with God. Those who disobeyed it were brutally persecuted. A reign of terror shook Judah's faith to the roots. Into this crisis stepped the unknown prophet of the Book of Daniel.

Like prophets before him, Daniel faced the problem of communicating a profound religious message to a simple people. To do so he used two literary devices: folktales and visions.

The first half of the book is devoted to folktales, the second half to visions. Both center around a Jewish hero named Daniel, who is taken prisoner in a foreign country. Since he is young and intelligent, he is assigned to the royal court. There he rises quickly to a position of power, much as Joseph did in Egypt.

Meanwhile, other court officials grow jealous of him. Aware that Daniel prays to God three times a day, they plot to have King Darius issue a decree making it a crime to pray to anyone but the king.

Of course, Daniel ignores the decree. He is condemned to death and thrown into a den of lions. But God is with Daniel, and the lions do not harm him. When the king sees this, he frees Daniel and honors him even more.

The point of the folktale is one of hope: God will save his people just as he saved Daniel from the lions.

The second half of the Book of Daniel deals with visions that Daniel had. Typical of the visions is this one. Daniel sees a mysterious figure, surrounded by clouds, coming toward him.

> *I saw what looked like a human being*
> *[Son of Man]. He was approaching me,*
> *surrounded by clouds, and he went to the one*
> *who had been living forever [God]*
> *and was presented to him.*
> *He was given authority, honor, and royal power,*
> *so that the people of all nations, races,*
> *and languages would serve him.*
> *His authority would last forever,*
> *and his kingdom would never end.*
> DANIEL 7:13–14

Jesus referred to this vision when he stood trial for his life. Asked if he were "the Messiah, the Son of the Blessed God," he replied, "I am, and you will all see the Son of Man seated at the right side of the Almighty and coming with the clouds of heaven!" (*Mark 14:61–62*).

The title Son of Man is the one Jesus used most often to refer to himself. We find it sixty-nine times in the New Testament. No other title could have better identified the person and mission of Jesus. He was, at once, a humble member of the Jewish nation and the exalted Son of God. To him was given "authority, honor, and royal power"; and his kingdom will never end.

The Book of Daniel concludes with a dramatic reference to the final judgment. God says to Daniel:

> *"All the people of your nation whose names*
> *are written in God's book will be saved.*
> *Many of those who have already died*
> *will live again:*
> *some will enjoy eternal life,*
> *and some will suffer eternal disgrace.*
> *The wise leaders*
> *will shine with all the brightness of the sky.*
> *And those who have taught many people*
> *to do what is right*
> *will shine like the stars forever."*
> DANIEL 12:1–3

The Nation Survives

Fired by the spirit of the Book of Daniel, loyal Jews came alive. Around 168 B.C. a full-scale resistance movement was mounted. It was led by three Jewish brothers called the Maccabees: Judas, Jonathan, and Simon.

Operating out of the hills, these freedom fighters battled the Syrians and eventually reclaimed the Temple. Modern Jews still celebrate this joyful event with the Feast of Lights, known as Hanukkah.

Eventually, Judas and Jonathan were killed in battle. It fell to their brother Simon to bring the revolt to a successful end, in 142 B.C.

The Maccabees operated out of caves like these, which still honeycomb the Palestinian countryside.

When Simon died, around 135 B.C., leadership passed to his son John. With him began the Hasmonean Era.

Hasmonean is the name given to the descendants of the Maccabees. During the era of the Hasmoneans, a new danger threatened the nation. It came from the Hasmoneans themselves. They introduced politics into religion, using the sacred office of high priest to gain political goals.

The clock began to strike midnight for the Hasmoneans in 63 B.C. In that year, Roman armies, led by Pompey, occupied Jerusalem.

Time finally ran out on the Hasmoneans around 37 B.C. when the Romans crowned Herod the Great king of Judah.

It was this ruler, with so many talents and so many weaknesses, who served as the bridge between the Old Testament and the New Testament eras.

Book of Sirach

The Book of Sirach rings down the curtain on the Old Testament period. Many Bibles list it (along with Psalms, Proverbs, Song of Songs, Ecclesiastes, Wisdom, and Job) as one of the seven "wisdom" books of the Hebrew Scriptures.

The Book of Sirach may be divided into two main sections: meditations on how to live, and eulogies (words of praise) of ancient heroes.

The tone of the meditations reminds us of a departing parent addressing a child.

> *Son, if you are going to serve the Lord,*
> *be prepared for times*
> *when you will be put to the test.*
> SIRACH 2:1

> *Give your help to the poor. . . .*
> *Be generous to every living soul. . . .*
> *Do not hesitate to visit the sick. . . .*
> *Whatever you do,*
> *remember that some day you must die.*
> SIRACH 7:32–33, 35–36

Typical of the eulogies is this one of Abraham:

> *Abraham was the great ancestor*
> *of many nations;*
> *his reputation was faultless.*
> *He kept the Law of the Most High*
> *and made a covenant with him. . . .*
> *And so the Lord made him a solemn promise*
> *that his descendants . . . would be countless,*
> *like the dust of the earth.*
> SIRACH 44:19–21

The Book of Sirach ends with this thought:

> *May God bless everyone*
> *who gives attention to these teachings. . . .*
> *Whoever lives by them*
> *will be strong enough for any occasion,*
> *because he will be walking*
> *in the light of the Lord. . . .*

> *Be joyfully grateful for the Lord's mercy,*
> *and never be ashamed to praise him.*
> *Do your duty . . . and the Lord,*
> *at the time he thinks proper,*
> *will give you your reward.*
> SIRACH 50:28–29; 51:29–30

Waiting and Praying

By their own admission, the Hebrew Scriptures are an "unfinished story." They end with many Jews, especially "the poor," waiting and praying for the Messiah.

Perhaps the most fitting conclusion to our study of the Hebrew Scriptures is this passage from *The Source* by James Michener:

Rabbi Asher
wandered among the gnarled olive trees;
his attention was arrested
by one so ancient
that its interior was rotted away,
leaving an empty shell
through which one could see;
but somehow the remaining fragments
had contact with the roots,
and the old tree was still vital,
sending forth branches that bore good fruit;

and as he studied this patriarch of the grove
Asher thought that it well summarized
the state of the Jewish people:
an old society
much of whose interior had rotted away,
but whose fragments
still held vital connection with the roots of God,
and it was through these roots of law
that Jews could ascertain the will of God
and produce good fruit.

Five Groups

As the sun set on the Old Testament, five groups of people emerged in Israel: Pharisees, Sadducees, Essenes, Zealots, and the poor.

Pharisees were made up of well-educated lay people. They believed the most important thing a Jew could do was to obey Jewish religious law. This law came from two sources: the Torah and the oral tradition, which they believed stretched all the way back to Moses. The Pharisees also believed that Israel was guided by God and did not need political rulers. Doctrinally, they believed in angels, the resurrection of the dead, and a final judgment.

Sadducees were made up, largely, of the wealthy upper class. Many chief priests were Sadducees. They observed only the Torah as binding. If it did not legislate on a point, Sadducees exercised freedom. This is why they accepted Roman occupation and adjusted to it. Doctrinally, they denied angels and the resurrection of the dead (Acts 23:8).

Essenes were made up of Jews who broke with conventional Judaism, regarding it as corrupt. Most of the information about them comes from the ancient Jewish historian Josephus and from the Dead Sea Scrolls. Essenes believed they were the true Israel, heirs to the new covenant (Jeremiah 31:31-34, Ezekiel 36:22-28). Doctrinally, they believed the human heart was a battle-ground of two conflicting spirits: goodness (light) and evil (darkness). Thus they preached, in a special way, personal sinfulness and divine forgiveness. Finally, they believed "the end" was near. In preparation for it they withdrew into desert communities like Qumran.

Zealots were made up of militant Jews, who scorned all of the above groups. They looked for a military messiah who would catapult Israel into first place among the nations of the world. Thus they were more of a militaristic movement than a religious group.

The poor made up the majority of the Jewish people. Their poverty kept them ignorant and made them outcasts. So they knew little about the Torah, the Temple, or religion. In their eyes, the Pharisees were too pious; the Sadducees, too political; the Essenes, too removed from life; and the Zealots, too militant. The poor had nothing to hope for but that God would someday send a messiah to rescue them.

Understanding Rebirth

Review

1. What two problems delayed the rebuilding of the Temple?

2. What two prophets arose to confront the crisis, and what was the basic message of each?

3. What two prophets arose to challenge the Hebrews' isolationism?

4. What point does the Book of Jonah make?

5. What kind of Jew is pictured in the Book of Ecclesiastes?

6. What serious problem does the Book of Job address? What is the book's message?

7. What did Antiochus IV try to do to the Jewish people? What situation did this produce?

8. What book addresses the situation created by Antiochus IV? Into what two main sections is the book divided?

9. What is the point of the story of Daniel in the lions' den?

10. In what two ways did Jesus link himself with Daniel's vision of the "figure surrounded by clouds"?

11. List and briefly explain the five groups of people in Israel as the Old Testament Era drew to a close.

12. What Jewish leader served as the bridge between Old and New Testament times?

13. What book rings down the curtain on Jewish history?

14. List the seven "wisdom" books.

Discuss

1. An ancient Chinese story concerns a man who had one son and one horse. One day the horse escaped to the hills. The neighbors said to the man, "God is punishing you." The man said, "How can you be so sure?" The next day the horse returned, bringing back ten wild horses. The neighbors said to the man, "God is rewarding you." The man said, "How can you be so sure?" The next day the man's son broke his leg while taming one of the horses. The neighbors said, "God is punishing him." The man said, "How can you be so sure?" The next day an enemy invaded the village and carried off all able-bodied young men. They left the son behind. This time the neighbors said nothing.

What is the point of the story? How is it similar to the point of the Book of Job? Recall a time when an apparent cross in your life turned out to be a blessing.

2. Someone updated the Book of Job, giving it a modern setting and calling it *J.B.* The character J.B. is an upright, wealthy businessman. One by one his children meet violent deaths. One is killed in the military; two are killed by a drunken driver; a fourth is

raped and murdered. Finally, the last child is killed in an air raid, which also destroys J.B.'s bank and fortune. Then J.B. contracts a horrible skin disease from atomic fallout. In spite of these tragedies, J.B. keeps his faith in God. Eventually, the play ends with J.B. being restored to health with the possibility of future wealth and children.

Explain why you think updating a Bible story like this helps/hinders God's revelation.

Activities

1. A fifteen-year-old Jewish boy, Elie Wiesel, was thrown into a Nazi concentration camp. One night the prisoners were celebrating the Jewish New Year (Rosh Hashanah). As the worship progressed, Elie became depressed. Suddenly, every fiber of his being cried out, "Why worship a God who allows six crematories [furnaces in which the Jews were burned] to operate day and night?" When the service ended, Elie was no longer a believer.

Imagine that you are Elie's best friend. Write a brief letter to him, telling how you (a Christian) think Jesus would respond to his question, "Why worship a God who allows six crematories to operate day and night?"

2. The Book of Jonah can be read in less than ten minutes. Read it with a friend. Then coauthor a briefer, updated version of the story. In place of Jonah, put a modern person to whom God has given a special mission.

3. Imagine that television is a part of the ancient world and that you are a talk show host. Your guests are a Sadducee, a Pharisee, an Essene, a Zealot, and a poor shepherd.

Select five people to play your guests. Moderate a discussion among them on their differences. Have them decide if they were faithful to the viewpoints held by each of the ancient groups.

Bible Reading

Pick a passage. After reading it, (1) summarize the main point, (2) tell how it relates to the chapter, and (3) list one or two thoughts that entered your mind as you read it.

1. Swords and picks   Nehemiah 4
2. Man overboard   Jonah 1
3. Seven cruel deaths   2 Maccabees 7
4. Satan attacks Job   Job 1:6–22
5. God rewards Job   Job 42

Prayer Journal

The Book of Job deals with the mystery of pain and suffering. Describe a time when you suffered. What role did prayer play in helping you cope with it? Here is one student's response.

> *I suffered greatly after my mom's death. I missed her terribly. Then one day I happened to notice a card under the glass top of my dresser. I saw it there for the first time a few weeks before mom went to the hospital, but I hadn't bothered to read it. I pulled it out and read it. Here is what it said:*
>
> *"For ev'ry pain we must bear,*
> *For ev'ry burden, ev'ry care,*
> *There's a reason.*
>
> *"For ev'ry grief that bows the head,*
> *For ev'ry teardrop that is shed,*
> *There's a reason.*
>
> *"For ev'ry hurt, for ev'ry plight,*
> *For ev'ry lonely, pain-racked night,*
> *There's a reason.*
>
> *"But if we trust God, as we should,*
> *It will turn out for our good;*
> *He knows the reason."*
> AUTHOR UNKNOWN
>
> *As I sat there, I could picture my mom, before going to the hospital, coming into my room and slipping the card beneath the glass, as if to say to me, "It's all right, Jon. Don't worry; he knows the reason."*

Gospel Time Chart

A.D.

—	Jesus born
26	Pilate made Procurator
27	John at Jordan
28	Jesus baptized
29	Jesus begins ministry
32	Jesus crucified
32	Jesus rises

Gospel World

Part Two

Christian Scriptures:
Gospels

9 The Promised One

The American writer Nathaniel Hawthorne was dead. On his desk lay the outline of a play he never got a chance to write. It centered around a person who never appeared on stage. Everyone talked about the person. Everyone dreamed about him. Everyone waited for him. But the person never appeared.

The Old Testament is like Hawthorne's unfinished play. It, too, centers around the coming of a great king, a messiah or savior, whom God had promised. For example, the prophets had foretold:

> The Lord says, "The time is coming
> when I will choose as king
> a righteous descendant of David. . . .
> He will be called
> 'The Lord Our Salvation.' "
> JEREMIAH 23:5–6

> He will rule as King David's successor,
> basing his power on right and justice
> from now until the end of time.
> ISAIAH 9:7

But the Old Testament ends without this "promised one" appearing.

It is against this background that we close the first half of the Bible, called the Old Testament, or Hebrew Scriptures, and open the second half, called the New Testament, or Christian Scriptures.

Composed of twenty-seven writings, the New Testament divides into four sections:

1. four Gospels,
2. the Acts of the Apostles,
3. twenty-one Letters, and
4. the Book of Revelation.

We now turn to this section of the Bible, beginning with the four Gospels.

The New Testament Begins

The four Gospels—Mark, Matthew, Luke, and John—are the result of a process that involved three important stages. These may be referred to as the *life* stage, the *preaching* stage, and the *written* stage.

The *life* stage was the actual life of Jesus. It is what Jesus did and said as he walked along the dusty roads of Galilee, teaching and healing the people. About this stage, Peter wrote, "With our own eyes we saw his greatness" (*2 Peter 1:16*).

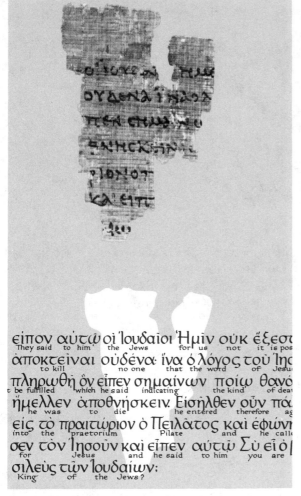

εἶπον αὐτῷ οἱ Ἰουδαῖοι Ἡμῖν οὐκ ἔξεσ
They said to him' the Jews for us not it is pos
ἀποκτεῖναι οὐδένα· ἵνα ὁ λόγος τοῦ Ἰη
to kill no one that the word of Jesu
πληρωθῇ ὃν εἶπεν σημαίνων ποίῳ θανά
t be fulfilled which he said indicating the kind of dea
ἤμελλεν ἀποθνῄσκειν. Εἰσῆλθεν οὖν πά
he was to die he entered therefore ag
εἰς τὸ πραιτώριον ὁ Πειλᾶτος καὶ ἐφώνη
into the praetorium Pilate and he call
σεν τὸν Ἰησοῦν καὶ εἶπεν αὐτῷ Σὺ εἶ ὁ
for Jesus and he said to him you are
σιλεὺς τῶν Ἰουδαίων;
King of the Jews?

People ask, "Do we have the original Gospel manuscripts?" The answer is no. We have only copies of the originals. The oldest known copy dates from A.D. 130. A fragment of that copy is shown here. Known as the Rylands Fragment, it contains a portion of John 18:31–33. The sketch shows how the fragment fits into the overall Greek manuscript.

The *preaching* stage began after Jesus' resurrection. On Pentecost, the Holy Spirit descended upon the followers of Jesus. Filled with the power of the Spirit, the Apostles began preaching to everyone the "Good News" about Jesus: He is the Promised One, the Messiah (Acts 2:31, 36). He has established God's kingdom on earth.

As the Apostles preached this Good News, they remembered what Jesus said in his lifetime: "This Good News about the Kingdom will be preached through all the world . . . and then the end will come" (*Matthew 24:14*). The Apostles thought they could complete the preaching of the Good News in their own lifetime. So they did not bother writing down what Jesus said and did.

Finally, when it became clear to the Apostles that they could not complete the preaching of the Good News in their lifetime, they decided to write it down for their successors.

This began the *written* stage. Luke refers to it when he says:

> *Many people have done their best*
> *to write a report of . . .*
> *what we have been told by those*
> *who saw these things . . .*
> *and who proclaimed the message.*
> *And so . . . because I have carefully studied*
> *all these matters from their beginning,*
> *I thought it would be good to write*
> *an orderly account for you.*
> LUKE 1:1–3

In conclusion, then, the four Gospels passed through three stages in their development:

1. *life* stage, what the disciples saw and heard,
2. *preaching* stage, what the Apostles preached,
3. *written* stage, what the evangelists recorded.

Four Gospel Portraits

Each of the four Gospels was written at a different time, in a different place, for a different group of people. Experts do not agree totally on when, where, and for whom each Gospel was written. But the following rundown is regarded by many as probable.

Mark wrote in Rome before A.D. 70 for Christians of a Gentile (non-Jewish) background.

Matthew wrote in Antioch (Syria) between A.D. 70 and A.D. 90 for Christians of Jewish background.

Luke wrote in Greece between A.D. 70 and A.D. 90 for Christians of Greek background.

John wrote in Ephesus (Asia Minor) after A.D. 90 for Christians of all backgrounds.

Because each evangelist (gospel writer) wrote for people of different backgrounds, each stressed different things about Jesus. As a result we have four different views, or "portraits," of Jesus.

Mark's portrait was influenced by the fact that he wrote mainly for Christians in Rome who were suffering persecution under the Roman emperor, Nero. Thus Mark stresses the suffering of Jesus. And if Jesus suffered, his disciples must not be surprised if they are called upon to suffer also (Mark 8:34–35). And so Mark's portrait of Jesus is that of the *suffering* Savior or Messiah.

Matthew's portrait of Jesus was influenced by the fact that he wrote mainly for Jews. They were deeply interested in how Jesus' teaching fitted in with Moses' teaching. Thus Matthew stresses how Jesus brought the teaching of Moses to fulfillment (Matthew 5:17). As a result, Matthew's portrait of Jesus is that of the *teaching* Savior.

Luke's portrait of Jesus was influenced by the fact that he wrote for Gentiles, especially the poor and outcasts of society. Thus Luke stresses Jesus' concern for the "second-class" citizens of society. For example, Luke records four episodes about women that are found nowhere else (Luke 7:11–17; 8:1–3; 15:8–10; 18:1–8). And so Luke's portrait of Jesus is that of the *compassionate* Savior.

Finally, John's portrait was influenced by the fact that he wrote for Christians of all backgrounds. Thus John stresses how Jesus came to make the lives of all people richer and fuller. "I have come," says Jesus, "that you might have life—life in all its fullness" (*John 10:10*). As a result, John's portrait of Jesus is that of the *life-giving* Savior.

And so the Gospels give us not one portrait of Jesus, but four.

This stained-glass window from the Cathedral of Chartres shows Matthew riding piggyback on Isaiah. It dramatizes an important biblical truth for medieval Christians: The New Testament rests upon the foundation of the Old Testament.

Synoptic Gospels

A TV director was planning a program called "New York City: A Tourist's View." He decided to present the city through the eyes of four different tourists approaching the city in four different ways:

1. by water in a boat,
2. by air in a plane,
3. by rail on a train,
4. by road in a car.

Thus the television viewer got not one but four different perspectives or portraits of New York City.

We have something like this in the four Gospels. We have not one portrait of Jesus, but four.

Moreover, just as three of the portraits of New York City (boat, train, and car) are somewhat similar, so three of the gospel portraits of Jesus are somewhat similar (Mark, Matthew, and Luke). In fact, these Gospels are so similar, *in parts,* that they are sometimes called the Synoptic Gospels.

The word *synoptic—syn* ("together") and *opsis* ("seeing")—indicates that these three Gospels are sometimes so similar that they can be placed side by side for study. Here is an example:

MARK

Six days later,
Jesus took with him
Peter, James, and John
and led them up a high mountain,
where they were alone.

As they looked on,
a change came over Jesus,
and his clothes
became shining white—
whiter than anyone in the world
could wash them.

Then the three disciples
saw Elijah and Moses
talking with Jesus.
Peter spoke up. . . .
MARK 9:2-5

MATTHEW

Six days later
Jesus took with him Peter
and the brothers James and John
and led them up a high mountain
where they were alone.

As they looked on,
a change came over Jesus;
his face was shining like the sun,
and his clothes
were dazzling white.

Then the three disciples
saw Moses and Elijah
talking with Jesus.
So Peter spoke up. . . .
MATTHEW 17:1-4

LUKE

About a week after
he said these things,
Jesus took Peter, John, and James
with him and went up a hill
to pray.

While he was praying,
his face changed its appearance,
and his clothes
became dazzling white.

Suddenly two men
were there talking to him.
They were Moses and Elijah,
who appeared in heavenly glory
and talked with Jesus. . . .
LUKE 9:28-31

Two Gospel Preludes

Let us now take a closer look at two of the Gospels: Matthew and Luke.

Both Matthew and Luke wanted to begin their story of Jesus with a brief introduction or *prelude* about Jesus' early years. This created a problem for them. None of Jesus' disciples were familiar with that part of Jesus' life. To remedy this situation, Matthew and Luke went to other sources for help.

1. *history:* what Mary's and Joseph's families and friends remembered about the early years of Jesus,
2. *prophecy:* what Old Testament prophets seemed to say about the early years of the Messiah,
3. *theology:* what the Holy Spirit inspired each writer to say about this period of Jesus' life.

Thus the preludes to Matthew's and Luke's Gospels are like tapestries woven from three threads: history, prophecy, and theology. These threads are woven together so artfully that it is hard to say which is which.

Let us now take a closer look at Luke's gospel prelude.

Luke's Prelude

NARRATOR *During the time when Herod was king of Judea . . . God sent the angel Gabriel to a town in Galilee named Nazareth. He had a message for a girl promised in marriage to a man named Joseph, who was a descendant of King David. The girl's name was Mary.*

ANGEL *Peace be with you! The Lord is with you and has greatly blessed you!*

NARRATOR *Mary was deeply troubled by the angel's message. . . .*

ANGEL *Don't be afraid, Mary; God has been gracious to you. You will become pregnant and give birth to a son, and you will name him Jesus. . . . The Lord God will make him a king, as his ancestor David was, and . . . his kingdom will never end!*

MARY *I am a virgin. How, then, can this be?*

ANGEL *The Holy Spirit will come on you, and God's power will rest upon you. For this reason the holy child will be called the Son of God. . . .*

MARY *I am the Lord's servant; may it happen to me as you have said.*

LUKE 1:5, 26–35, 38

Two remarkable things stand out in this passage. First, the angel identifies Jesus with the "Promised One" foretold by the prophets.

The Lord God will make him a king, as his ancestor David was, and . . . his kingdom will never end!

The second remarkable thing is the angel's explanation of how Mary will conceive.

The Holy Spirit will come on you, and God's power will rest upon *you.*

The expression *rest upon* is rarely found in the Bible. One place it is found, however, is in the Book of Exodus. There it describes the mysterious cloud that covered the "meeting tent" in which the ark (housing the tablets of the Commandments) was kept. The cloud then filled the "meeting tent" with "the Lord's presence" (*Exodus 40:34*).

Luke deliberately compares Mary's body with the "meeting tent" and her womb with the ark. Luke's point? In Mary, God will make himself present among his people in a marvelous new way: not in *symbol* (tablets in the ark) but in *person* (Jesus in the womb).

Jesus Is Born

Darrel Doré was inside a room on an oil rig in the Gulf of Mexico. Suddenly the rig capsized and crashed into the sea. The lights in the room flickered and went out. As the rig sank into the sea, it filled with water—except for a big air bubble in the corner of the ceiling.

Doré plunged his head inside the air bubble. For twenty-two hours, he shivered and prayed inside the fragile bubble. Then, when he had just about given up hope, a remarkable thing happened. A light appeared in the darkness. It was a light on a diver's helmet. Rescue had come.

The diver's rescue of Doré helps illustrate the role Jesus played in the rescue of the human race. Like Doré, the human race was on its way to death (spiritual death). Then a light appeared in the darkness: the star of Bethlehem. Rescue had come.

The rescue of the human race involved a couple, named Mary and Joseph. They were engaged to be married. Before the marriage, however, Mary "found out she was going to have a baby by the Holy Spirit" (*Matthew 1:18*). This caused Joseph deep anguish, until he learned that Mary had indeed conceived by the Holy Spirit. Commenting on all this, Matthew says:

> *Now all this happened in order*
> *to make come true*
> *what the Lord had said through the prophet,*
> *"A virgin will become pregnant and have a son,*
> *and he will be called Immanuel"*
> *(which means, "God is with us").*
> *So when Joseph woke up, he married Mary,*
> *as the angel of the Lord had told him to.*
> MATTHEW 1:22–24

Two points are of special interest in this episode from the lives of Mary and Joseph.

The first is their engagement. Unlike modern engagements, ancient engagements had the force of marriage. Many times the two young people did not know each other, because the marriage was arranged by their parents—sometimes even before they were born. The purpose of the engagement was to give the young people a chance to get to know each other before coming together as husband and wife. If the young man died during the engagement period, the young woman was his legal widow.

The second point of interest is Matthew's reference to the title "Immanuel," which the prophet used of Jesus. It makes the same point Luke made in his annunciation narrative: In Jesus, "God is with us" now in *person,* not just in *symbol* (tablets in ark).

Matthew's explanation of Mary's pregnancy sets the stage for Jesus' birth. Here is how Luke describes this great event.

> *At the time Emperor Augustus*
> *ordered a census to be taken*
> *throughout the Roman Empire. . . .*
> *Everyone, then, went to register himself,*
> *each to his own home town.*
>
> *Joseph went from the town of Nazareth*
> *in Galilee to the town of Bethlehem in Judea,*
> *the birthplace of King David.*

> *Joseph went there because he was a descendant*
> *of David. He went to register with Mary. . . .*
>
> *While they were in Bethlehem,*
> *the time came for her to have her baby.*
> *She gave birth to her first son, wrapped him*
> *in cloths and laid him in a manger—*
> *there was no room for them to stay in the inn.*
>
> *There were some shepherds in that part*
> *of the country who were spending the night*
> *in the fields, taking care of their flocks.*

An angel of the Lord appeared to them,
and the glory of the Lord shone over them.
They were terribly afraid,
but the angel said to them, "Don't be afraid!
I am here with good news for you. . . .
This very day in David's town
your Savior is born—Christ the Lord!". . .

So they hurried off
and found Mary and Joseph
and saw the baby lying in the manger. . . .
The shepherds went back, singing praises
to God for all they had heard and seen.

LUKE 2:1, 3–11, 16, 20

Three things are remarkable about the description of Jesus' birth.

First, Luke, again, identifies Jesus with the "Promised One." Jesus is "Christ the Lord." Literally, this means Jesus is "the Messiah the Lord." The Hebrew word *Messiah* is translated into Greek by the word *Christos,* which is translated into English by the word *Christ.*

The second point is the way Jesus enters the world. He enters, not as the son of a powerful king, born in a beautiful palace, in one of the mightiest nations on earth. Rather, he enters as the son of a poor carpenter, born in a cave, in one of the weakest nations on earth. Moreover, the first people to visit Jesus are not the rich and the powerful, but the poor and the powerless.

Third, Luke notes the time of year when the birth takes place. He does not give the month or the day, or even the hour. He goes about it much more subtly. He says, "Some shepherds . . . were spending the night in the fields, taking care of their flocks."

Normally, to protect their flocks from wild animals and the cold, shepherds herded them into caves or pens for the night. One time, however, when they did not do this was during the lambing season. This was to keep the newborn lambs from being trampled to death in a crowded area.

All this suggests that Jesus was possibly born during lambing season. This would have been a beautiful time for Jesus to be born. For like the lambs born in Bethlehem and towns around Jerusalem—lambs that were destined for sacrifice in the Temple—Jesus, the "Lamb of God," was also destined for sacrifice.

Luke's description of Jesus' birth leaves us singing the same song that Zechariah sang at the birth of John the Baptist.

"[God] has come to the help of his people
and has set them free.
He has provided for us a mighty Savior,
a descendant of his servant David . . .
promised through his holy prophets long ago."

LUKE 1:68–70

Caves still pockmark Israel's countryside.
A cave like this may have provided shelter
for Jesus' birth.

Understanding the Promised One

Review

1. In what sense is the Old Testament (Hebrew Scriptures) an unfinished book?

2. What is another name for the gospel writers?

3. List and explain the three stages by which the Gospels developed.

4. List the probable dates, places, and audiences for each of the four Gospels.

5. List and briefly explain the gospel portrait of Jesus that each gospel writer paints for us.

6. List the Synoptic Gospels, and explain why they are given this name.

7. How do Matthew and Luke begin their Gospels? What problem did this create for them? Explain their threefold solution of the problem.

8. Explain the two points that stand out in the annunciation narrative.

9. What was the purpose and force of ancient Jewish engagements?

10. What point does Matthew make by his Immanuel prophecy?

11. What three things are especially remarkable about Luke's description of the birth of Jesus? Explain.

Discuss

1. While visiting the Holy Land, a man bought a nativity set. It was made up of tiny figures carved from olive wood: Jesus, Mary, Joseph, the shepherds. The airport security officer x-rayed each piece, explaining to the man, "We can't take chances. We must make sure there's nothing explosive in them." The man smiled to himself and thought, "That nativity set contains the most explosive power in the world."

What power did the man have in mind? How can that power be released?

2. A missionary in Africa had an African artist design a nativity set for Christmas. He was taken aback when he saw that all the figures had black features and were dressed in African garb. But as he thought about it, he said to himself, "That's better than designing them with Jewish features and Jewish garb."

Discuss the pros and cons for keeping the features of the figures historically accurate. How do you feel about this question?

3. A missionary entered a Peruvian church on Christmas. It was packed with Indian children holding squirming lambs. The Mass was chaotic. The missionary's homily could hardly be heard above the baa-a-as of the lambs. After Mass, the annoyed missionary asked an Indian friend, "What does bringing lambs to church have to do with Christmas?" His friend said,

"The first people to visit Jesus were shepherds, who didn't want to leave their newborn lambs unattended. So they brought them along. We're shepherds, and that's how we celebrate Christmas." The missionary suddenly realized that the baa-a-as of the lambs had preached a better homily than he had.

Explain the last sentence. What is the most important thing to remember in worshiping God?

Activities

1. A church in Texas ran a Christmas ad in the local paper. It showed three candles with the words "Come Home for Christmas." The ad read:

If you are Catholic, and have stopped going to church, this invitation is for you. Whether you are hurt, angered, or have just lost interest, we invite you home for Christmas. Your Catholic family misses you. We cannot promise to agree on everything. What family does! But we still find Christ and his love in the community of the Church, the Bible, and the Eucharist. We believe you can too.

Why is this ad a good/bad idea? Compose a similar ad for your church, to be run in the local paper. Write it from the viewpoint of a younger brother or sister inviting an older brother or sister to "come home" for the holidays.

2. Design a Christmas card with a spiritual message. Make it different from most cards. For example, compose a few lines similar to these by Jim Auer: "Christmas is a good time to get a little crazy. After all, God did. He became a human being. That's pretty crazy." If you wish, you can use Auer's lines and find a good drawing or photo to fit them.

Bible Reading

Pick a passage. After reading it, (1) summarize its main point, (2) tell how it relates to the chapter, and (3) list one or two thoughts that entered your mind as you read it.

1. Eternal Son   Proverbs 8:22–31
2. Light amid darkness   Isaiah 9:2–7
3. Eternal Word   John 1:1–18
4. Greater than angels   Hebrews 1
5. Long live the King!   Psalm 72

Prayer Journal

One way to bring the Gospel alive is to meditate on it. First, pick some biblical event and read it slowly. Second, imagine you are present at the event: What do you see and hear? How do you feel? Here is a sample meditation on Luke 2:8–14, the angel's appearance to the shepherds on Christmas Eve.

My name is Zack. What I am about to tell you is a true story. My cousin Ann and I were sitting around a campfire, guarding our sheep. Suddenly a ball of fire lit the sky above us. It was so bright it woke the sheep, but they didn't panic. They just looked at the sky. Then beautiful singing began. I never heard anything like it before. A minute later, an angel appeared, saying, "Don't be afraid! I am here with good news. . . . This day in David's town your Savior was born." Then, pointing to a light in a cave in the distance, the angel said, "You will find a baby lying in a manger." With that the angel vanished. Then the ball of fire moved toward the cave. Ann and I followed it. The music made us feel as though we were walking on a cloud. The air was cold, but our hearts were warm. At last we reached the cave and went inside.

Finish the meditation. What did Ann and Zack see and hear? How did they feel? First, read Luke 2:15–20. Then let your imagination run wild.

10 Pre-ministry

In his book *Roots*, Alex Haley describes the ancient ceremony by which his ancestors in Africa were named. It took place eight days after birth and made the child a member of the tribe. The highpoint came when the father took the child in his arms.

He lifted the infant, and as all watched,
whispered three times into his son's ear
the name he had chosen for him.
It was the first time the name
had ever been spoken as the child's name,
for Omorro's people felt that each human being
should be the first to know who he was.

That night the father completed the ceremony.

Out under the moon and the stars, alone . . .
he walked to the edge of the village,
lifted his baby up with its face to the heavens,
and said softly,
"Fend kiling dorong leh warrata ka iteh tee"
(Behold—the only thing greater than yourself).

This beautiful episode helps us appreciate better a similar ceremony that happened eight days after Jesus' birth.

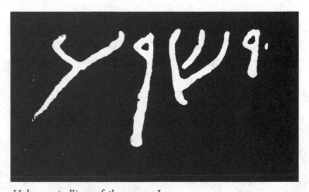

Hebrew spelling of the name Jesus.

Jesus Is Identified

Every Jewish boy was circumcised eight days after birth. This ceremony was so sacred that it could be performed even on the Sabbath. At this time the child was also named. Luke writes:

A week later, when the time came for the baby
to be circumcised, he was named Jesus,

107

*the name which the angel had given him
before he had been conceived.*

Luke continues:

> *The time came for Joseph and Mary
> to perform the ceremony of purification,
> as the Law of Moses commanded.
> So they took the child to Jerusalem
> to present him to the Lord.*
> LUKE 2:21–22

Three sacred actions surrounded the birth of every firstborn Jewish male: circumcision, presentation, and purification of the mother (Genesis 17:10, Exodus 13, Leviticus 12).

Circumcision initiated the child into the community of God's people.

Presentation consecrated the child to God, in thanksgiving for God's protection of Israel's firstborn during the final plague. The ceremony took place a month after the child's birth.

Purification welcomed the mother back into full participation in the worshiping community.

Jesus' presentation occasioned the inspired witness of two old Jews, Simeon and Anna. Both had been praying all their lives for the promised Messiah. Seeing Jesus, Simeon took him in his arms and gave thanks to God, saying:

> *"Now, Lord, you have kept your promise. . . .
> With my own eyes
> I have seen your salvation. . . . :
> A light to reveal your will to the Gentiles
> and bring glory to your people Israel."*
> LUKE 2:29–30, 32

Mary and Joseph were "amazed at the things Simeon said about him." Then Simeon turned to Mary and said:

> *"This child is chosen by God for the destruction
> and the salvation of many in Israel.
> He will be a sign from God
> which many people will speak against. . . .
> And sorrow, like a sharp sword,
> will break your own heart."*
> LUKE 2:34–35

In a similar way, Anna "gave thanks to God and spoke about the child to all who were waiting for God to set Jerusalem free" (*Luke 2:38*).

Three points emerge from the witness of Simeon and Anna. Jesus' future ministry will—

1. extend beyond Israel to the Gentiles,
2. split Israel into two groups: saved and lost,
3. bring pain to his mother.

Magi Visit Jesus

Another significant event took place sometime later. Magi from the East (wise men who studied the stars) came to Jerusalem inquiring about Jesus.

MAGI   *Where is the baby born to be the king
of the Jews? We saw his star
when it came up in the east,
and we have come to worship him.*

NARRATOR   *When King Herod heard about this,
he was very upset, and so was
everyone else in Jerusalem.
He called . . .
the teachers of the Law.*

HEROD   *Where will the Messiah be born?*

TEACHERS   *In the town of Bethlehem in Judea.
For this is what the prophet wrote:
"Bethlehem in the land of Judah,
you are by no means the least
of the leading cities of Judah;
for from you will come a leader
who will guide my people Israel."*

NARRATOR   *And so the visitors left. . . .
When they saw the child
with his mother Mary,
they knelt down and worshiped him.
They brought out their gifts
of gold, frankincense, and myrrh,
and presented them to him.
Then they returned to their country
by another road, since God
had warned them in a dream
not to go back to Herod.*
MATTHEW 2:2–6, 9, 11–12

Like the other events of Jesus' early years, the story of the Magi is drawn from three sources:

1. history (old people's remembrances),
2. prophecy (Old Testament prophecies),
3. theology (Matthew's inspiration).

We can detect "threads" from each of these three sources in the story of the Magi.

For example, *history* tells us about wise men from the East, called Magi. Historian John M. Scott says:

The Magi were not kings. . . .
They were the masters of kings.
The kings ruled the people,
but the wise men directed the kings.
They alone could communicate
with Ahuramazda, the god of light.
No king began war without consulting them.
In the name of science and religion,
they held first rank in the nation.

Similarly, threads from Old Testament *prophecies* seem to be woven into the Magi story. For example, the prophet Micah said:

Bethlehem Ephrathah,
you are one of the smallest towns in Judah,
but out of you I will bring a ruler for Israel.
MICAH 5:2

So, too, the psalmist wrote:

The kings of Arabia . . . will bring him offerings.
All kings will bow down before him;
all nations will serve him.
PSALM 72:10–11

Likewise, the prophet Balaam says in the Book of Numbers:

I look into the future,
And I see the nation of Israel.
A king, like a bright star,
will arise in that nation.
Like a comet he will come from Israel.
NUMBERS 24:17

That brings us to the third "thread," Matthew's personal *inspiration* from God. This is the most important thread. It is the one that weaves the other two together into the beautiful "tapestry" that we call the "Story of the Magi."

One final point. Early Christians attached deep significance to the Magi's three gifts: gold, frankincense, and myrrh.

Gold was the "king of metals." Therefore, it made an ideal symbol of Jesus' *kingship*.

King Herod

Herod the Great was enraged when the Magi left without telling him where Jesus was. So he ordered a massacre of "all the boys in Bethlehem and its neighborhood who were two years old and younger" (*Matthew 2:16*). Jesus escaped, however, because Joseph had taken him to Egypt (Matthew 2:13-14).

The massacre was the act of a sick man. An ancient historian, Josephus, tells us that not long after this order Herod attempted suicide. Rumors of the attempt caused loud wailing throughout his palace. When Herod's son (jailed by his father) heard the cries, he mistook them to mean that his father was dead. So he tried to bribe his jailers to release him. When Herod heard about this, he had the boy executed on the spot.

Now Herod's depression grew deeper. His own death was close, and he knew it. What pained him was the thought that his death would cause joy in Judea. To forestall this, he devised an incredible plan. Josephus says:

> *Having assembled the most distinguished men from every village from one end of Judea to the other, he ordered them to be locked in the hippodrome in Jericho.*

Herod decreed that they be executed at the moment he himself died. His sick mind reasoned that their death would dispel any joy in Judea over his own death. The order was never carried out.

The date of Herod's death is given as 4 B.C. This looks as though he died before Jesus' birth. Actually, Jesus was born before A.D. 1. Our present B.C.-A.D. calendar was designed in the sixth century by Dionysius Exiguus. He erred in his calculations by five to seven years. This means Jesus was probably born sometime between 7 B.C. and 5 B.C. Since it would be too troublesome to correct all the wrong dates, they are kept as they are.

Herod was buried in the Herodium (shown here). This artificially shaped minimountain is located outside Bethlehem. It was one of several fortress-palaces built by Herod the Great. Living quarters and fortifications are located inside the craterlike top (smaller photo).

One final point. Herod the Great is to be distinguished from Herod Antipas, his son, and from Herod Agrippa, his grandson.

Herod Antipas is the "Herod" who beheaded John the Baptist (Mark 6:21-28) and the "Herod" who questioned Jesus before his crucifixion (Luke 32:7).

Herod Agrippa is the "Herod" who jailed Peter and died a wretched death shortly afterward (Acts 12:1, 23).

Frankincense was used in religious worship. The aroma and smoke, coiling heavenward, spoke of divinity and therefore made an ideal symbol of Jesus' *divinity.*

Myrrh was used to prepare the dead for burial. Myrrh, therefore, spoke of human weakness and made an ideal symbol of Jesus' *humanity.*

Fifteen hundred years ago, an early Christian writer named Peter Chrysologus summed up the Magi story this way:

> *The Magi gaze in deep wonder at what they see:*
> *heaven on earth, earth in heaven,*
> *man in God, God in man. . . .*
> *As they look they believe and do not question,*
> *as their symbolic gifts bear witness:*
> *gold for a king, incense for God,*
> *and myrrh for one who is to die.*

Finally, we may note that the Magi story serves as a kind of twofold preview of what lies ahead for Jesus:

1. many Jews (like Herod) will reject him,
2. many Gentiles (like the Magi) will accept him.

Jesus Grows Up

The Gospels say little of Jesus' boyhood in Nazareth. Luke sums it up in one sentence: "Jesus grew both in body and in wisdom, gaining favor with God and men" (*Luke 2:52*).

Jesus' youth, however, was probably not too different from that of most Jewish boys. An ancient Jewish book, the Talmud, says of the Jewish boy:

> *At five he must begin sacred studies;*
> *at ten he must set himself*
> *to learning the tradition;*
> *at thirteen he must know the whole law*
> *of Yahweh and practice its requirements.*

Today, the religious ceremony of Bar Mitzvah ("Son of the Law") celebrates the thirteen-year-old boy's entry into early adulthood. He must now "know" and "practice" the "whole law." This explains why Jesus went to Jerusalem for the Passover when he was twelve (going on thirteen). He had reached early adulthood and was practicing the whole law.

Bar Mitzvah makes a Jewish boy a "son of the Law." It also qualifies him to be one of the ten people (minyan) required to hold a synagogue service.

After the celebration, the huge caravan of people from Galilee began the long trip home. Mary and Joseph had traveled a whole day before they realized that Jesus was not with them. So they hurried back to Jerusalem to look for him.

NARRATOR	*On the third day* *they found him in the Temple,* *sitting with the Jewish teachers,* *listening to them* *and asking questions.* *All who heard him were amazed* *at his intelligent answers.* *His parents were astonished* *when they saw him.*
MARY	*Son, why have you done this to us?* *Your father and I have been* *terribly worried trying to find you.*
JESUS	*Why did you have to look for me?* *Didn't you know that I had to be* *in my Father's house?*
NARRATOR	*But they did not understand* *his answer. So Jesus went back* *with them to Nazareth,* *where he was obedient to them.* *His mother treasured* *all these things in her heart.*

LUKE 2:46–51

One detail, especially, stands out in this episode. It is Jesus' question, "Didn't you know that I had to be in my Father's house?" It suggests the possibility that Jesus had a special religious experience during his Temple visit—perhaps an insight into his future mission.

Jesus Is Baptized

Linda Marshall, daughter of the famous chaplain of Congress, Peter Marshall, was about to take a shower. She had one foot in the shower and the other foot on the bathroom rug.

The Boy Jesus

Jesus probably did what most boys his age did. He climbed hills with friends, tracked foxes (Luke 9:58), and helped shepherds (John 10:1-4).

Jesus learned his father's trade (Mark 6:3). Like all fathers and sons, he and Joseph took days off together. On some of these, they hiked to the Sea of Galilee to watch the fishermen work their nets. Jesus may even have gone out with the fishermen on their boats.

The Sabbath was special for Jesus. It began on Friday night at sunset with a loud trumpet blast. Work stopped, and prayer began. On Sabbath morning, Jesus went with Mary and Joseph to the synagogue. There, the minister in charge appointed members of the congregation to read from the Hebrew Scriptures. No doubt, Joseph and Jesus were called upon regularly.

But amid the ordinariness of daily life in Nazareth, something wonderful and mysterious was happening inside the mind and heart of Jesus. His own human awareness of himself and his heavenly Father was developing in a beautiful way.

As she stood in this awkward position, she thought to herself, "This is a good picture of my life."

Linda had long wanted to commit her life to God, but she could never quite do it. She always kept one foot in and one foot out. Now it seemed the moment had finally come for her to decide.

Linda paused for a long time. Then she took a deep breath and said aloud, "I choose you, Lord." With that she stepped into the shower. It was like a baptism.

If we can relate to Linda's hard choice, we can relate to the hard choice John the Baptist set before people when he appeared preaching and baptizing along the Jordan River. John confronted people as no one had confronted them before.

> *It was the fifteenth year*
> *of the rule of Emperor Tiberius;*
> *Pontius Pilate was governor of Judea,*
> *Herod was ruler of Galilee. . . .*
> *At that time the word of God came to John*
> *son of Zechariah in the desert.*
> *So John went throughout the whole territory*
> *of the Jordan River, preaching,*
> *"Turn away from your sins and be baptized."*
> LUKE 3:1–3

Luke pinpoints the date of John's appearance several ways, to show its importance.

John's expression "turn away from your sins" translates the Hebrew word that means "to return from traveling down a wrong road and to set out anew on the right road." In other words, people should admit their sinful ways and correct them.

As a sign that they are sincere, John tells people to be baptized. He warns them, however, that good intentions are not enough: "Do those things that will show that you have turned from your sins" (*Luke 3:8*). Thus, John makes it clear that his baptism is only the first step of a journey.

> *"I baptize you with water*
> *to show that you have repented,*
> *but the one who will come after me*
> *will baptize you with the Holy Spirit and fire.*
> *He is much greater than I am;*
> *and I am not good enough*
> *even to carry his sandals."*
> MATTHEW 3:11

The point is clear. John's baptism is a *baptism of repentance,* a rejection of one's old life. Jesus'

baptism, on the other hand, is a *baptism of rebirth,* a reception of a new life.

One day, John was taken by surprise by something he had not expected. There, wading through the water to be baptized, was Jesus. What should he do?

> *John tried to make [Jesus] change his mind.*
> *"I ought to be baptized by you," John said,*
> *"and yet you have come to me!"*
> *But Jesus answered him, "Let it be so for now."*
> MATTHEW 3:14–15

And so Jesus was baptized, just like the rest of the people.

> *While he was praying, heaven was opened,*
> *and the Holy Spirit came down upon him*
> *in bodily form like a dove.*
> *And a voice came from heaven,*
> *"You are my own dear Son.*
> *I am pleased with you."*
> LUKE 3:21–22

Jordan River today.

Deeper Meaning

Three images stand out in this remarkable scene: the sky, the dove, and the voice.

The first image is the *sky opening* above Jesus. To understand this image, we need to know how ancient people viewed the universe. They saw it as three worlds stacked on top of each other, like pancakes. God lived in the top world; they lived in the middle world; and the dead lived in the bottom world.

The boundary between God's world and their world was the sky, which they conceived to be a crystallike dome (Genesis 1:6). The boundary between their world and the world of the dead was the ground they walked on.

After Adam's sin, the middle world became more and more evil. Holy people prayed to God to come down from his world and do something about their world.

> *Why don't you tear the sky open*
> *and come down?*
> ISAIAH 64:1

> *O LORD, tear open the sky*
> *and come down.*
> PSALM 144:5

It is against this background that we should interpret Luke's image of the *sky opening*. God is "tearing open the sky" and coming down into the world to set it right. A *new era* in human history is dawning.

The second image is the *dove hovering* over Jesus in the water. This image recalls the power of God hovering over the waters at the dawn of creation.

> *In the beginning . . . the power of God*
> *was moving over the water.*
> *Then God commanded, "Let there be light"—*
> *and light appeared.*
> GENESIS 1:1–3

Jewish rabbis likened the power of God hovering over the waters to a dove. Luke uses this image to teach that Jesus' baptism is the start of a *new creation*. The words of Isaiah are realized at last.

> *The LORD says, "I am making a new earth. . . .*
> *The events of the past*
> *will be completely forgotten.*
> *Be glad and rejoice forever in what I create."*
> ISAIAH 65:17–18

The third image is the *voice speaking* from heaven: "You are my own dear Son. I am pleased with you." Jesus is portrayed as being the firstborn son of the new creation. He is the "new Adam" of the "new creation." Paul says:

> *"The first man, Adam,*
> *was created a living being";*
> *but the last Adam [Jesus]*
> *is the life-giving Spirit. . . .*
> *The first Adam,*
> *made of earth, came from the earth;*
> *the second Adam came from heaven. . . .*
> *Just as we wear the likeness*
> *of the man made of earth [the first Adam],*
> *so we will wear the likeness*
> *of the Man from heaven [the second Adam].*
> 1 CORINTHIANS 15:45, 47, 49

This final image contains an important message for us today. Because we wear both the likeness of the "man of earth" and the "Man from heaven," we experience an inner tension in our lives between the flesh and the spirit.

Paul experienced this tension in his own life, saying, "I don't do what I would like to do, but instead I do what I hate" (*Romans 7:15*).

Even Jesus experienced this inner tension as we shall now see.

Jesus Is Tested

Doug Alderson wrote an article in *Campus Life*. In it, he explained why he took off on a two-thousand-mile, summer-long hike down the Appalachian Trail.

> *I had just graduated from high school.*
> *I had many questions. My goals in life?*
> *My future? Was there a God?*
> *I thought the answers might lie*
> *in the beautiful wilderness ahead.*

There had to be more to life than money,
TV, parties, and getting high.
In a sense, my hike was a search
for inner peace, a journey to find myself.

Doug said the long hours on the trail gave him a chance to get to know himself better and to plan his future.

Five months later he returned home—a changed person. Even his dog eyed him suspiciously, as if to say, "Where have you been? What have you done? You look different."

Doug was different. He found what he was searching for: "peace from within, and peace from God." He summed up his experience this way: "I was more my own person. I liked what I saw in myself."

Doug Alderson belongs to that long line of people in history who have gone off alone for a period of time to take inventory of themselves and to ask questions about the meaning of life. Moses did it; the prophets did it; John the Baptist did it.

It comes as no surprise, therefore, to find that Jesus did it, too. He went off into the desert for forty days to be alone with his thoughts and to commune with his Father.

NARRATOR   *After spending forty days*
and nights without food,
Jesus was hungry.
Then the Devil came to him.

DEVIL   *If you are God's Son, order these*
stones to turn into bread.

JESUS   *The scripture says,*
"Man cannot live on bread alone,
but needs every word
that God speaks."

NARRATOR   *Then the Devil took Jesus*
to Jerusalem, the Holy City,
[and] set him on the highest point
of the Temple.

DEVIL   *If you are God's Son,*
throw yourself down,
for the scripture says, "God will give
orders to his angels about you;
they will hold you up with their hands,
so that not even your feet
will be hurt on the stones."

JESUS   *But the scripture also says,*
"Do not put the Lord your God
to the test."

NARRATOR   *Then the Devil took Jesus*
to a very high mountain
and showed him all the kingdoms
of the world in all their greatness.

DEVIL   *All this I will give you,*
          if you kneel down and worship me.

JESUS   *Go away, Satan!*
          The scripture says,
          "Worship the Lord your God
          and serve only him!"
          MATTHEW 4:2–10

Jesus' temptations (test) in the desert have a deeper meaning than what first appears on the surface. To understand this meaning, think of them as a movie preview. A preview tells just enough about a movie to get people interested in it, but not enough to spoil the story. Jesus' temptations do something similar. They preview the answers to three important questions about Jesus:

1. his *identity* (Who is he?),
2. his *mission* (What did he come to do?),
3. his *style* (How will he go about doing it?).

But the temptations show something more. They show that Jesus reacted to the devil in a totally different way than we do. He did not hesitate or waver. No one ever showed such firmness in the face of temptation.

Jesus' reaction to temptation shows that he is more than just another human. There is something special about him. The devil gives a clue to this "specialness" when he says, "If you are *God's Son.*" Jesus is not just another human being. He is *God's Son* become man. Years later, Paul described Jesus this way:

He always had the nature of God,
but he . . . became like man
and appeared in human likeness.
PHILIPPIANS 2:6–7

And so the temptations preview the answer to our first question, Who is Jesus? Jesus is both *man* and *God.*

Jesus' Identity

Jesus' temptations show that he felt inside himself the same inner tension between flesh and spirit that we feel. He experienced the same inner conflict between right and wrong that we experience. In other words, his temptations show that he was truly *human,* as we are.

Jesus' Mission

The temptations also preview the answer to the question, What did Jesus come to do? Recall two things we learned earlier.

First, Jesus' baptism revealed that a *new creation* or *re-creation* of the world was taking place. Second, right after the first creation, the

This mountain overlooks Jericho. Tradition says this is the desert spot where Jesus spent forty days. A modern Greek monastery wraps itself around the mountain. Here monks continue to fast and pray in imitation of Jesus.

devil tempted Adam, the first man, and caused him to sin. That sin brought spiritual death to all of Adam's descendants. Paul writes:

> *Sin came into the world through one man,*
> *and his sin brought death with it.*
> *As a result,*
> *death has spread to the whole human race*
> *because everyone has sinned.*
> ROMANS 5:12

Now, the devil repeats the process. He tempts Jesus, the first man of the *new* creation, and tries to get him to sin, also. But Jesus stands firm.

Jesus' victory over the devil restores life to the human race. "So then, as the one sin condemned all [people], in the same way the one righteous act sets all [people] free and gives them life" (*Romans 5:18*). That is exactly the way Paul explains Jesus' mission.

> *Just as all people die*
> *because of their union with Adam,*
> *in the same way all will be raised to life*
> *because of their union with Christ. . . .*
> *For the scripture says, "The first man,*
> *Adam, was created a life-giving being";*
> *but the last Adam [Christ]*
> *is the life-giving Spirit.*
> 1 CORINTHIANS 15:22, 45

In other words, Jesus' mission is to be the *new* Adam of the *new* creation. He has come to right the *first* Adam's wrong. He has come to undo his sin and restore life to the human race.

Jesus' Style

Finally, Jesus' temptations preview the way he will carry out his mission.

First, Jesus' refusal to turn stones into bread shows that he will not use his marvelous power for his own comfort or benefit. Rather, Jesus will sweat, hunger, and suffer to accomplish his work on earth.

Second, Jesus' refusal to throw himself down from the Temple and let the angels protect him previews that he has not come to be served but to serve. Later, he will tell his disciples:

> *"If one of you wants to be first,*
> *he must be the slave of all.*
> *For even the Son of Man*
> *did not come to be served;*
> *he came to serve."*
> MARK 10:44–45

Finally, Jesus' refusal to kneel before the devil, even in exchange for the whole world, previews that he will not compromise or negotiate with evil. This temptation implies, correctly, that at that moment the world belonged to the devil to give to whomever he wished. Jesus' refusal shows that God is God, right is right, wrong is wrong. Jesus will suffer—even die—at the hands of evil, rather than negotiate with it.

And so by rejecting the devil's temptations, Jesus previews three principles that will characterize the style he will follow in carrying out his mission:

1. he will suffer, rather than avoid pain;
2. he will serve, rather than be served;
3. he will die, rather than negotiate with evil.

After the temptations, Jesus left the desert and reentered the world he came to save.

Understanding Pre-ministry

Review

1. List and explain the three ceremonies that surrounded the birth of Jewish males in biblical times.

2. What three points emerged from the inspired witness of Simeon and Anna when Jesus was taken to the Temple as a baby?

3. List and illustrate the three threads from which the Magi story is woven. Which is the most important, and why?

4. Explain the symbolism that early Christians attached to the Magi's gifts to Jesus.

5. List the three "Herods" mentioned in the Bible. Give one important biblical event for which each was responsible.

6. In what year was Jesus probably born? Explain.

7. Why did Jesus go to Jerusalem to celebrate the Passover when he was a boy?

8. Explain the point or purpose of John's baptism. How did it differ from the one Jesus prescribed?

9. Explain the meaning of the three images that accompanied John's baptism of Jesus.

10. Explain what Jesus' temptations suggest (preview) concerning (a) his identity, (b) his mission, (c) the manner in which he will carry out his mission.

Discuss

1. Explain how the following statements relate to temptation:

Every evil to which we do not succumb is a benefactor. (Ralph Waldo Emerson)

There is a silly idea about that good people don't know what temptation is. (C. S. Lewis)

If the camel once gets his nose in the tent, his body will soon follow. (Arab proverb)

2. Albert Wiggam wrote: "I feel sorry for the person who has never gone without dinner to buy a book of poems, a ticket to a concert, a little statuette or a picture or a pretty rug or chair for his home."

What is his point? Share with the group one sacrifice you made to achieve something or buy something for yourself or another.

3. The Bible mentions fasting over seventy times. Often it is mentioned in connection with praying. In other words, prayer and fasting are joined.

Why add fasting to praying for something? What was the longest time you went without food? What was the occasion for it? Why are "hunger strikes" so effective? Can you recall such a strike by someone?

Activities

1. Henry Van Dyke wrote a fascinating short story called "The Other Wise Man." It concerns a fourth person, Artaban, who was supposed to accompany the other wise men to Bethlehem. Try to find a copy of the story in the library to learn what gift he was bringing and why he never reached Bethlehem.

Imagine you are the "other" wise man. What gift would you bring to Jesus? Write a brief paragraph explaining your choice.

2. William Sydney Porter (O. Henry) wrote a short story called "The Gift of the Magi." It concerns two young people, Jim and Dela, who buy each other Christmas gifts. Try to locate the story in the library and find out what the gifts were and the "surprise" ending to each gift.

Describe one of the best gifts you ever received for Christmas or a birthday. What made it one of your best?

3. Circumcision might be compared to Christian baptism. Interview your parents or your sponsors about your baptism. Who baptized you? Where? When? Who attended? What kind of day was it? Did you cry? What other name did they consider calling you? Try to get a photocopy of your baptism.

4. Andrew Burgh of Evanston, Illinois, said to those gathered for his Bar Mitzvah celebration: "My Bar Mitzvah is the time when I become a Jewish adult and take on more responsibilities toward the Jewish community." Andrew then read a letter he wrote to the Prime Minister of Israel protesting the war in Lebanon, which was going on at that time. He ended his letter, saying: "Instead of centerpieces and candy and nuts for my Bar Mitzvah party, I have asked my family to send money to the Kiryat Sanz Laniado Hospital, where Jews hurt in the war are being treated."

Interview a Jewish boy (telephone or face-to-face) about Bar Mitzvah. Where and when is it made? What goes on? Is there a similar ceremony for girls? Write out the responses, and comment on the interview. What sacrament is Bar Mitzvah similar to? Explain.

5. Check the lyrics to the song hit "We Are the World" by Michael Jackson and Lionel Richie.

What temptation of Jesus is referred to? What mistake is made in the reference?

Bible Reading

Pick a passage. After reading it, (1) summarize its main point, (2) tell how it relates to the chapter, and (3) list one or two thoughts that entered your mind as you read it.

1. Angels will protect you   Psalm 91
2. Don't test your God   Deuteronomy 6:10–25
3. Not on bread alone   Deuteronomy 8:1–10
4. New creation   Isaiah 65:17–25
5. New song   Psalm 144

Prayer Journal

Like Jesus in the desert, all of us have been tempted. Describe a temptation experience in your life. Here is an experience turned in by one student.

My biggest temptation experience occurred in the eighth grade. One day I stole a cassette recorder and headphones from my school. That night my conscience wouldn't let me sleep. I kept thinking about the wrong I'd done to the other students and to God.

After a sleepless night, I decided to return the equipment. I figured this was the only way to make amends for my actions. I built up my courage and made an appointment with the principal. I confided in her totally. She promised that if I returned everything, nothing would happen.

Out in the street, the sun was going down and its rays touched me. I felt a warm glow inside me and all around me. I have yet to experience anything quite like that moment. It was a great feeling to know that I had come back to God of my own free will, after having broken with him.

11 *Miracle Ministry*

Paride Taban was just a schoolboy when a religious persecution broke out in his country in the Sudan, Africa. Since he was Catholic, he fled to Uganda. There he entered a seminary and became a priest.

Eventually, the situation in the Sudan improved and young Father Taban returned home. But the Catholics of his homeland could not believe that he was actually a priest. Father Taban says, "The people looked hard at me and asked, 'Do you mean to say, black man, that you are a priest? We can't believe it.'"

These people had never seen a black priest before. Their priests had always been white and had given them medicine and clothing. Father Taban was from the Madi tribe and was poor. He had no "things" to give them.

To make matters worse, Father Taban had to introduce his Catholics to the new changes of Vatican II. They said to one another, "This young black man turns our altar around and celebrates Mass in our own language. He cannot be a real priest."

Father Taban's experience of opposition from his own people helps us understand a similar experience that Jesus had early in his ministry.

Jesus Meets Opposition

After his stay in the desert, Jesus went north to Galilee to the lakeside town of Capernaum. There he preached that God's kingdom (re-creation of the world) was at hand. His words stirred up excitement. Soon, people from nearby towns invited Jesus to preach in their synagogues. It was during this tour of preaching that Jesus returned to his hometown in Nazareth.

> *On the Sabbath he went as usual*
> *to the synagogue. He stood up*
> *to read the Scriptures and was handed*
> *the book of the prophet Isaiah.*
> *He unrolled the scroll and found the place*
> *where it is written,*
>
> *"The Spirit of the Lord is upon me,*
> *because he has chosen me*
> *to bring good news to the poor.*
> *He has sent me to proclaim liberty*
> *to the captives*
> *and recovery of sight to the blind,*
> *to set free the oppressed*
> *and announce that the time has come*
> *when the Lord will save his people."*

Jesus rolled up the scroll, gave it back
to the attendant, and sat down.
All the people . . . had their eyes fixed on him,
as he said to them,
"This passage of scripture has come true today,
as you heard it being read."
They were all well impressed with him
and marveled at the eloquent words
that he spoke.
LUKE 4:16–22

For centuries, Jews had gathered in synagogues to read the Scriptures and to pray for the coming of the Messiah and God's kingdom. Now, Jesus tells his friends and neighbors that *he* is God's answer to their prayers.

When the full impact of his words hit home, a ripple of whispering broke out: "Is this not Joseph's son? Is he not one of us?"

Within minutes the ripple of whispering turned into a wave of talking: "What are we to think? Is he saying he's the Messiah? What's gotten into him?"

Suddenly, the wave exploded into a storm of protests: "He blasphemes! He blasphemes!" The people "rose up, dragged Jesus out of town, and . . . meant to throw him over the cliff, but he walked through the middle of the crowd and went his way" (*Luke 4:29–30*).

Luke's words bring the starry-eyed Christian down to earth with a thud. They recall the prophecy Simeon spoke to Joseph and Mary when Jesus was presented in the Temple.

> *"This child . . . will be a sign from God*
> *which many people will speak against."*
> LUKE 2:34

Jesus left Nazareth with a preview of what lay ahead for him. He also left with a new awareness of what his ministry involved. It involved exposing himself to opposition—violent opposition.

Stone fragments from an ancient synagogue. The word Nazareth *appears on the second line of the fragment on the left.*

Jesus Works Miracles

Someone said, "There was a time when Christians believed because of Jesus' miracles. Now, they believe in spite of them." Not everyone agrees with that statement, but most agree with the point behind it. People today are products of a scientific age. And one of their unspoken laws is this: "Everything can be explained!" By definition, people tend to rule out the mysterious.

But when it comes to the life of Jesus, the mysterious must be confronted head on. It cannot be ruled out or ignored.

The New Testament uses three different words to refer to Jesus' miracles: *teras, dynamis,* and *semeion.* Each of these Greek words (the New Testament was written in Greek) provides some insight into what a miracle really is.

Teras means "a marvel." It stresses the idea that a miracle is something that makes people marvel. It is something that astonishes them,

amazes them, flabbergasts them. They do not know what to make of it.

Dynamis means "a power." It is the word from which *dynamite* comes. It stresses the idea that a miracle is something powerful. It can restore sight to a blind person, hearing to a deaf person, life to a dead person.

Semeion means "a sign." It stresses the idea that a miracle is like a flashing red light. The important thing is not the flashing red light, but what it *signifies.* In other words, a miracle points to something beyond a blind person seeing again. It points to the miracle's *significance:* what Jesus wanted to say through it.

Semeion is the word that the evangelist John used most often. For John, Jesus' miracles had two levels: the *sense* level (what was *seen*) and the *sign* level (what was *signified*). It is this meaning that is stressed in this chapter.

Let us now take a closer look at Jesus' miracles to see what they signified, that is, what Jesus wanted to say through them.

Miracles Are Announcements

Why did Jesus work miracles? Was it because he felt sorry for people who were crippled or blind? Was it because these people asked him to be healed?

Obviously, Jesus cured people for both of these reasons. He was moved by their wretched condition. He was also moved by their pleas for help. But there were two deeper purposes for which Jesus worked miracles.

First, miracles were *announcements.* They announced that Jesus is the Promised One, who is inaugurating God's kingdom (re-creation).

Second, miracles were *invitations.* They invited people to believe in Jesus and to become members (re-creations) in God's kingdom.

Let us now look at several of Jesus' miracles to see how they achieved the first of these

purposes: to announce that Jesus is the Promised One, who is inaugurating God's kingdom.

Healing Miracles

Concert pianist Marta-Korwin Rhodes was in Warsaw when the city was attacked by the Nazis. Instead of fleeing, she stayed to work in the hospitals. One night she came upon a soldier sobbing. The sight moved her deeply. She placed her hands on the young man's head and began to pray. Almost instantly, he stopped crying and fell asleep.

What caused this? Was it the touch of her hands that told him she cared? Was it God's grace working through her prayer? Or was it a combination of both?

Jesus used touch and prayer to heal people. For example, Mark describes Jesus' healing of a deaf-mute.

> *Jesus took him off alone, away from the crowd,*
> *put his fingers in the man's ears, spat,*
> *and touched the man's tongue.*
> *Then Jesus looked up to heaven,*
> *gave a deep groan, and said to the man,*
> *"Ephphatha," which means, "Open up!"*
> *At once the man was able to hear,*
> *his speech impediment was removed,*
> *and he began to talk without any trouble.*
> MARK 7:33–35

This brings us to our first question: How did these miracles announce that Jesus is the Promised One who is inaugurating God's kingdom?

Jesus himself answered that question. One day, some friends of John the Baptist came to ask Jesus if he were the Promised One. Jesus replied:

> *"Tell John what you have seen and heard:*
> *the blind can see, the lame can walk . . .*
> *the deaf can hear,*
> *the dead are raised to life,*
> *and the Good News is preached to the poor."*
> LUKE 7:22

To understand Jesus' answer, we need to go back to the Hebrew Scriptures. The prophet Isaiah had foretold that the coming of the Promised One would be accompanied by certain signs. These signs would be as follows:

> *The blind will be able to see,*
> *and the deaf will hear.*
> *The lame will leap and dance,*
> *and those who cannot speak will shout for joy.*
> ISAIAH 35:5–6

In other words, by his response to John's friends, Jesus reveals that he is the one of whom Isaiah spoke.

And so the first reason why Jesus healed people was to announce that he is the Promised One, who is inaugurating God's kingdom.

This brings us to a second kind of miracle Jesus worked.

Who is this Jesus?

Expulsion Miracles

The movie *The Exorcist* is about a young person possessed by an evil power. It was based on a true case of a fourteen-year-old who lived in Mount Rainier, Maryland, in 1949. The young person's life was a living hell until the evil power was expelled.

Although expelling evil powers is rare today, it was not that uncommon in biblical times. For example, once Jesus was in a synagogue. Suddenly a man with an evil spirit began to shout:

> MAN   *What do you want with us,*
> *Jesus of Nazareth?*
> *Are you here to destroy us?*
> *I know who you are:*
> *you are God's holy messenger!*
>
> JESUS   *Be quiet*
> *and come out of the man!*
>
> NARRATOR   *The demon threw the man down*
> *in front of them*
> *and went out of him*
> *without doing him any harm.*
> *The people were all amazed . . .*
> *and the report about Jesus spread*
> *everywhere in that region.*
> LUKE 4:34-37

"What does all this mean?" the people asked themselves as they left the synagogue.

Sometime later, Jesus answered the question himself. It happened when someone said he expelled demons by the power of "Beelzebul, the chief of the demons." Jesus responded:

> *"No, it is rather by means of God's power*
> *that I drive out demons,*
> *and this proves that the Kingdom of God*
> *has already come to you."*
> LUKE 11:20

And so, Jesus presented his power over demons as a second way to announce he is the Promised One, who is inaugurating the kingdom of God.

This brings us to yet a third group of miracles that Jesus worked.

Nature Miracles

The Sea of Galilee is six hundred feet below sea level. It is entirely surrounded by hills and ravines. The ravines act as wind tunnels. As warm air rises around sunset, cool air rushes through the ravines to replace it. The result is amazing. Within minutes, a quiet lake turns into an angry, white-capped sea. This unusual phenomenon tallies perfectly with "the storm at sea," described in Luke's Gospel.

NARRATOR   *One day Jesus got into a boat*
with his disciples.

JESUS   *Let us go across to the other side*
of the lake.

NARRATOR   *. . . Suddenly a strong wind*
blew down on the lake,
and the boat began to fill with water. . . .

DISCIPLES   *Master! Master!*
We are about to die!

NARRATOR   *Jesus got up*
and gave an order to the wind
and to the stormy water;
they quieted down,
and there was a great calm. . . .

DISCIPLES   *Who is this man?*
He gives orders
to the winds and waves,
and they obey him!
LUKE 8:22–25

"He calmed the raging storm, and the waves became quiet." Psalm 107:29

To understand the *deeper meaning* of this miracle, we need to go back to the first sin. Recall that as a result of it, evil invaded not only the human heart but also all of creation.

Soil that once produced fruit now produced thorns. Water that once irrigated fields now flooded and destroyed them. Age that once produced wisdom and beauty now produced ugliness and death.

In other words, sin alienated nature from people. The harmony that once existed between them was destroyed.

It is against this background that we must view Jesus' calming the storm at sea. It shows that the rebellion of nature that began with the first sin is now at an end. Jesus showed his power over nature.

And so Jesus presented his power over nature as yet a third sign that he is the Promised One, who is inaugurating God's kingdom on earth. God, in the person of Jesus, has indeed "torn open the sky," entered our world, and is re-creating it.

This brings us to the second *deeper purpose* for which Jesus worked miracles.

Miracles Are Invitations

Bruce Marshall wrote a humorous story about someone who prayed for a miracle so great that people could no longer doubt the truth of God and religion. The miracle—and here is the humorous part—is to have a sinful nightclub lifted off its foundation and carried away to a deserted island off the coast of Scotland.

The miracle takes place, but instead of converting people, it has the opposite effect. The nightclub owners turn the whole thing into a big publicity stunt. The story ends with the person realizing that it takes more than a miracle to bring people to faith.

John makes a similar point in his Gospel. One day, Jesus told a blind man to wash in the Pool of Siloam. The man did, and his sight came back.

Jesus said to the blind man, "Go and wash your face in the pool of Siloam" (John 9:7). The man did and "came back seeing." Today, small boys bathe in the same Pool of Siloam.

When certain religious leaders heard about this, they refused to believe that Jesus had healed the man. Jesus said to them:

*"I came to this world to judge,
so that the blind should see
and those who see should become blind."*
JOHN 9:39

The point is clear. No one, not even Jesus, can compel belief. Believing involves much more than seeing signs and hearing words. It also involves opening our hearts to what we see and hear.

This brings us to the second *deeper purpose* for which Jesus worked miracles. Beside using them as *announcements,* Jesus also used them as *invitations.* He employed them to invite people to believe and become members (new creations) in God's kingdom. How so? Consider this fact.

The healing of the blind, the curing of the deaf, the raising of the dead—these were not permanent cures. The blind person's sight would dim again with age, the deaf person's hearing would fade again, and the dead person would die again. What, then, was the *deeper meaning* behind these miracles?

The healing of the blind is a *sign* inviting people to open their eyes to what Jesus did. The curing of the deaf is a *sign* inviting people to open their ears to what Jesus said. Finally, the raising of the dead is a *sign* inviting people to be reborn—to begin new lives as "new creations" in God's kingdom.

And so the second purpose for which Jesus used miracles was to invite people to believe and to enter God's kingdom.

People Respond to Jesus

Many Palestinian farmers sowed their seed on top of the soil and then plowed it under. It was a common occurrence for some seed to blow onto footpaths that sometimes crisscrossed fields or to blow into thick patches of thornbushes that bordered the fields. Some seed also fell on the thin skin of soil that sometimes hid large, flat rocks just below the soil's surface.

Jesus used this familiar situation as the background for an important parable: the parable of the sower.

One day a man sowed seed in his field. Some fell on a footpath. Birds snatched it up immediately. Some fell on the thin skin of soil hiding rocks. It sprouted quickly but died when the sun dried the moisture in the thin skin. Some blew into thorn patches. It took root but did not bear

Path People

Sir Kenneth Clark is a British television celebrity. In his book *The Other Half: A Self-Portrait,* Clark describes a religious experience he had in the church of San Lorenzo in Italy. It was so intense that he considered making some changes in his life.

After the experience passed, however, so did Sir Kenneth's considerations about making the changes. Looking back on the incident, he wrote of his decision not to change.

> *I think I was right: I was too deeply imbedded*
> *in the world to change course.*
> *But that I had "felt the finger of God,"*
> *I was quite sure.*

Clark's response reminds us of the seed that fell on the footpath. That seed stands for those who hear God's word, "but the Devil comes and takes the message away."

This leads us to the second situation Jesus talked about in his parable.

fruit because the thorns choked it. Jesus explained the parable this way:

> *"The seeds that fell along the path*
> *stand for those who hear;*
> *but the Devil comes*
> *and takes the message away. . . .*
> *The seeds that fell on rocky ground*
> *stand for those who hear the message*
> *and receive it gladly. . . .*
> *But when the time of testing comes,*
> *they fall away.*
> *The seeds that fell among thorn bushes*
> *stand for those who hear;*
> *but the worries and riches and pleasures*
> *of this life crowd in and choke them,*
> *and their fruit never ripens.*
> *The seeds that fell in good soil*
> *stand for those who hear the message*
> *and . . . bear fruit."*
>
> LUKE 8:12–15

To see how Jesus' parable works in real life, let us look at four true stories. Each illustrates one of the situations Jesus describes.

Rock People

Two brothers, Clarence and Robert, committed their lives to Jesus when they were young. Later, Clarence became active in the civil rights movement. Robert became a lawyer, with political dreams.

One day Clarence turned to Robert for help in a legal problem. Robert begged off, saying that involvement in the problem could hurt his political future. Clarence was stunned. He confronted Robert about his commitment to Jesus. Robert responded, "I follow Jesus, but not all the way to the cross. I'm not getting myself crucified." Clarence said, "Robert, you're not a follower of Jesus; you're only a fan of his."

Robert's situation can be compared to the seed that fell on rocky ground. It stands for those who hear Jesus' message "and receive it gladly. But when the time of testing comes, they fall away."

This brings us to the third situation described in the parable.

Thorn People

A high school girl in Philadelphia wrote the following comments as part of a homework assignment.

> *I got this strange feeling in class*
> *when we were discussing the parable*
> *about the farmer who planted the seed.*
> *It was like Jesus was speaking right to me.*
>
> *At the end of last year,*
> *I had this really good talk with my counselor.*
> *She helped me see a lot of things differently,*
> *and I made several resolutions for this year.*
>
> *Then, yesterday, it really hit me.*
> *I hadn't followed up on a single resolution.*
> *I had let all of them get lost in a lot*
> *of other things.*

The girl's comments are like the seed that fell among thorns. It stands for those who hear Jesus' words, "but the worries and riches and pleasures of this life crowd in and choke them."

And that brings us to the fourth and final situation Jesus described.

Soil People

In his book *Basic Christianity,* John R. Stott describes an incident that happened when he was a young man. One Sunday night, he knelt down at his bedside and committed his life totally to Jesus Christ. The next day he wrote:

> *Yesterday really was an eventful day. . . .*
> *Behold, he stands at the door and knocks.*
> *I have heard*
> *and now he has come into my house.*
> *He has cleansed it and now rules it.*

Later on, Stott wrote these words:

> *I really have felt an immense new joy. . . .*
> *It is the joy of being at peace with the world*
> *and being in touch with God.*
> *I never really knew God before.*

John's total commitment to Jesus can be compared to the seed that fell on good soil. It stands for those "who hear the message . . . and bear fruit."

Obstacles to Responding

A *Peanuts* cartoon shows Charlie Brown standing inside his house. He is all bundled up to go out to play in the snow. That's his problem. He is so bundled up that he can't get through the door.

Had this cartoon been around in his time, Jesus might have used it to teach about God's kingdom. To enter it, people must be willing to strip away whatever keeps them from passing through the door to it.

Jesus stressed this point when a rich young man came to him and asked what he must do to enter into eternal life. Jesus replied, "Keep the commandments." The youth replied that he did.

JESUS   *If you want to be perfect,*
               go and sell all you have and
               give the money to the poor . . . ;
               then come and follow me.

NARRATOR   *When the young man heard this,*
               he went away sad,
               because he was very rich.

JESUS   *[to his disciples]*
               I assure you . . . it is much harder
               for a rich person to enter
               the Kingdom of God
               than for a camel to go through
               the eye of a needle.
               MATTHEW 19:21–24

Some people try to soften Jesus' words, suggesting that "the eye of a needle" was a narrow gate through which a camel could barely squeeze. Others suggest the Greek word *kamilon* ("cable"), not *kamelon* ("camel"), was what Jesus meant. But most people think Jesus' imagery fits the oriental practice of exaggerating to make a point.

What is the point? Put in simplest terms, it is this: Wealth and material things are big obstacles to accepting Jesus' invitation to follow him.

In conclusion, the parable of the sower and the parable of the rich young man are *mirror* parables. That is, they act as mirrors into which we can look to get a better picture of ourselves. They make us ask:

Which of the four people in the parable of the sower are we most like? How closely do we resemble the rich youth? How willing are we to strip away everything that keeps us from entering the door of God's kingdom?

Jesus the Storyteller

Jesus took everyday scenes, like a man casting a net into the sea, and turned them into striking parables. Parables were simple stories drawn from this life to teach people about things beyond life.

Parables were ideally suited to help Jesus teach the people of his day about such things as God's kingdom and the Messiah. How so?

First, many people expected God's kingdom to be a worldly one that would catapult Israel into first place among the nations. They also expected the Messiah to be a worldly king, like David. Jesus had to correct these notions before revealing his own identity and mission. This explains why, early in his ministry, he guarded against anything that would reinforce these false notions.

Thus, after healing a leper, Jesus told him, "Don't tell anyone about this" (*Mark 1:44*). Jesus had to reeducate the people about the Messiah and the kingdom first. This required tact and had to be done gradually. Parables were ideally suited for this. They made their point subtly and delicately, without crushing or disillusioning the people.

Second, God's kingdom was so far beyond people's everyday experience that Jesus could not speak about it directly. Paul said of the kingdom: "What no one ever saw or heard, what no one ever thought could happen, is the very thing God prepared for those who love him" (*1 Corinthians 2:9*). Parables taught about God's kingdom by using simple stories that allowed people to stretch their minds gradually to embrace ideas that were bigger than those they were used to.

Finally, parables revealed the status of people's hearts. They invited people to discover themselves as they really were: open or closed to truth. Since a parable did not make its point directly, it gave people the option of accepting or rejecting the deeper meaning to which it pointed. Hearers were free to admit the teaching or to close their ears and eyes to it. Thus, parables acted as a kind of test to see if a person's heart was open or closed. Concerning people with closed hearts, Jesus said to his disciples:

*"So the prophecy of Isaiah applies to them:
'This people will listen and listen,
but not understand;
they will look and look, but not see,
because their minds are dull,
and they have stopped up their ears
and have closed their eyes.
Otherwise, their eyes would see,
their ears would hear,
their minds would understand,
and they would turn to me, says God,
and I would heal them.'
As for you, how fortunate you are!
Your eyes see and your ears hear."*
MATTHEW 13:14-16

Understanding Miracle Ministry

Review

1. How did Jesus' preaching experience at Nazareth preview what lay ahead for him?

2. What three words does the New Testament use to refer to Jesus' miracles? What does each mean? How does each contribute to the understanding of what a miracle is?

3. What are the two major purposes for which Jesus used miracles?

4. Explain how the following acted as *signs* announcing the arrival of God's kingdom: healing miracles, expulsion miracles, nature miracles.

5. Explain how the following acted as *signs* inviting people to believe: Jesus' healing of the blind and the deaf, his raising of the dead.

6. Using the parable of the sower as an example, list and explain the four ways people responded to Jesus' preaching.

7. Give three reasons why parables were ideally suited to teach the people of Jesus' time about God's kingdom and the Messiah.

8. What is the point of the story of the rich young man?

9. Using the parable of the sower as an example, explain what a *mirror* parable is.

Discuss

1. "If Jesus were to come today, people would not crucify him. They would ask him out to dinner, hear what he had to say, and make fun of him" (Carlyle).

Do you agree with that statement totally, partially, hardly at all? Explain.

2. An artist said, "If we are to believe the life Jesus lived, the pictures that were painted of him just didn't fit the man."

What did the artist mean? What do the following Scripture passages suggest about Jesus' physical body: Mark 1:39; Luke 4:1–2, 6:12, 9:58? Can you think of reasons why Jesus might have been physically attractive?

3. Four friends—Terri, Tom, Matt, and Mary—made a retreat together. Terri didn't like it. Tom liked it; it inspired him to begin praying daily. Matt and Mary liked it, too. Matt decided to work at a boys' club on Saturdays. Mary decided to spend more time with her family. Two months later, the four friends met for lunch. The retreat came up again. Terri still disliked it. Matt and Mary confessed they had abandoned their retreat resolutions. Matt missed Saturday football too much. Mary didn't like being called "antisocial" by her friends. Tom, alone, persevered in his resolution.

Which of the four friends was like the seed that fell on the path? The thorns? The rock? The good soil? Explain.

4. Suppose Jesus came to earth today in America, rather than in the first century in Palestine.

Do you think his parents would live—
  a. in a small town,
  b. in the inner city, or
  c. in a migrant worker camp?

When Jesus grew up, do you think he would live with—
  a. fishermen on the Gulf of Mexico,
  b. street people in Washington, D.C., or
  c. ordinary people anywhere?

Do you think Jesus would—
  a. be a pastor in a small, poor church,
  b. beg on street corners, or
  c. do odd jobs anywhere?

Would Jesus do most of his preaching—
  a. in shopping centers,
  b. at rock concerts and on college campuses, or
  c. on radio and TV?

From what three groups would Jesus pick his twelve Apostles?

  a. salespeople   **d.** minority workers
  b. the jobless   **e.** college students
  c. disc jockeys   **f.** professional athletes

Activities

1. Team up with some friends and do a pantomime of the parable of the sower. Act out the fate of the seeds that fell on the path, the rock, the thorns, the good soil. For an encore, pantomime some lesser-known parables and have the class try to identify them.

2. You are a reporter for the *Jerusalem Daily News*. Do a feature story on one or several of Jesus' miracles. Interview the person healed, eyewitnesses, and Jesus himself.

3. A London newspaper carried this ad in the early 1900s: "Wanted: Persons for dangerous journey. Small wages, bitter cold, long months of complete darkness, constant danger, safe return doubtful, honor and recognition if successful."

Why do you think over five thousand applicants answered the ad?

Sir Ernest Shackleton chose twenty-eight men from the five thousand for his polar expedition. All returned safely to honor and recognition.

Today, there is a need for courageous, dedicated people in Christian ministry: priests, nuns, brothers, lay missionaries.

Imagine you operate an advertising agency. A bishop commissions you to design an ad challenging high school graduates to enter Christian ministry as a life's work. The ad is to run full-page (8½" × 11"), with photos and not more than fifty words of copy. Design the ad.

4. Interview two adults you know well. Ask them if they think it is easier or harder to follow Jesus today than when they were young? Have them give reasons for their answers. Record their answers. Write out your own response to this question.

5. Miracles still happen today. The *Reader's Digest* (April 1982) contains an article about a young soldier's miraculous cure. The article is entitled "Vittorio Micheli's Pilgrimage to Lourdes."

Look up the article in the library and prepare a report on it for the group.

6. *The Exorcist* is based on a true story. It was talked about in the February 11, 1974, *Newsweek* magazine. The magazine also discussed exorcisms in general. Get the magazine in a library and prepare a report for the group.

Bible Reading

Pick a passage. After reading it, (1) summarize its main point, (2) tell how it relates to the chapter, and (3) list one or two thoughts that entered your mind as you read it.

1. I see walking trees	Mark 8:22–26
2. The "Rock" sinks	Matthew 14:22–31
3. Who touched me?	Luke 8:40–56
4. Case of the two sons	Matthew 21:28–32
5. Blinder than the blind	John 9

Prayer Journal

One day Jesus healed a paralyzed person whom friends had lowered through an opening in the roof (Luke 5:17–26). Imagine you are that person. Describe your feelings. Here is one person's prayerful meditation on the miracle.

As my friends lowered me through the opening, I felt everyone's eyes fixed on me. There was one pair of eyes, however, that I felt more than all the others. They were the eyes of Jesus.

Suddenly I began to feel bad about my life, because I had the feeling that this man called Jesus knew everything about me. Then Jesus spoke. His voice could shake a house yet calm a frightened child. He told me my sins were forgiven.

All of a sudden, I felt a strange sensation sweep through my body. Even my legs tingled. Then he told me to get up and walk. And I did! People crowded around me, and I had the feeling that I was reborn.

I ran off to shout the news to my family. But I forgot to thank him. By the time I realized it, he was gone. I resolved to tell others about this remarkable man. I told everyone who would listen— even those who would not listen. I hoped in this way I thanked him.

Instead of imagining you are the paralyzed person in Luke 5:17–26, you may prefer to imagine you are the deaf-mute in Mark 7:31–37, the sick woman in Luke 8:43–48, the dead girl in Mark 5:35–43, or one of the Apostles in the storm in Mark 4:35–41.

12 *Teaching Ministry*

Before Super Bowl XVI, the *New York Post* interviewed linebacker Reggie Williams of the Cincinnati Bengals. Reggie has been partially deaf from childhood. He told the reporter that his early teachers dismissed him as a poor learner. When he got to the third grade, however, a teacher named Miss Chapman took an interest in him. She discovered his disability and helped him. That help changed his life. Eventually, he graduated in the top 5 percent of his high school class and attended Dartmouth University. "If Miss Chapman hadn't helped me," Reggie said, "I don't know where I'd be today."

Miss Chapman's concern for Reggie Williams gets at the heart of Jesus' teaching.

Love As I Love

If we picked one word to sum up Jesus' teaching, it would be the word *love*. "My commandment is this," said Jesus. "Love one another, just as I love you" (*John 15:12*).

There are two reasons why love forms the heart of Jesus' teaching.

First of all, Jesus made it the *sign* of God's kingdom on earth. He told his disciples, "If you have love for one another, then everyone will know that you are my disciples" (*John 13:35*). In other words, when people see the love Jesus' disciples have for one another, they know that God's kingdom is alive and well in their hearts.

Second, love is the *power* by which God's kingdom on earth grows. It is the *power* by which we reverse the "chain reaction of evil" that started with the first sin, and replace it with a "chain reaction of good." Consider this example.

A man was boarding a crowded bus. Suddenly someone shoved ahead of him, almost knocking him down. He turned to the person and said in *mock* sincerity, "Forgive me! I didn't mean to shove you!" The other person was taken aback and said with *true* sincerity, "I'm sorry. That was really rude of me."

Now the man was taken aback. The other person had responded to his counterfeit display of love as if it were real. And for the moment the other person was dramatically changed.

Later, as the man thought about the incident, he was surprised how his false kindness changed the other person. Then it hit him. That's what love is all about. It sets in motion a *power* by which a "chain reaction of evil" can be arrested and changed into a "chain reaction of good." It releases an energy that can re-create the world.

Because love forms the heart of Jesus' teaching, he made it the point of one of his most important parables.

The Good Samaritan

The road from Jerusalem to Jericho rolls and twists downward. Sometimes it coils around huge boulders and cliffs. In Jesus' time, it was a favorite haunt for robbers and outlaws.

A letter from A.D. 171 complains of the amount of crime along the road. There are also stories of travelers who paid protection money to local thugs for safe passage over the road.

It was this infamous road that provided Jesus with the realistic setting for his parable of the good Samaritan.

LAWYER	*Teacher, what must I do to receive eternal life?*
JESUS	*What do the Scriptures say? How do you interpret them?*
LAWYER	*"Love the Lord your God with all your heart, with all your soul, with all your strength, and with all your mind"; and "Love your neighbor as you love yourself."*
JESUS	*You are right; do this and you will live. . . .*
LAWYER	*Who is my neighbor?*
JESUS	*There was once a man who was going down from Jerusalem to Jericho when robbers attacked him, stripped him, and beat him up, leaving him half dead. It so happened that a priest was going down that road; but when he saw the man, he walked on by on the other side.*

*In the same way
a Levite also came there,
went over and looked at the man,
and then walked on by
on the other side.*

*But a Samaritan
who was traveling that way
came upon the man,
and when he saw him,
his heart was filled with pity.
He went over to him,
poured oil and wine on his wounds
and bandaged them;
then he put the man
on his own animal
and took him to an inn,
where he took care of him.*

*The next day
he took out two silver coins
and gave them to the innkeeper.*

SAMARITAN   *Take care of him,
and when I come back this way,
I will pay you
whatever else you spend on him.*

JESUS   *[to lawyer]
In your opinion,
which of these three acted
like a neighbor toward the man
attacked by robbers?*

LAWYER   *The one who was kind to him.*

JESUS   *You go, then, and do the same.*
LUKE 10:25–37

In this parable, Jesus paints portraits of three different people: a priest, a Levite, a Samaritan.

The *priest* was probably on his way to Jerusalem to worship in the Temple. Apparently he thought the man by the roadside was dead. This explains why he walked on by. If a priest touched a dead person, he became ritually unclean and was temporarily banned from the Temple (Numbers 19:11–13). So the priest chose not to get involved.

The *Levite* was something like a modern deacon. It is not clear why he walked on by. Perhaps his reason was the same as the priest's. Or perhaps he feared the man was only pretending to be hurt and would attack him when he leaned over to help. So the Levite, too, chose not to get involved.

Finally, there was the *Samaritan*. Making the Samaritan the hero of his parable would have shocked Jesus' listeners. They shunned Samaritans as "no goods" who had compromised their faith. Samaritans were banned from the Temple. Their religious contributions were refused, and their testimony was not accepted in a court of law.

But Jesus knew what he was doing by making a Samaritan a hero. He wanted to teach his Jewish listeners that love knows no boundaries. It reaches out to everyone. It does not walk on by. It stops to help, regardless of who the person is.

Jesus' parable turned the world of his listeners upside down. It made them rethink their attitudes toward other people. It also laid the groundwork for Jesus' most revolutionary teachings about love: *People are to love their enemies.* Jesus taught this in one of the most famous scenes in the Gospels.

The Sermon on the Mount

One day Jesus and some disciples were on a hillside outside Capernaum. When the people in the surrounding towns heard about it, they streamed out to the hillside. Jesus was deeply moved and began to teach them.

*"Happy are those
who are merciful to others;
God will be merciful to them! . . .
Happy are those who work for peace;
God will call them his children!
Happy are those who are persecuted
because they do what God requires;
the Kingdom of heaven belongs to them! . . .*

*"You are like light for the whole world. . . .
Your light must shine before people,
so that they will see the good things you do
and praise your Father in heaven. . . .*

*"You have heard that it was said,
'Love your friends, hate your enemies.'
But now I tell you: love your enemies
and pray for those who persecute you,
so that you may become sons of your Father
in heaven.
For he makes his sun to shine
on bad and good people alike. . . .*

*Be perfect—just as your Father in heaven
is perfect."*
MATTHEW 5:7, 9–10, 14, 16, 43–45, 48

These words of Jesus rank among the most
powerful that he ever spoke. They challenge
people to love their enemies and to pray for those
who cause them suffering and harm. Just as the
sun shines on bad and good people alike, so their
love should shine on bad and good people alike.
No person should fall outside the boundary of
their love, not even enemies.

A beautiful illustration of this teaching of Jesus
was reported widely by the media some years
ago. *Newsweek* magazine began its report this
way:

> *When Gerald Lipke awakened that morning,
> the first thing he did was turn on the radio.
> Jerry, who is 11, likes to listen to the news
> while he is dressing for school. That morning
> the news was bad: United Air Lines Flight 629
> with 44 persons aboard had exploded
> and crashed the night before in Colorado.*

It turned out that someone had placed a
bomb on flight 629. Jerry's parents were on the
flight and were killed. Later the students of Saint
Gabriel's School (Jerry's school) asked their
pastor for a prayer service. The pastor asked Jerry
if this would be okay. Jerry said it would. Then
he added, "Could we also say a prayer for the
man who killed my mother and father?"

That story of Jerry Lipke sums up the teaching
of Jesus about love:

Love is a sign of God's kingdom on earth.
Love is the power by which God's kingdom
grows.
Love extends to even our enemies.

This brings us to Jesus' second most important
teaching.

*"He will leave the other ninety-nine grazing
on the hillside and go and look for the lost
sheep."* Matthew 18:12

Forgive As I Forgive

On Christmas Eve, a prison commander passed out Bibles to American POWs in Vietnam. He said they were for Christmas Day only. The prisoners resolved to make the best of their opportunity. Using toilet tissue for paper, wire for pens, and a mixture of ashes for ink, they began to copy passages from the Bible.

One of the passages they copied was the parable of the lost sheep. They saw themselves as lost sheep, separated from the flock, unable to find their way back. All they could do was wait patiently for the Good Shepherd to find them and lead them home. A second parable they copied was the best-known story Jesus ever told.

The Prodigal Son

This story is about a young son who demanded his inheritance in advance of his father's death. The father gave it to him, and the boy left home. In no time he spent his whole inheritance.

NARRATOR   *Then a severe famine*
spread over that country,
and he was left without a thing.
So he went to work for one
of the citizens of that country,
who sent him out to his farm
to take care of the pigs.
He wished he could fill himself
with the bean pods the pigs ate,
but no one
gave him anything to eat.
At last he came to his senses.

SON   *All my father's hired workers*
have more than they can eat,
and here I am about to starve!
I will get up and go to my father
and say, "Father, I have sinned
against God and against you.
I am no longer fit
to be called your son; treat me
as one of your hired workers."

NARRATOR   *So he got up*
and started back to his father.

He was still
a long way from home
when his father saw him;
his heart was filled with pity,
and he ran, threw his arms
around his son, and kissed him. . . .

FATHER   *Hurry! Bring the best robe*
and put it on him.
Put a ring on his finger
and shoes on his feet.
Then go and get the prize calf
and kill it, and let us celebrate
with a feast! . . .

NARRATOR   *In the meantime*
the older son . . . heard the music. . . .

ELDER SON   *What's going on?*

SERVANT   *Your brother*
has come back home,
and your father has killed
the prize calf,
because he got him back safe. . . .

NARRATOR   *The older brother was so angry*
that he would not go
into the house;
so his father came out
and begged him to come in. . . .

ELDER SON   *Look, all these years*
I have worked for you
like a slave,
and I never disobeyed your orders.
What have you given me?
Not even a goat for me
to have a feast with my friends!
But this son of yours wasted
all your property on prostitutes,
and when he comes back home,
you kill the prize calf for him!

FATHER   *My son,*
you are always here with me,
and everything I have is yours.
But we had to celebrate . . .
because your brother was dead,
but now he is alive;
he was lost,
but now he has been found.
LUKE 15:14–32

This parable contains two remarkable things. The first is the son's demand for his share of the

The Last Judgment

Sheep and goats graze together during the day. At night, however, they are separated. The goats are herded off to a warm place, because they cannot stand the cold. Jesus used this image of separation as the background for an important parable.

The parable portrays the end of time, when the "Son of Man" returns to reign over God's kingdom. He separates the people of the world into two groups, "as a shepherd separates the sheep from the goats." Then he addresses the group on his right.

KING   *Come and possess the kingdom*
which has been prepared for you
ever since the creation of the world.
I was hungry and you fed me,
thirsty and you gave me a drink;
I was a stranger and
you received me in your homes,
naked and you clothed me;
I was sick
and you took care of me,
in prison and you visited me.

GOOD   *When, Lord, did we ever*
see you hungry and feed you,
or thirsty and give you a drink? . . .

KING   *I tell you,*
whenever you did this for
one of the least important
of these brothers of mine,
you did it for me!
MATTHEW 25:34-37, 40

Then, the king condemns the bad people on his left for not feeding him, giving him a drink, clothing him, receiving him, and visiting him. He ends by saying, "Whenever you refused to help one of the least important ones, you refused to help me" (*Matthew 25:45*). He then sends them off "to eternal punishments," but the good he leads into "eternal life."

Jesus' point is clear. During the daylight of life, loving and unloving people will live side by side. But when evening comes, they will be separated.

inheritance. This was a cruel demand to make. To insist upon one's inheritance before one's parents died was, in effect, to rob them of their "social security." Jesus' listeners were shocked at the demand. They were even more shocked when the father granted it.

The other remarkable thing is the father's response to the son's return home. The father does three things that surprised Jesus' listeners.

First, he embraces his son. Embracing the boy shows that his father welcomes him back fully. No sign of affection is held back from him.

Second, the father puts shoes on his son's feet. Putting shoes on the boy's feet shows that the father forgives him fully. In biblical times, shoes were a sign of a free person; slaves went barefooted. Putting shoes on his son's bare feet takes away the sign that says he is somebody's slave and gives him the sign that says he is somebody's son.

Finally, the father gives his son a ring. Putting a ring on the boy's finger shows that the father restores him fully to the status he had before he left home. For, undoubtedly, the ring was a signet ring, containing the family seal. To have it was to possess the power to act in the family's name.

And so the embrace, the shoes, and the ring show that the father welcomes his son back totally, forgives him fully, and restores him completely to the status that he had before he left home.

The second half of the parable focuses on the older son. It contrasts the father's lavish forgiveness with the older son's lack of forgiveness. The older son will not even go into the house to celebrate, even though the father begs him to go in.

The parable ends without telling us what the older son did. Did he finally go inside and celebrate? Or did he stay outside in the darkness?

The reason Jesus does not tell us what the older son did is because of who the two sons stand for. The older son stands for the religious leaders of Jesus' time. The younger son stands for the sinners and outcasts of the time.

The sinners and outcasts are responding to Jesus' call to repent their sins. Jesus, in turn, is forgiving them. And this angers many religious leaders, like scribes and Pharisees, who think sinners and outcasts do not deserve to be saved (Luke 15:1–2).

And so Jesus tells the parable in such a way that each scribe and Pharisee must write his own ending to the story. Each realizes he is the older brother and must decide whether to forgive his younger brother. Each realizes that he must decide whether to go inside and dance or stay outside and sulk.

Herein lies Jesus' teaching for all of us. We, too, are to forgive others, as God has forgiven us.

Nor is it enough to forgive others once or twice. Jesus made this clear on another occasion when Peter asked him, "Lord, if my brother keeps on sinning against me, how many times do I have to forgive him? Seven times?" Jesus responded, "No, not seven times, but seventy times seven, because the Kingdom of heaven is like this" (*Matthew 18:21–23*).

This brings us to a third and final important teaching of Jesus.

Pray As I Pray

One night Dr. Martin Luther King was in bed. He was about to doze off when the phone rang. A voice on the other end said, "Listen, nigger, we've taken all we want from you. Before next week, you'll be sorry you ever came to Montgomery." Dr. King hung up. Suddenly, all his fears came crashing down upon him. His courage began to melt. He did not know what to do or where to turn. Then he bowed his head and prayed. No sooner had he begun his prayer than he felt the presence of God as he had never experienced it before.

Dr. King's prayer introduces us to the third great teaching of Jesus: *Pray as I pray.*

And how did Jesus pray? His prayer may be summed up this way: he prayed often; he prayed in different settings; he prayed in different ways. Let us take a look at each.

"So he got up and started back to his father."
Luke 15:20

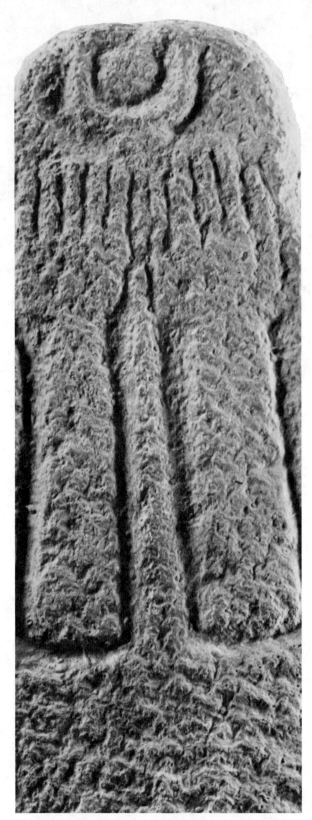

This 3,500-year-old Canaanite stone relief portrays hands uplifted in prayer.

Jesus Prays Often

Jesus prayed at set times each day, as every good Jew did. Recall that Daniel "knelt down at the open windows and prayed to God three times a day" (*Daniel 6:10*).

But the Gospels make it clear that Jesus also prayed at other times, in addition to the regular set times each day. Consider a few examples.

At his *baptism,* Jesus was praying when the sky opened "and the Holy Spirit came down upon him" (*Luke 3:22*).

During his *ministry,* Jesus often rose "long before daylight" and went off to "lonely places, where he prayed" (Mark 1:35, Luke 5:16).

Before *choosing* his twelve Apostles, Jesus spent the whole night in prayer (Luke 6:12).

Before *asking* his disciples the question "Who do you say I am?" Jesus prayed (Luke 9:18).

Before he was *transfigured,* Jesus prayed on a hilltop (Luke 9:28).

Before *teaching* his disciples how to pray, Jesus was found at prayer (Luke 11:1).

On the eve of his *suffering,* Jesus prayed in the Garden of Gethsemane (Luke 22:41).

On the *cross,* Jesus prayed (Luke 23:34).

These examples give an idea of the frequency and the time when Jesus prayed, apart from the regular prayer times each day.

Jesus Prays in Different Settings

In his book *Walden,* Henry David Thoreau, the famous naturalist, says of his wilderness cabin:

I had three chairs in my house,
one for solitude, two for friendship,
three for society.

Thoreau's statement is a reference to the three facets of our personality. We humans are like triangles. We have three sides: a private side, a friendship side, and a community side.

Sometimes we need privacy. Sometimes we need the support of family and friends. And sometimes we need the support of the larger community.

What is true of our psychological needs is also true of our spiritual needs. There are times when we need to pray alone. There are times when we need to pray with family and friends. There are times when we need to pray with the larger community.

The Gospel shows that Jesus prayed in all three of these settings.

First, he prayed privately, going off by himself to meditate and speak to his heavenly Father.

Second, he prayed with his family each day around the meal table and on religious holidays. He also prayed with close friends, for example, at the time of his transfiguration (Luke 9:28).

Third, Jesus prayed with the community. For example, Luke says, "On the Sabbath he went *as usual* to the synagogue" to pray (*Luke 4:16*).

Thus, Jesus' prayer took into account each of the three psychological and spiritual sides of his personality: private, friendship, and communal.

Jesus Prays in Different Ways

In *The Inner Game of Tennis,* W. Timothy Gallwey points out that when we watch a tennis match, we see only the *outer* game: what happens on the court. We do not see the *inner* game: what happens in the players' minds.

What is true of tennis is also true of prayer. Prayer has an outer dimension and an inner dimension. The Gospels tell us about both of these dimensions of Jesus' prayer.

Outwardly, Jesus prayed in different ways. For example, he prayed kneeling down (Luke 22:41). He prayed lying face down (Matthew 26:39). He prayed with his eyes uplifted (Mark 7:34, John 17:1). He prayed out loud (Matthew 26:42). He prayed with perseverance (Matthew 26:44–45).

Inwardly, Jesus also prayed in different ways: *free* prayers and *fixed* prayers. His *free* prayers came spontaneously from the heart in his own words (John 17:1). He also prayed *fixed* prayers that had been a part of the Jewish faith for centuries. For example, on the cross, Jesus prayed Psalm 22 (Mark 15:34).

Significantly, when Jesus' followers asked him to teach them to pray, he taught them a new *fixed* prayer.

The Lord's Prayer

One day Jesus was praying in a certain place.
When he had finished,
one of his disciples said to him,
"Lord, teach us to pray."
LUKE 11:1

Jesus responded by teaching them the Our Father, or Lord's Prayer.

Our Father, who art in heaven,
hallowed be thy name; thy kingdom come;
thy will be done on earth as it is in heaven.
Give us this day our daily bread;
and forgive us our trespasses as we forgive
those who trespass against us;
and lead us not into temptation,
but deliver us from evil.
ADAPTED FROM MATTHEW

Two things stand out in this prayer. The first thing is the word *Father*. The word for *Father* (in Aramaic, the language Jesus spoke) is *Abba*. Palestinian children still use this word to address their fathers. *Abba* is a title of affection, like our word *daddy*. In other words, Jesus taught us to address God with the same affection and trust that a small child addresses its father.

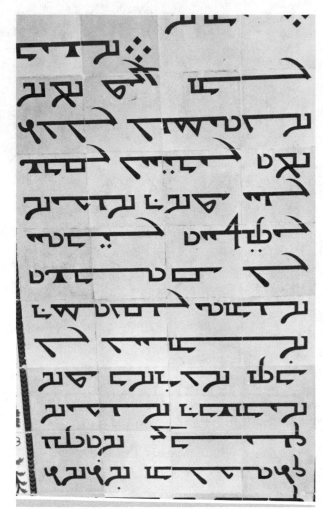

The Lord's Prayer in Aramaic, the language Jesus spoke.

The second thing that stands out in the Lord's Prayer is its double perspective. It contains three *your* petitions:

1. hallowed be *your* name,
2. *your* kingdom come,
3. *your* will be done.

It also contains three *our* petitions:

1. give *us our* daily bread,
2. forgive *us our* trespasses,
3. deliver *us* from evil.

The three *your* petitions deal with the same event: the coming or completion of God's kingdom in its fullness. Each petition approaches it from a slightly different angle.

The three *our* petitions shift the focus from the completion of God's kingdom to the needs of God's people as they work for the completion of the kingdom.

We are now ready to look at the final thing the Gospels teach about prayer.

Four Kinds of Prayer

The Gospels reveal four different kinds of prayer. People sometimes refer to them by the word *acts,* which is formed by taking the first letter of each of the four kinds of prayer found in the Gospels: *a*doration, *c*ontrition, *t*hanksgiving, and *s*upplication.

Adoration acknowledges God as God. For example, we find Thomas falling on his knees and saying to Jesus, "My Lord and my God!" (*John 20:28*).

Contrition acknowledges people as sinners in need of God's mercy. For example, the blind beggar cries out, "Jesus! Son of David! Have mercy on me!" (*Luke 18:38*).

Thanksgiving acknowledges God's many gifts to his children. For example, Jesus himself prayed, "Father, Lord of heaven and earth! I thank you . . ." (*Luke 10:21*).

Finally, *supplication* acknowledges the need for God's help. For example, Jesus taught his disciples, "Ask, and you will receive; seek, and you will find; knock, and the door will be opened to you" (*Luke 11:9*).

In conclusion, the Gospels teach people to pray as Jesus prayed:

1. often;
2. in different settings: alone, with family and friends, and with the community;
3. in different outer ways: kneeling, lying down, with uplifted eyes, out loud, with perseverance;
4. in different inner ways: free prayers and fixed prayers;
5. with different kinds of prayer: adoration, contrition, thanksgiving, supplication, especially the Lord's Prayer.

Watch and Pray

Ancient wedding celebrations lasted for days. A high-point in the celebration was the arrival of the bridegroom at the house of the bride. Bridesmaids carrying lighted oil lamps waited to welcome him. It is against this background that Jesus told a parable that deals with an important question: When will God's kingdom reach completion and the "Son of Man" return?

Jesus answered the question by describing ten bridesmaids waiting to meet the bridegroom. Five were wise and had a full supply of oil in their lamps. Five were foolish and had only a limited supply. When the bridegroom was delayed in coming, the bridesmaids fell asleep. As they slept, the oil supply of the foolish bridesmaids almost burned out. Suddenly a voice shouted, "Get ready! Here comes the bridegroom!"

FOOLISH BRIDESMAIDS   *[to wise]*
Let us have some of your oil,
because our lamps are going out.

WISE BRIDESMAIDS   *No, indeed, there is not enough*
for you and for us.
Go to the store
and buy some for yourselves.

NARRATOR   *So the foolish girls went off*
to buy some oil;
and while they were gone,
the bridegroom arrived.
The five girls who were ready
went in with him
to the wedding feast,
and the door was closed.
Later the other girls arrived.

FOOLISH BRIDESMAIDS   *Sir, Sir! Let us in!*

BRIDEGROOM   *Certainly not! I don't know you.*
MATTHEW 25:8-12

The point of Jesus' parable is this. The hour when God's kingdom reaches completion and the "Son of Man" returns will take all people by surprise. The wise will be ready; the foolish will not. Those who are ready will enter the wedding feast (heaven) with the bridegroom (Jesus). Those who are not ready will remain in everlasting darkness.

Understanding Teaching Ministry

Review

1. Explain how love is (a) the *sign* of God's kingdom and (b) the *power* by which God's kingdom reaches completion.

2. In the parable of the good Samaritan, why didn't the priest become involved? Why was the Samaritan a surprise hero for Jesus' listeners? Why did Jesus make the Samaritan the story's hero?

3. What challenging teaching about love did Jesus present to his hearers in the Sermon on the Mount?

4. What criterion will be used to separate good people from bad people in the Last Judgment?

5. In the parable of the prodigal son, why was it unforgivable for the son to ask for his share of the inheritance in advance? Of what were the *embrace*, the *ring*, and the *shoes* signs? Who did the elder son stand for in real life? What teaching does Jesus make through this parable?

6. List four important occasions when Jesus prayed.

7. List the three *settings* in which Jesus prayed.

8. What do we mean by the *inner* and the *outer* dimension of Jesus' prayer? Give an example of each.

9. List the three *your* petitions of the Lord's Prayer. With what event do they deal? List the three *our* petitions. To whom do they refer?

10. List and explain the four different kinds of prayer referred to in the Gospel.

11. With what question does the parable of the bridesmaids deal? In real life, who/what do the following stand for: wise maids, foolish maids, coming of the bridegroom, bridegroom, wedding feast?

Discuss

1. In the 1970s a New York woman was stabbed to death while her own neighbors watched and did nothing. Commenting on the episode, a newspaper reporter said, "We ought to tear the parable of the good Samaritan out of our Bibles. No one lives it any longer."

Why would you agree/disagree with the reporter?

2. After the New York stabbing, a team of university psychologists performed this experiment. An actor boarded a subway train, posing as an invalid with a cane. After the train left the station, he fell to the floor. They repeated the experiment sixty-five times.

Next the actor posed as a drunk, reeking with alcohol. After the train left the station, he too fell to the floor. This experiment was repeated thirty-eight times.

How many times do you think people helped the invalid? The drunk? Why the difference? Is this difference a valid reason for helping or not helping?

3. Why do you agree/disagree with this statement: "It's easier to forgive an enemy than a friend" (Austin O'Malley).

4. In the movie *The Karate Kid,* Mr. Miyagi asks Daniel for one good reason why he should teach him karate. Daniel says, "Is revenge a good reason?" To this Mr. Miyagi says, "The person who pursues revenge should dig two graves."

What did Mr. Miyagi mean?

Activities

1. A high school student in Chicago wrote:

Last summer, my dad asked me to support our family. You see, his company went on strike at the start of the summer. I was the only one in our family with a job. My father told me he would be proud of me if I could do this. Dad's words really hit me. I was glad he turned to me in this time of need.

Each week my check went to pay for family bills. Some of my friends asked me where all my money was going. All I told them was that it was going for a good purpose. They wouldn't have understood had I told them the true situation.

Describe a time when you acted as a good Samaritan.

2. Describe a time when someone acted as a good Samaritan toward you.

3. Sometimes we treat people outside our family better than we do our own family. Ask two or three family members to evaluate you on the following:

> 4 = always
> 3 = usually
> 2 = sometimes
> 1 = rarely

_____	**a.**	Take care of room
_____	**b.**	Do chores without being reminded
_____	**c.**	Bring friends home
_____	**d.**	Observe time deadlines
_____	**e**	Tell parents where I go
_____	**f.**	Tell parents what I do
_____	**g.**	Phone when I will be late
_____	**h.**	Obey promptly
_____	**i.**	Obey cheerfully
_____	**j.**	Show affection externally
_____	**k.**	Apologize when appropriate
_____	**l.**	Accept correction without sulking
_____	**m.**	Give thanks for help given me
_____	**n.**	Try to see others' viewpoint
_____	**o.**	Discuss differences calmly

Now evaluate yourself, and compare your grades to those your family gave you. Discuss the results with your family. Write out a brief report of your discussion.

Bible Reading

Pick a passage. After reading it, (1) summarize its main point, (2) tell how it relates to the chapter, and (3) list one or two thoughts that entered your mind as you read it.

1. The town sinner   Luke 7:36–50
2. Jottings in the dirt   John 8:1–11
3. Crooked judge   Luke 18:1–8
4. Excuses! Excuses!   Luke 14:15–24
5. The greatest lover   John 15:1–17

Prayer Journal

A practical method of prayer is called the *three-minute replay.*

First minute: Replay your day. Pick out a *high* point: a good thing you did. Talk to God the Father about it. Then thank him for it.

Second minute: Replay your day again. This time pick out a *low* point: a bad thing you did. Talk to Jesus about it. Then ask him to forgive you.

Third minute: Look ahead to tomorrow to a *critical* point: a hard thing you must do. Talk to the Holy Spirit about it. Then ask for light and courage to deal with it as you should.

Here is a sample three-minute replay.

High Point: I heard from a friend.

"Father, today I got a card from an old friend. Thank you for friends. They make life so much more enjoyable."

Low Point: I yelled at my mother.

"Jesus, you taught us to love. Forgive me for not showing love today to someone who deserves it most, my mother."

Critical Point: I have a problem with my dad.

"Holy Spirit, I want to do right, but I'm not always sure what it is. Help me know how to act toward Dad, who is under stress and is drinking a lot lately."

Tonight, do a three-minute replay of your day. Write it out, following the model above.

13 Death and Resurrection

Toward the end of his life, Dr. Martin Luther King said to his followers, "We've got some difficult days ahead. But it doesn't matter with me now. . . . Like anybody, I would like to live a long life; longevity has its place. But I'm not concerned about that now. I just want to do God's will."

Jesus began to speak to his followers in a similar way toward the end of his life. He said:

"The Son of Man will be handed over to men
who will kill him.
Three days later, however,
he will rise to life."
But they did not understand
what this teaching meant,
and they were afraid to ask him.
MARK 9:31–32

Jesus Clashes with Authorities

Jewish leaders opposed Jesus from the beginning. For example, early in his ministry Jesus said to a paralyzed man, "Your sins are forgiven." When the religious leaders heard this, they flew into a rage. "How does he dare talk like this? This is blasphemy! God is the only one who can forgive sins!" (*Mark 2:7*).

On another occasion, Jesus drove a demon out of a man. Again the religious leaders protested, saying, "He drives out demons only because their ruler Beelzebul gives him power to do so" (*Matthew 12:24*).

On still another occasion, the leaders jumped all over Jesus because his disciples did not practice the religious rite of washing their hands before they ate. Although this rite was not prescribed by Scripture, the leaders said it should be followed rigidly. Now it was Jesus' turn to grow a bit heated. He said sharply:

"How right Isaiah was
when he prophesied about you! . . .

*'These people . . . honor me with their words,
but their heart is really far away from me. . . .
They teach man-made rules
as though they were my laws!' ''*

MARK 7:6–7

Finally, the day came when Jesus used some of his strongest language against the leaders.

*"You hypocrites! You give to God
one tenth even of the seasoning herbs . . .
but you neglect to obey
the really important teachings of the Law,
such as justice and mercy. . . .*

*"Blind guides! You strain a fly
out of your drink, but swallow a camel! . . .
You are like whitewashed tombs,
which look fine on the outside
but are full of bones
and decaying corpses on the inside."*

MATTHEW 23:23–24, 27

Plot against Jesus' Life

And so the gap between Jesus and the religious leaders grew wider with each passing month. Finally, a showdown developed. It came when news spread that Jesus had raised Lazarus from the dead (John 11:1–44).

The leaders sensed that the situation was getting out of hand. They also feared that Jesus' growing popularity among the masses might mushroom into a revolt.

LEADERS   *What shall we do? . . .
If we let him go on in this way,
everyone will believe in him,
and the Roman authorities
will take action and destroy
our Temple and our nation! . . .*

NARRATOR   *From that day on
the Jewish authorities made plans
to kill Jesus. So Jesus did not
travel openly in Judea. . . .
The time for
the Passover Festival was near,
and many people went up
from the country to Jerusalem. . . .*

PEOPLE   *What do you think?
Surely [Jesus] will not come
to the festival, will he?*

JOHN 11:47–48, 53–56

The answer was not long in coming. Suddenly, word buzzed around the city that Jesus was on his way to Jerusalem.

Jesus Enters Jerusalem

As Jesus approached the main gate of the city, crowds of people ran out to meet him. When they saw him riding on a donkey, they got even more excited.

*People spread their cloaks on the road
while others cut branches from the trees*

*Modern pilgrims celebrate Jesus' Passion
(Psalm) Sunday entry into Jerusalem.*

and spread them on the road.
The crowds walking in front of Jesus
and those walking behind began to shout,
"Praise to David's son!
God bless him who comes in the name
of the Lord! Praise be to God!"
MATTHEW 21:8-9

When Jesus arrived at the Temple, he was shocked at what he saw. The Court of the Gentiles looked like a carnival site. Men were selling animals and birds for sacrifice. Jesus kicked over their tables and shouted:

"It is written in the Scriptures that God said,
'My Temple will be called a house of prayer.'
But you are making it a hideout for thieves!"
MATTHEW 21:13

To understand Jesus' sharp words, we need to know that the prices of the animals and birds sold in the Court of the Gentiles were often five times the normal amount. The poor, especially, were the victims of these inflated prices.

Jesus' actions angered the religious leaders. The next day they confronted him. Jesus used the opportunity to tell a parable that referred directly to them.

The Vineyard Tenants

JESUS
There was once a landowner
who planted a vineyard,
put a fence around it,
dug a hole for the wine press,
and built a watchtower.
Then he rented the vineyard
to tenants and left home
on a trip.

When the time came
to gather the grapes,
he sent his slaves to the tenants
to receive his share of the harvest.
The tenants grabbed his slaves,
beat one, killed another,
and stoned another.

Again the man sent other slaves,
more than the first time,

and the tenants treated them
the same way.

Last of all he sent his son to them.
"Surely they will respect my son,"
he said.
But when the tenants saw the son,
they said to themselves,
"This is the owner's son.
Come on, let's kill him,
and we will get his property!"
So they grabbed him,
threw him out of the vineyard,
and killed him.

Then Jesus turned to the religious leaders.

JESUS
Now, when the owner
of the vineyard comes,
what will he do to those tenants?

LEADERS
He will certainly kill
those evil men
and rent the vineyard out
to other tenants,
who will give him his share
of the harvest. . . .

JESUS
And so I tell you,
the Kingdom of God will be taken
away from you
and given to a people
who will produce the proper fruits.

NARRATOR
The chief priests
and the Pharisees . . . knew
that he was talking about them,

"A landowner . . . built a watchtower"
(Matthew 21:33). *Such towers served as look-out posts against thieves and wild animals.*

so they tried to arrest him.
But they were afraid
of the crowds,
who considered Jesus to be
a prophet.
MATTHEW 21:33–46

This is one of the most remarkable and best-constructed parables Jesus ever told. Consider three points about it, especially.

First, it is a beautiful summary of Scripture. This emerges from a closer study of its "cast of characters."

Landowner:	God
Vineyard:	Israel
First renting:	old covenant
Tenants:	religious leaders
Slaves:	early prophets

Other slaves:	later prophets
Owner's son:	Jesus
Second renting:	new covenant
New tenants:	Jesus' Apostles

Second, Jesus' question to the Jewish leaders forces them to condemn themselves: He will "kill those evil men and rent the vineyard out to other tenants." In other words, the Jewish leaders (former tenants) will be thrown out. Jesus' twelve Apostles (new tenants) will become the new leaders of God's chosen people.

Third, Jesus is the son of the vineyard owner (God). He is not just another prophet, like Elijah and Isaiah. He is someone far greater.

Shortly after his confrontation with the Jewish leaders, Jesus told Peter and John, "Go and get the Passover meal ready" (*Luke 22:8*).

The Temple

Reconstruction of the Temple.

Jews considered the Jerusalem Temple to be the holiest place on earth. Novelist James Michener gives us an insight into the love Jews had for Jerusalem and the Temple in his book *The Source*. He describes the inner feelings of an old woman as she journeys a great distance, on foot, to the city and the Temple.

> *She longed for Jerusalem*
> *as bees long for spring to open the flowers*
> *or as lions trapped in the valley*
> *hunger for the hills. . . .*
> *It was the golden city, the site of the temple,*
> *the focus of worship, the target of longing.*

If the Temple (shown here) was the holiest place on earth, the holiest room in the Temple was the holy of holies, which housed the ark of the covenant. Surrounding the Temple structure, which only certain priests entered on special occasions, were four courts:

Court of the Priests,
Court of the Men,
Court of the Women,
Court of the Gentiles.

Separating the Court of the Gentiles from the other courts was a barrier with warning signs, like the one shown here. Discovered in 1871, it bears this chilling inscription: "Let no Gentile go beyond this barrier. Whoever is caught doing so will have himself to blame for his death, which will follow."

Jesus Celebrates the Last Supper

The story *Town Beyond the Wall* deals with the power of friendship. In the story, the power flows not from the friend directly, but from the *memory* of the friend. Michael survives torture because Pedro, his absent friend, is alive in his memory. Michael's memory does more than recall his friend from the past. It brings his friend into the present.

That story touches on an important biblical truth. For ancient Jews, "remembering" involved more than recalling a past religious event. It involved bringing the event into the present and reliving it.

Thus, when Jews celebrated ("remembered") the Passover, they did more than recall the event that freed them from Egypt. They brought that event into the present, by faith, and relived it.

It is with this understanding that Jesus and his disciples gathered to celebrate the Passover meal.

Normally, Jews ate only two meals daily: one about 10 A.M., the other late in the afternoon. The Passover meal, however, was eaten at night, after the appearance of the first stars. Thus everyone celebrated the meal at the same time as one family.

When the stars appeared, Jesus, acting as the father, began the Passover ceremonies. He began, however, in a strange way. Departing from Passover practice, he poured water into a basin and began to wash the feet of each Apostle. For Jews, washing another's feet was humiliating. Only slaves washed another's feet. Thus Jesus' action created a deep impression. When Jesus finished, he sat down and said:

> *"I, your Lord and Teacher,*
> *have just washed your feet.*
> *You, then, should wash one another's feet.*
> *I have set an example for you."*
> JOHN 13:14–15

Greek Orthodox Christians commemorate the washing of the feet, which Jesus performed at the Last Supper.

Then Jesus prepared the cup of wine that began all Passover meals, saying:

> *"Take this and share it among yourselves.*
> *I tell you that from now on*
> *I will not drink this wine*
> *until the Kingdom of God comes."*
> LUKE 22:17–18

Red wine was normally used at Passover meals. It recalled the blood-marked doorposts in Egypt and the covenant blood at Mount Sinai.

Next, the food was set before Jesus: wild herbs, unleavened bread, and sauce into which the bread and herbs were dipped. Finally came the lamb.

The bitter herbs recalled the bitter years of slavery. The clay-colored sauce recalled the bricks the Hebrews made under the hot sun. The unleavened bread recalled the haste of Israel's departure from Egypt. There was not enough time to let the next day's bread rise before baking it.

It was now time to eat the food that was arranged in front of Jesus.

This Is My Body

A reverent silence fell over the Apostles as they watched Jesus take the bread in his hands. Looking up to heaven,

> *he . . . gave thanks to God, broke it,*
> *and gave it to them, saying,*
> *"This is my body, which is given for you.*
> *Do this in memory of me."*
> LUKE 22:19

The Apostles would have been struck by Jesus' reference to his body. Perhaps some of them recalled that day in a synagogue in Capernaum, when Jesus said:

> *"I am the living bread*
> *that came down from heaven. . . .*
> *The bread that I will give [you] is my flesh."*
> JOHN 6:51

The Apostles took the bread and ate it. As they did, they sensed that something marvelous and mysterious was taking place.

This Is My Blood

After the rest of the food had been eaten, Jesus prepared the cup of wine that concluded all Passover meals. Again, a reverent silence fell over the Apostles as they watched Jesus raise his eyes to heaven and pray over the cup. Then he passed it to them, saying:

> *"This cup is God's new covenant
> sealed with my blood,
> which is poured out for you."*
> LUKE 22:20

The Apostles would have been struck by Jesus' reference to the "new covenant" and the words "sealed with my blood." Perhaps some of them recalled God's promise: "I will make a new covenant with the people of Israel" (*Jeremiah 31:31*). And perhaps they recalled the old covenant when Moses sprinkled blood and said, "This is the blood that seals the covenant which the LORD has made with you" (*Exodus 24:8*).

As the Apostles drank from the cup, their minds were filled with questions: Was this the moment God had promised? Was this the new covenant? What did Jesus mean when he said, "sealed with my blood"? It was a solemn moment.

Mark concluded this account of the Last Supper with these words:

> *Then they sang a hymn
> and went out to the Mount of Olives.*
> MARK 14:26

Archaeologists date the remains of this stepped-street, near the traditional site of the upper room, back to about the first century. Jesus and his disciples could have passed this way en route to the Mount of Olives.

Jesus Is Arrested

On the slope of the Mount of Olives stands a grove of eight ancient olive trees. Nobody knows how old the trees are. But experts agree that they probably mark the spot where Jesus began his passion (suffering before his death).

When Jesus and the Apostles arrived at the Mount of Olives, sorrow came over Jesus. He went off alone into the darkness, "threw himself on the ground," and prayed:

> *"Father, my Father!
> All things are possible for you.
> Take this cup of suffering away from me.
> Yet not what I want, but what you want."*
> MARK 14:36

Jesus' prayer echoes the spirit of the Lord's Prayer: "Our Father . . . thy will be done."

Then Jesus returned to his disciples. Finding them asleep, he woke them, saying, "Keep watch and pray." Then he disappeared into the darkness again.

After a short while, he returned. Minutes later "a crowd armed with swords and clubs" entered the Garden of Gethsemane (*Mark 14:43*). Judas was with them. When Judas kissed Jesus, Jesus turned to him and said, "Judas, is it with a kiss that you betray the Son of Man?" (*Luke 22:48*).

When it was clear what was happening, the disciples fled. Jesus was left standing alone.

Peter Denies Jesus

The armed crowd took Jesus to the high priest's residence. Peter followed at a distance. Later he entered the courtyard of the residence. Someone spotted him and accused him of being a disciple. Peter denied it, not once but three times. Then a rooster crowed, and Peter remembered what Jesus had said earlier.

> *"Before the rooster crows . . .*
> *you will say three times*
> *that you do not know me."*
> MARK 14:72

Peter went out into the darkness and "wept bitterly" (*Matthew 26:75*).

This moving scene was recorded first by Mark. No doubt he preserved it for pastoral reasons. Writing for Christians under persecution in Rome, he wanted to warn them of the danger of denying their faith under pressure.

More importantly, he wanted to assure them that if they did deny their faith, they could hope to be forgiven as Peter was.

Jesus Stands Trial

After being taken before the high priest, Jesus was imprisoned for the few remaining hours of darkness. When dawn broke, he was led off to be questioned by the Jewish Council, a body of Israel's most important religious leaders. When all was ready, the questioning began.

COUNCIL	*Tell us, are you the Messiah?*
JESUS	*If I tell you, you will not believe me;* *and if I ask you a question,* *you will not answer.* *But from now on the Son of Man* *will be seated at the right side* *of Almighty God.*
COUNCIL	*Are you, then, the Son of God?*
JESUS	*You say that I am.*
COUNCIL	*We don't need any witnesses!* *We ourselves have heard* *what he said!*

LUKE 22:67–71

At this, the high priest in charge tore his robe and shouted, "Blasphemy!" Then turning to the Council, he said, "You have just heard his blasphemy! What do you think?" They answered, "He is guilty and must die" (*Matthew 26:65–66*). Then they led Jesus off to be tried by Pilate.

Archaeologists found this dedication stone at Caesarea-on-the-Sea.

The first line reads TIBERIEUM, the second (PON)TIUS PILATUS, the third (PRAEF)ECTUS IUDA(EAE).

The stone is part of a larger statement of dedication to Tiberius Caesar by Pontius Pilate, Prefect of Judea.

Modern pilgrims retrace the route Jesus took to Golgotha on the first Good Friday.

The Council leaders told Pilate, "We caught this man misleading our people, telling them not to pay taxes to the Emperor and claiming that he himself is the Messiah, a king" (*Luke 23:2*). Thus, the case they made before Pilate shifted from a religious one to a political one.

True, Jesus had criticized the nation's leaders, but on religious, not political, grounds. He had also discussed taxation, but did not oppose it (Matthew 22:15–22). Finally, he was called a king, but refused the title in a political way (John 6:15).

Pilate sized up the situation as a religious squabble among Jews. He tried to remove himself from the case by sending Jesus to Herod (Luke 23:7). But this failed, so Pilate tried another tactic.

PILATE [to the crowd]
*According to the custom you have,
I always set free a prisoner
for you during the Passover.
Do you want me to set free
for you the king of the Jews?*

CROWD *No, not him!
We want Barabbas! . . .*

NARRATOR *[Again Pilate's tactic failed.
So he tried yet another one.
He had Jesus whipped.]*

*The soldiers made a crown
out of thorny branches
and put it on his head;
then they put a purple robe
on him [and abused him].*

*[The soldiers returned Jesus
to Pilate, and Pilate presented
Jesus to the crowd.]*

PILATE *Look! Here is the man!*

NARRATOR *When the chief priests
and the Temple guards saw him,
they shouted, "Crucify him!
Crucify him!". . .
Then Pilate handed Jesus over
to them to be crucified.*
JOHN 18:39–19:6, 16

Jesus Is Crucified

The soldiers led Jesus away to a place called Golgotha, meaning "the place of the skull." They began the execution by giving Jesus some wine mixed with myrrh, a drug. But Jesus refused it.

*Then they crucified him and divided his clothes
among themselves, throwing dice to see
who would get which piece of clothing. . . .
They also crucified two bandits with Jesus,
one on his right and the other on his left.*

*People passing by shook their heads
and hurled insults at Jesus:
"Aha! You were going to tear down the Temple
and build it back up in three days! . . ."*

*At noon
the whole country was covered with darkness,
which lasted for three hours.
At three o'clock Jesus cried out . . . "My God,
my God, why did you abandon me?". . .*

With a loud cry Jesus died.

*The curtain hanging in the Temple
was torn in two, from top to bottom.
The army officer who was standing there*

in front of the cross saw how Jesus had died.
"This man was really the Son of God!" he said.
MARK 15:24, 27, 29, 33–34, 37–39

Three points stand out in Mark's description of Jesus' crucifixion.

First, in spite of his tremendous pain on the cross, Jesus prayed. And the prayer he chose was Psalm 22, which begins, "My God, my God, why did you abandon me?" Written six hundred years before the Romans devised death by crucifixion, this psalm mirrors Jesus' situation perfectly.

> *My God, My God,*
> *why have you abandoned me? . . .*
>
> *All who see me make fun of me . . .*
> *and shake their heads. . . .*
> *My strength is gone,*
> *gone like water spilled on the ground.*
>
> *All my bones are out of joint;*
> *my heart is like melted wax.*
> *My throat is as dry as dust, and*
> *my tongue sticks to the roof of my mouth. . . .*
>
> *A gang of evil men is around me . . .*
> *they tear at my hands and feet. . . .*
> *My enemies look at me and stare.*
> *They gamble for my clothes. . . .*
>
> *O LORD, don't stay away from me!*
> *Come quickly to my rescue!*
> PSALM 22:1, 7, 14–19

The second thing that stands out is Mark's reference to the Temple and the tearing of the Temple curtain. Early Christians interpreted the torn curtain to be a sign indicating the end of the Temple and of Old Testament sacrifice (Hebrews 10:9). The New Testament sacrifice and the new temple are being born on the cross. Jesus' own body is to be the new temple (Ephesians 1:22–23). Jesus' own death is to be the new sacrifice (Hebrews 9:14, 10:9).

The final point is the Roman soldier's act of faith in Jesus. Looking up at Jesus, he exclaims, "This man was really the Son of God!" Thus he becomes the first in an endless parade of people who will look up at the figure of Jesus on the cross, believe, and win eternal life. Jesus foretold this earlier, saying, "The Son of Man must be lifted up, so that everyone who believes in him may have eternal life" (*John 3:14–15*).

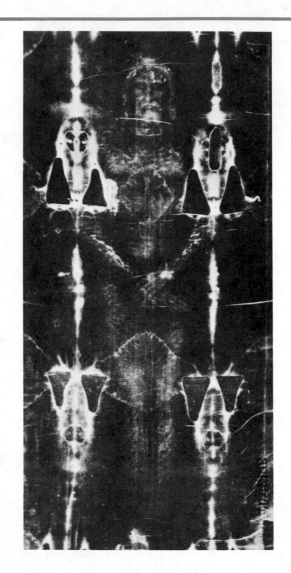

Image of Jesus?

Many Christians believe the Shroud of Turin (shown here) is the burial wrapping of Jesus (John 20:5). It measures three feet by fourteen feet. Close study shows bloodstains around the wrists, feet, head, and side. Whip marks are also visible on the body. The linen wrapping first attracted attention in 1898 when a photograph showed it to be a photographic negative.

Some think the imprint could be a vaporgraph caused by a chemical reaction. Others think it could be a thermograph caused by heat radiation. Scientific experiments show it is not a painting. The man whose image it bears must have been crucified before A.D. 300, because crucifixion was outlawed by the Roman state after that time.

Jesus Is Raised

A man was drifting in a canoe reading a book. He glanced down and saw a water beetle crawling up the side of the canoe. Halfway up, it stuck its talons into the wood and died. The man went back to reading his book.

Later he glanced down again. The beetle had dried, and its back was cracking open. As he watched, something emerged from the opening: first a moist head, and then wings. It was a beautiful dragonfly. The man took his finger and nudged the dried-up shell. It was like an empty tomb.

This beautiful death-resurrection example from nature helps us appreciate better what happened on the first Easter Sunday.

NARRATOR   *As Sunday morning was dawning,*
            Mary Magdalene and the other Mary
            went to look at the tomb.
            Suddenly
            there was a violent earthquake;
            an angel of the Lord
            came down from heaven,
            rolled the stone away,
            and sat on it.
            His appearance was like lightning,
            and his clothes were white as snow.
            The guards were so afraid
            that they trembled
            and became like dead men.
            The angel spoke to the women.

ANGEL   *. . . I know you are looking for Jesus,*
            who was crucified. . . .
            Tell his disciples,
            "He has been raised from death,
            and now he is going to Galilee. . . ."

NARRATOR   *So they left the tomb in a hurry,*
            afraid and yet filled with joy,
            and ran to tell his disciples.
            Suddenly Jesus met them.

JESUS   *Peace be with you. . . .*
            Do not be afraid.
            Go and tell my brothers
            to go to Galilee,
            and there they will see me.
            MATTHEW 28:1–5, 7–10

Wheellike stones once sealed ancient tombs by being rolled down an inclined track. Such stones often weighed as much as a ton.

Meanwhile, the soldiers guarding the tomb told the chief priests all that had happened. The chief priests paid them to say that someone stole the body while they were dozing. Such an explanation may have been credible at first, but it diminished in impact as weeks stretched into months, and months into years. Arnold Lunn tells why in his book *Now I See.*

Lunn says that if the disciples had stolen the body, they would have been the first to know that Jesus did not rise, that he simply died the death of a deluded fanatic. Then Lunn asks this question:

> Is it conceivable that these twelve men
> would have persisted to the end in maintaining
> an elaborate conspiracy of falsehood . . . ?
>
> Is it conceivable that men
> would have faced death with radiant courage
> in their efforts to propagate a doctrine
> which they knew to be false?

The answer to that question is perfectly obvious. It is "No!"

Disciples' Reaction

The disciples' first reaction to the resurrection was disbelief. They called it "nonsense" (*Luke 24:11*). But then other appearances of Jesus began to take place.

In A.D. 135, Rome's Emperor Hadrian covered the traditional sites of Golgotha and Jesus' tomb with a massive pavement. Two centuries later, Constantine removed it and built the first Church of the Holy Sepulcher. This stairwell wall belongs to the present church. The carved graffiti were left by pilgrims nearly one thousand years ago.

One of the most dramatic episodes occurred on Easter Sunday evening. Two disciples were returning on foot to their home in Emmaus. As they walked along, they talked about the tragic weekend.

Suddenly a stranger (Jesus) approached them and asked to walk along with them. They welcomed him and began telling him about Jesus and the tragedy of his death. They told him about the women who went to the tomb, found it empty, and came back in a state of hysteria, saying Jesus had risen. But they themselves could not accept this.

JESUS
How foolish you are,
how slow you are to believe
everything the prophets said!
Was it not
necessary for the Messiah
to suffer these things
and then enter his glory?

NARRATOR
And Jesus explained to them
what was said about himself
in all the Scriptures,
beginning with the books of Moses
and the writings
of all the prophets.

As they came near the village
to which they were going,
Jesus acted as if
he were going farther;
but they held him back.

DISCIPLES
Stay with us;
the day is almost over
and it is getting dark.

NARRATOR
So he went in to stay with them.
He sat down to eat with them,
took the bread,
and said the blessing;
then he broke the bread
and gave it to them.
Then their eyes were opened
and they recognized him,
but he disappeared
from their sight. . . .

They got up at once
and went back to Jerusalem.
LUKE 24:25–31, 33

Jerusalem Appearance

Besides appearing to the women and to the Emmaus disciples, Jesus also appeared to other followers. The first appearance occurred Easter Sunday night. A group of disciples was gathered together behind locked doors, because they were afraid of trouble with the Jewish authorities. Suddenly, Jesus stood in their midst.

JESUS
Peace be with you.

NARRATOR
After saying this, he showed them
his hands and his side.
The disciples were filled with joy
at seeing the Lord.

JESUS
Peace be with you.
As the Father sent me,
so I send you.
Receive the Holy Spirit.
If you forgive people's sins,
they are forgiven;
if you do not forgive them,
they are not forgiven.
JOHN 20:19–23

Many Bible readers see here the origin of the sacrament of Reconciliation. It is a beautiful Easter gift to those who had deserted Jesus in the Garden of Gethsemane. They are forgiven, and they are commissioned to forgive others.

The fullness of the Holy Spirit will be poured out upon *all* of Jesus' followers on Pentecost. Then it will take place in a highly visible way for all the world to see.

Galilean Appearances

Jesus made two other appearances to his closest disciples. Both appearances took place in Galilee, where he had instructed the disciples to go. The first appearance ranks among the most delightful episodes in the Gospels.

One night, while waiting for Jesus, Peter and some of the others decided to go fishing. They got into their boats and headed out. Maybe their minds were not on their work. Maybe it was just a bad night, but they did not catch a single

The Risen Body

A feature of Jesus' appearances to his disciples after his resurrection is their inability to recognize him.

For example, when Jesus appeared to Mary Magdalene, "she did not know that it was Jesus" (*John 20:14*). When Jesus appeared to a group of followers in Jerusalem, they thought "they were seeing a ghost" (*Luke 24:37*). When Jesus appeared to the disciples on the seashore, they "did not know that it was Jesus" (*John 21:4*).

All this speaks of the nature of resurrection and the resurrected body.

Jesus' resurrection was not a restoration of life, such as happened to Jairus' daughter, the widow's son, and Lazarus. The term *resurrection* designates something no human being has yet experienced. It is not a return to a former life, but a quantum leap forward into an infinitely higher form of life.

In other words, the body of Jesus that God raised from the dead on Easter Sunday morning was radically different from the body that was buried on Good Friday afternoon. Paul illustrates the difference with this comparison:

When you plant a seed in the ground . . .
what you plant is a bare seed . . .
not the full-bodied plant
that will later grow up. . . .
This is how it will be
when the dead are raised to life.
When the body is buried, it is mortal;
when raised, it will be immortal.
When buried, it is ugly and weak;
when raised, it will be beautiful and strong.
When buried, it is a physical body;
when raised, it will be a spiritual body.
1 CORINTHIANS 15:36-37, 42-44

Is it any wonder that Jesus' disciples failed to recognize him when he first appeared to them?

fish—all night! As they approached shore in the morning, they saw a stranger standing on the beach. They did not pay any attention to him until he shouted, "Throw your net on the right side of the boat."

The net had hardly sunk into the water when it began filling up with fish. As they struggled to retrieve it, John looked again at the stranger. This time he gasped, "It's the Lord!"

When the disciples hauled their boat onto the beach, they saw that Jesus had prepared a fire. On it lay some freshly cooked fish; off to the side was some bread. They sat down on the sand and ate breakfast. When they finished, Jesus did something unusual and beautiful. He turned to Peter.

Three times Jesus asked him, "Peter, do you love me?" Three time Peter answered, "Yes, Lord!" And three times Jesus responded to Peter, "Feed my sheep!" Peter's threefold affirmation of love erased from his heart his threefold denial of Jesus. And Jesus' threefold response to Peter commissioned him to be the shepherd of the flock of Jesus' followers (John 21).

The final Galilean appearance took place on a hill, probably Mount Tabor. Matthew uses it to conclude his Gospel.

Jesus drew near and said to them,
"I have been given all authority
in heaven and on earth.
Go, then, to all peoples everywhere
and make them my disciples:
baptize them
in the name of the Father, the Son,
and the Holy Spirit,
and teach them to obey everything
I have commanded you.
And I will be with you always,
to the end of the age."
MATTHEW 28:18–20

Mount Tabor in Galilee.

Understanding Death and Resurrection

Review

1. List three gospel episodes that show the growing tension that developed between Jesus and Israel's religious leaders.

2. List the four courts into which the Temple was divided.

3. List and explain three important points contained in the parable of the vineyard tenants.

4. Explain the biblical idea of "remembering." What was strange about the way Jesus began the Passover meal? Why did he make this change? Explain the meaning of the red wine, bitter herbs, clay-colored sauce, and unleavened bread. What three remarks of Jesus over the bread and the cup of wine struck the Apostles? What previous events did each recall?

5. For what twofold reason did Mark probably preserve the account of Peter's denial of Jesus?

6. What remark of Jesus during his hearing before the Jewish Council led to its decision that he must die?

7. What two tactics did Pilate use to try to avoid trying Jesus?

8. List and briefly explain the three points that deserve special note with regard to Jesus' crucifixion.

9. Who were the first followers of Jesus to learn that he was risen?

10. How did the religious authorities explain the empty tomb?

11. What common reaction did Jesus' followers have when they first saw Jesus risen? How might we explain it?

12. At what appearance did Jesus (a) give his disciples the power to forgive others, (b) commission Peter to lead his followers, (c) commission his followers to preach and baptize all nations?

Discuss

1. Jesus suffered four ways: physically, mentally, emotionally, and spiritually. For example, (a) he anguished in the garden, (b) he sweat blood in the garden, (c) he was betrayed by Judas, (d) he was denied by Peter, (e) he was crowned with thorns, (f) he was whipped, (g) he felt abandoned by God.

Identify the kind of pain Jesus suffered in each of the above examples. Which pain do you think was hardest to bear? Why?

2. Jesus took bread, thanked God, broke and gave the bread to his Apostles, saying, "This is my body. Do this in memory of me."

To what three parts of the Mass do "took bread," "thanked God," and "broke and gave bread" refer?

3. Jesus' followers "buried Jesus' body" (*Luke 23:52–53*); they "ate Jesus' body" (*Luke 22:19*), and they "are Christ's body" (*1 Corinthians 12:27*).

What three "bodies of Jesus" are referred to above? What name do we give to each body? When did each body come into existence?

4. President Kennedy was killed November 22, 1963. A few days later, a preschooler told her teacher excitedly, "The president is dead. They buried him! He's really dead." The teacher walked the child to a window box, where the children had planted seeds a week earlier. Digging up a decaying seed with a tiny sprout growing from it, the teacher said, "The president only seems dead; something is happening to him—something similar to what is happening to this seed."

What did the teacher mean? How does the seed example strengthen the idea of resurrection?

Activities

1. Each panel below portrays a gospel event that pertains to the Eucharist. Identify each event and tell how the panel relates to it. (For clues see chapters 2 and 4 in John and chapters 22 and 24 in Luke.)

2. Interview four Catholic adults, asking them why they go to Mass. Record their responses.

3. Invite a non-Catholic friend to attend Sunday Mass with you. Write a brief report on how your friend (a) responded to your invitation and (b) responded to the Mass.

4. Jesus said at the Last Supper, "Do this in memory of me" (*Luke 22:19*). What motivates you to go to Mass? Briefly describe the best Mass you ever attended.

5. Listen to a recording of Bach's *Passion* or a recording of Handel's *Messiah*. Jot down the thoughts that came to you as you listened.

6. Jesus prayed for those who crucified him, "Forgive them, Father! They don't know what they are doing" (*Luke 23:34*). Describe a time when you prayed for or forgave someone who seriously hurt or wronged you.

7. Write a brief paragraph explaining what convinces you most that Jesus really rose from the dead.

Bible Reading

Pick a passage. After reading it, (1) summarize its main point, (2) tell how it relates to the chapter, and (3) list one or two thoughts that occurred to you while you read it.

1. The wounded healer	Isaiah 52:13–53:8
2. He prayed for us	John 17
3. Over 500 saw him	1 Corinthians 15:1–12
4. Whose wife is she?	Mark 12:18–37
5. Seeds and stars	1 Corinthians 15:35–58

Prayer Journal

A Jewish detective stands alone in a Washington, D.C., church. A priest has been murdered while hearing confessions. The detective looks at the blood seeping from under the confessional door into the aisle of the church. The detective sits down and shakes his head. Then he lifts his eyes to a huge crucifix on the wall. He studies it for a while. Then he speaks to Jesus.

> *Who are you? God's son? No, you know I don't believe that. I just asked to be polite. . . . I don't know who you are, but you are Someone. . . . Do you know how I know? From what you said. When I read, "Love your enemy," I tingle. . . . No one on earth could ever say what you said. No one could even make it up. . . . The words knock you down. . . . Who are you? What is it that you want from us?*
> WILLIAM BLATTY, *Legion*

Study a crucifix prayerfully for a few minutes. When you feel ready, talk to Jesus in your own words, just as the detective did. Write out a part of your conversation.

Acts Time Chart

A.D.

Part Three

Christian Scriptures:
Acts/Letters/Revelation

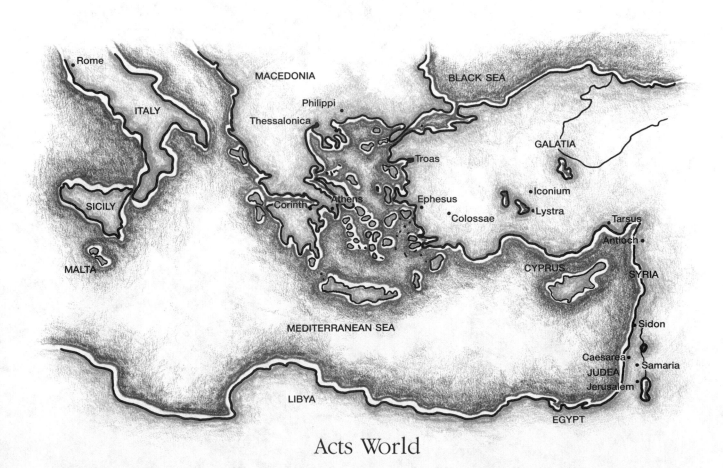

Acts World

14 *The Holy Spirit*

A giant television tower rises above the skyline of East Berlin. Just below the tip of the tower is a revolving restaurant. Communist officials intended it to be a showpiece to the West. But a fluke in design turned it into an embarrassment. Whenever the sun hits the tower a certain way, it turns into a huge, shimmering cross. Officials tried to repaint the tower to blot out the cross, but to no avail.

Something similar happened in Jerusalem after Jesus' crucifixion. Officials hoped Jesus' death would blot out the Christian movement. But instead, it did just the opposite. Christianity spread so spectacularly that by A.D. 64, it was established in faraway Rome. It was so established that the Roman emperor, Nero, made it the target of an all-out persecution.

How did Christianity, in thirty short years, grow from a tiny mustard seed into a towering tree? That amazing story is told in the Acts of the Apostles.

Jesus Goes to His Father

Luke wrote the Acts of the Apostles as a follow-up to his Gospel. It tells what happened to Jesus' followers in the thirty years that followed the ascension. Luke begins, saying of Jesus:

NARRATOR *Before he was taken up [to heaven],*
he gave instructions
by the power of the Holy Spirit
to the men he had chosen
as his apostles. . . .

JESUS *Do not leave Jerusalem, but wait*
for the gift I told you about,
the gift my Father promised.
John baptized with water,
but in a few days you will be
baptized with the Holy Spirit. . . .
When the Holy Spirit
comes upon you, you will be filled
with power, and you will be
witnesses for me in Jerusalem,
in all of Judea and Samaria,
and to the ends of the earth.

NARRATOR *After saying this, he was taken*
up to heaven as they watched him,

167

> *and a cloud hid him*
> *from their sight.*
> *They still had their eyes fixed*
> *on the sky as he went away,*
> *when two men dressed in white*
> *suddenly stood beside them.*

MEN   *Galileans, why are you standing*
> *there looking up at the sky?*
> *This Jesus, who was taken*
> *from you into heaven,*
> *will come back in the same way*
> *that you saw him go to heaven.*
> ACTS 1:2, 4–5, 8–11

Two things stand out in this account. First, there is Jesus' instruction about the Spirit. When the Holy Spirit comes, he will make the Apostles witnesses for Jesus. They will witness not only in Jerusalem, but also in Judea and Samaria and to the ends of the earth. This instruction underscores what Jesus said in his lifetime.

> *"When I go, you will not be left all alone. . . .*
> *The Helper, the Holy Spirit,*
> *whom the Father will send in my name,*
> *will teach you everything and make you*
> *remember all that I have told you. . . .*
> *He will speak about me.*
> *And you, too, will speak about me,*
> *because you have been with me*
> *from the very beginning."*
> JOHN 14:18, 26; 15:26–27

The second thing to note is the instruction about Jesus' return. He will come back "the same way" he left. The Apostles had no idea when this would be, but they expected it would take place in their own lifetime (2 Peter 3:9).

Preparing for the Spirit

In the days ahead, the disciples prepared for the Spirit's coming. "They gathered frequently to pray as a group, together with the women and with Mary the mother of Jesus and with his brothers" (*Acts 1:14*).

The way the disciples prepared is important. They prayed. Just as Jesus prepared for his ministry by going into the desert to pray, so Jesus'

followers prepared for their ministry by prayer. This points to something we will see again and again in the Acts of the Apostles. The life of Jesus' followers parallels the life of their Master.

While praying and waiting, the disciples decided to choose someone to replace Judas as one of "the Twelve." The qualification was simple. He had to be associated closely with Jesus from Jesus' baptism to his ascension.

The disciples eventually narrowed the field to two candidates. "Then they drew lots to choose . . . and the one chosen was Matthias" (*Acts 1:26*).

Drawing lots to decide something was not unusual with Jews (Joshua 18:6, Judges 20:9). It was a way to put the outcome in God's hands. If God had a preference about something, drawing lots was a good way to let him show it. For Jews, God's will was more important than life itself.

The Spirit Comes

A small boy got a toy sailboat for his birthday. He was so excited he could not sit still. He ran around the house showing it to everybody. Finally, he ran to the window, looked at the sky, and said, "O God! Have you seen my boat?"

A long pause followed, as if the boy were waiting for God to answer. Then the boy turned and asked his mother, "What is God like?" But before his mother could answer, he shouted, "I know! He's like the wind!"

Ancient Jews would have applauded the boy's insight. They, too, saw a parallel between the wind and God. The unseen wind's breathlike touch and its stormlike force spoke to Jews of God's own unseen presence and power. The prophets used the wind as an image of God's Spirit (Ezekiel 37:9–10). So did Jesus (John 3:8).

Another image of God that Jews often used was fire. This probably grew out of Moses' experience of God in the burning bush (Exodus 3:3–6) and the people's experience of God at

Mount Sinai, when God came "down on it in fire" (*Exodus 19:16–18*).

It is against this background of wind and fire that the Pentecost event must be read. At that time, the disciples gathered together in a house in Jerusalem.

> *Suddenly there was a noise from the sky*
> *which sounded like a strong wind blowing,*
> *and it filled the whole house*
> *where they were sitting.*
> *Then they saw what looked like*
> *tongues of fire which spread out*
> *and touched each person there.*
> *They were all filled with the Holy Spirit*
> *and began to talk in other languages,*
> *as the Spirit enabled them to speak.*
> ACTS 2:2–4

This noise and uproar attracted a crowd out in the street. The amazed onlookers exclaimed:

> *"Some of us are from Rome,*
> *both Jews and Gentiles converted to Judaism,*
> *and some of us are from Crete and Arabia—*
> *yet all of us hear them*
> *speaking in our own languages*
> *about the great things that God has done!"*
> *Amazed and confused, they kept asking*
> *each other, "What does this mean?"*
> ACTS 2:10–12

Two points about the Pentecost event should be underscored.

First, Pentecost was a major Jewish feast: a thanksgiving celebration, combining gratitude for the year's harvest with gratitude for the Sinai covenant. Meaning "fiftieth," Pentecost occurred fifty days after Passover. On Pentecost, Jews from all over came to the Temple. This explains why the people speaking different languages were in Jerusalem.

Second, the Pentecost event reverses the Tower of Babylon event. Concerning the world situation before that event, the Book of Genesis says everyone spoke "one language" (*Genesis 11:1*). When God saw the pride of the people building the tower, he "mixed up the language of all the people" and "scattered them all over the earth" (*Genesis 11:9*).

The coming of the Holy Spirit on Pentecost reverses this situation. After the Spirit's coming, the people of different languages in Jerusalem understand what the disciples are saying.

The point is clear. What sin split apart, the Spirit unites. Thus the Holy Spirit makes it clear that what happened in Jerusalem on the first Christian Pentecost is meant not just for Jews alone, but for all peoples of all nations. God is re-creating the world that sin de-created.

Filled with the Spirit

Following the Spirit's coming, the Apostles go outside to speak to the crowd in the street. Peter acts as their spokesperson.

> *"Fellow Jews . . .*
> *this is what the prophet Joel spoke about. . . .*
> *'God says:*
> *I will pour out my Spirit on everyone . . .*
> *and they will proclaim my message.*
> *I will perform miracles in the sky above*
> *and wonders on the earth below . . . before*
> *the great and glorious Day of the Lord comes.*
> *And then, whoever calls out to the Lord*
> *for help will be saved.' "*

ACTS 2:14, 16–21

"I will pour out my Spirit on everyone."   Acts 2:17

Peter's reference to the Day of the Lord is important. It designates that moment in history when Jews believed God would intervene to raise his chosen people above all nations.

Much as Christians think of history as being divided into *before Christ* and *after Christ,* so Jews thought of it as being divided into *before the Day of the Lord* and *after the Day of the Lord.*

Peter sees Pentecost as the *beginning* of the long-awaited Day of the Lord. That *day* (an unspecified period of time) will *end* with Jesus' return (Acts 1:11). Peter continues:

> *"Jesus of Nazareth was a man*
> *whose divine authority*
> *was clearly proven to you*
> *by all the miracles and wonders*
> *which God performed through him.*
> *You yourselves know this,*
> *for it happened here among you. . . .*
> *[But] you killed him*
> *by letting sinful men crucify him. . . .*
>
> *"[And now] he has been raised*
> *to the right side of God, his Father,*
> *and has received from him*
> *the Holy Spirit, as he had promised.*
> *What you now see and hear*
> *is his gift that he has poured out on us. . . .*
> *Jesus, whom you crucified,*
> *is the one that God has made Lord and Messiah!"*

ACTS 2:22–23, 33, 36

When the people heard Peter's explanation, they were deeply moved. "What shall we do?" they asked.

PETER   *Each one of you must turn away*
           from his sins and be baptized
           in the name of Jesus Christ,
           so that your sins will be forgiven;
           and you will receive God's gift,
           the Holy Spirit. . . .

NARRATOR   *Many of them*
           believed his message
           and were baptized,
           and about three thousand people
           were added to the group that day.
           They spent their time
           in learning from the apostles,
           taking part in the fellowship,
           and sharing
           in the fellowship meals
           and the prayers.

ACTS 2:38, 41–42

Peter recalls four important events in the life of Jesus.

First, he cites Jesus' miracles. They were signs of God's power at work in Jesus, as he set up God's kingdom on earth.

Second, Peter cites Jesus' death on the cross. All people share the responsibility for it.

Third, he cites Jesus' resurrection and ascension to the right hand of the Father. Jesus returns to his Father, from whence he came (John 1:14–18).

Fourth, he cites Jesus' receiving and sending of the Holy Spirit. This fulfills the promise Jesus made to his followers (John 15:7).

These events—Jesus' miracles, death, resurrection and ascension, and sending of the Holy Spirit—affirm that Jesus is "Lord and Messiah."

Peter's words moved the people. Nearly three thousand were baptized. Baptism formed these people into a single *body,* which we call the *Church.*

The Church is more than just a *body of people* sharing a common belief. It is the *body of Christ* sharing a common life. "The church is Christ's body" (*Ephesians 1:23*). "[Christ] is the head of his body, the church; he is the source of the body's life" (*Colossians 1:18*).

And so Pentecost is rightly called the birthday of the Church, the visible manifestation and extension of Christ's risen body into space and time.

Acts and Luke

Ancient writers used the word *Acts* to refer to the feats of great leaders. Thus we have *The Acts of Hercules, The Acts of Hannibal,* and *The Acts of Alexander.* The Acts of the Apostles models itself after these writings.

Luke, shown here, is the author of the Acts of the Apostles. He is mentioned in three letters of Paul: Colossians 4:14, 2 Timothy 4:11, and Philemon 24. Two facts emerge from these references. First, Luke was a doctor. Second, Luke occasionally traveled with Paul. A third fact—that Luke was a Gentile—may be inferred from Colossians 4:11-14.

A question arises. Where did Luke get his information for Acts? Here we must distinguish between the first half of Acts and the second half.

The first half deals mainly with three Christian communities: Jerusalem, Caesarea-on-the-Sea, and Antioch. Luke probably got much of his information from Christians living in these communities.

The second half deals mainly with Paul's journeys and preaching. Luke possibly got much of this information from traveling and talking with Paul. The "we" sections (where Luke says, *"We* did this," or *"We* went there") are cited as evidence of this. (See Acts 16:10-17, 20:5-16, 21:1-18, 27:1-28:16 for "we" sections.)

Mosaic of Luke.

Understanding the Holy Spirit

Review

1. Who wrote the Acts of the Apostles, and what does it contain?

2. What two instructions did Jesus give his disciples before he ascended into heaven?

3. How did the disciples prepare for the Spirit's coming?

4. Who did the disciples choose to replace Judas? What method did they use to choose him, and why?

5. What two biblical signs of God's presence are used to indicate the coming and the presence of the Holy Spirit?

6. What does the word *Pentecost* mean? Why was it so called? What did Jews celebrate or commemorate on this feast?

7. Explain the relationship between the Tower of Babylon story and Christian Pentecost.

8. What key events did Peter review for the people on Pentecost? What do they affirm about Jesus? How did the people respond to Peter's words?

9. When we say that Pentecost is the "birthday of the Church," what do we mean?

10. List two biographical facts about Luke, giving the source of each. How does the first half of Acts differ from the second half? Where did Luke get the information to write the first half? The second half?

Discuss

1. Iranians held 52 Americans hostage for 444 days in the early 1980s. One night one of the hostages, Kathryn Koob, awoke with a start. She had the feeling that someone had just entered the room. She writes: "But no one was there. Instantly I was reminded of the Holy Spirit the Comforter. And with the sense of his presence came a very real knowledge that I had a source of strength." Kathryn said that before the experience she was terrified; after it she had a deep peace.

Did you ever experience anything similar to this? What might indicate that Kathryn's experience was from God and not from her imagination?

2. Confirmation is the sacrament of the Holy Spirit. Robert Tuzik discusses one of its purposes this way: "Often people tell candidates for confirmation that at baptism their parents made the decision to initiate them into the church, and now at confirmation they must restate or renew this baptismal commitment" (*Liturgy 80*).

If confirmation is a personal "restatement" of our baptismal commitment, what would be a good age for receiving it? Explain.

3. Robert Tuzik also says of confirmation, "It is a sacrament of spiritual maturity wherein the candidate is strengthened to do the work of Christ in the world and make it a better place" (*Liturgy 80*).

What can we do, in a practical way, to make the world a better place to live in?

Activities

1. Take two paper cups and a cigarette lighter. Hold the lighter under one of the cups so that the flame touches it. What happens? Now fill the other cup with water and hold the lighter under it so that the flame touches it. What happens?

Comparing the cup to the disciples and the water to the Holy Spirit (*John 7:38–39*), explain how the experiment dramatizes what happened on Pentecost when the disciples were filled with the Holy Spirit.

2. God said of Pentecost, "I will pour out my Spirit on everyone" (*Acts 2:17*). God adds that when this happens, young people will "see visions"—visions of a better world.

List three visions of a better world that you have. Pick one of the visions and tell what you can do right now to begin to help bring it about.

3. Listen to Marty Haugen's "Burn Bright" from his recording *With Open Hands.*

Afterward create a collage showing how you see the Holy Spirit burning in the lives of certain people today.

Bible Reading

Pick a passage. After reading it, (1) summarize its main point, (2) tell how it relates to the chapter, and (3) list one or two thoughts that entered your mind as you read it.

1. One Spirit, many gifts   1 Corinthians 12:1–11
2. Taught by the Spirit   1 Corinthians 2:7–16
3. Gifts of the Spirit   Isaiah 11:1–9
4. Fruits of the Spirit   Galatians 5:16–26
5. Life in the Spirit   Romans 8:1–17

Prayer Journal

A plane carrying a South American rugby team crashed into deep snow on a mountaintop. Miraculously sixteen out of forty-five boys survived and lived seventy days in subzero weather until rescue came. Their greatest source of strength was nightly prayer sessions. One memorable night, a boy named Arturo, who was normally hard to get along with, led the others in prayer. "He spoke with such feeling that the others were struck with a new affection for him." When he finished, he began to sob. When the others asked why, Arturo said it was because he felt so close to God.

Describe a moving prayer experience you had, alone or in a group; or if you prefer, describe a time when you felt close to God. Be specific: when, where, what, why?

15 *Local Witness*

Peter Matthiessen and a friend were hiking in India. Outside of a small village, they came upon a crippled girl dragging herself along a road. The child's nose and mouth scraped across the gravel.

After they had passed the child, Peter's companion said to him, "In Bengali . . . beggars will break their children's knees to achieve this pitiable effect for business purposes."

Peter was shocked. And so are we. It makes us realize that poverty makes people do terrible things.

Beggars, like those in Bengali, were common in biblical times. Begging was the only way many cripples could survive.

The Church Witnesses in Jerusalem

One day Peter and John were on their way to the Temple. At the Temple door they met a crippled man. He sat there day after day begging money.

NARRATOR	*When he saw Peter and John going in, he begged them to give him something.*
PETER	*I have no money at all, but I give you what I have: in the name of Jesus Christ . . . I order you to get up. . . .*
NARRATOR	*At once the man's feet and ankles became strong; he jumped up, stood on his feet, and started walking around. Then he went into the Temple with them, walking and jumping and praising God. The people there saw him walking and . . . were all surprised and amazed.*

ACTS 3:3, 6–10

The cure of the cripple spread like wildfire. Within minutes everyone in Jerusalem was talking about it. Everyone now knew that the same healing power that was present in Jesus was present in the young Church. As a result, "sick people were carried out into the streets . . . and they were all healed" (*Acts 5:15–16*).

The reaction of the Jewish Council was predictable. They ordered the Apostles to stop preaching and healing. But the Apostles refused.

APOSTLES   *We must obey God, not men.*
The God of our ancestors
raised Jesus . . .
to his right side as Leader
and Savior,
to give the people of Israel
the opportunity to repent
and have their sins forgiven.
We are witnesses to these things—
we and the Holy Spirit,
who is God's gift
to those who obey him.

NARRATOR   *When the members of the Council*
heard this, they were so furious
that they wanted to have
the apostles put to death.
But one of them,
a Pharisee named Gamaliel,
who was a teacher of the Law
and was highly respected
by all the people,
stood up in the Council.

He ordered
the apostles to be taken out. . . .

GAMALIEL   *Fellow Israelites, be careful*
what you do to these men. . . .
Leave them alone!
If what they have planned
and done is of human origin,
it will disappear,
but if it comes from God,
you cannot possibly defeat them.
You could find yourselves
fighting against God.

NARRATOR   *The Council*
followed Gamaliel's advice.
ACTS 5:29–35, 38–39

and wonders among the people.
But he was opposed by some men
who were members
of the synagogue of the Freedmen. . . .
They seized Stephen
and took him before the Council.
Then they brought in some men
to tell lies about him.
"This man," they said, "is always talking
against our sacred Temple
and the Law of Moses. . . ."

The High Priest asked Stephen,
"Is this true?"
ACTS 6:8–9, 12–13; 7:1

Stephen began his defense by tracing the history of God's dealings with Israel. He showed how many of Israel's ancestors resisted God's Spirit. For example, jealous brothers rejected Joseph and sold him into slavery. Angry Israelites rejected Moses and tried to push him aside. Then Stephen looked right at the Council and said, "You are just like your ancestors: you too have always resisted the Holy Spirit!" (*Acts 7:51*).

The Council members were enraged. They seized Stephen, dragged him outside the city, and stoned him. This action was not that of an undisciplined mob. On the contrary, the Council interpreted Stephen's remarks as blasphemy. The Law said of a blasphemer, "Show him no mercy. . . . Stone him to death!" (*Deuteronomy 13:8, 10*).

Stephen's last words, "Do not remember this sin against them!" show that as in life, so in death, he tried to imitate his Master (*Luke 23:34*).

The death of Stephen, the first Christian martyr, touched off a tidal wave of persecution. A positive result of all this was that many disciples

Persecution Breaks Out

For a while it looked as though a peaceful coexistence might be worked out between Jewish authorities and Jesus' followers. But it was not to be. A young deacon named Stephen won the admiration of the people, and they flocked to hear him and be healed by him.

Stephen, a man richly blessed by God
and full of power, performed great miracles

Archaeologists link this cornerstone to the Freedmen's synagogue, whose members attacked Stephen.

fled to Judea and Samaria. There they preached the Good News about Jesus (Acts 8:4). Thus, almost by accident, the second phase of Jesus' commission to his disciples began.

> *"When the Holy Spirit comes upon you,*
> *you will be filled with power,*
> *and you will be witnesses for me*
> *in Jerusalem, in all of Judea and Samaria,*
> *and to the ends of the earth."*
>
> ACTS 1:8

The Church Witnesses outside Jerusalem

One of the outstanding witnesses in Judea and Samaria was another young hero named Philip. Going first to Samaria, he preached the Good News about Jesus. "The crowds paid close attention . . . and saw the miracles that he performed. . . . So there was great joy in that city" (*Acts 8:6, 8*).

Word of Philip's success in Samaria brought Peter and John to the area to see for themselves.

> *When they arrived,*
> *they prayed for the believers*
> *that they might receive the Holy Spirit.*
> *For the Holy Spirit*
> *had not yet come down on any of them;*
> *they had only been baptized*
> *in the name of the Lord Jesus.*
> *Then Peter and John*
> *placed their hands on them,*
> *and they received the Holy Spirit.*
>
> ACTS 8:15–17

By prayer and the laying on of hands, Peter and John confirmed the new Christians, sharing with them the gift of the Spirit which they themselves received on Pentecost.

The Holy Spirit continued to bless and guide the preaching of Philip. For example, one day he encountered "an important official in charge of the treasury of the queen of Ethiopia" (*Acts 8:27*). Philip heard him reading these words of Isaiah:

The Temple Declines

Jesus loved the Temple. He called it his "Father's house" (*John 2:16*). He also taught in it daily (Matthew 26:55).

Jesus' followers also loved the Temple. Only gradually did they realize the significance of what happened in the Temple when Jesus died: "The curtain hanging in the Temple was torn in two" (*Matthew 27:51*). Only gradually did they abandon the Temple after Jesus' resurrection and begin gathering in each other's homes to celebrate the Eucharist (Philemon 2). Only by degrees did they understand fully that they were the new "living temple" of God (Ephesians 2:20-22).

The Romans destroyed the Temple in A.D. 70. All that remains of it today is a retaining wall that once formed part of the plaza on which it stood. Shown here, the wall is a shrine for modern Jews. It is referred to as the Wailing Wall or, preferably, the Western Wall.

When Israeli tanks rumbled into Jerusalem's Old City in 1967, it was the first time, except for a brief period in A.D. 135, that Jews regained control of the Temple site since A.D. 70.

Ancient road in Samaria.

"He was like a sheep that is taken to be slaughtered. . . . He did not say a word" (*Acts 8:32*). Philip asked him if he understood what he was reading. The official said that he did not. Thereupon, Philip explained the passage to him and how it referred to Jesus. The official believed and was baptized.

Excited by Philip's success in Samaria, Peter began a whirlwind preaching mission of cities in Judea. It was during this tour that something remarkable happened at Caesarea-on-the-Sea.

Gentile Pentecost

One of the Roman officers in Caesarea was a centurion named Cornelius. He was a good man who not only prayed but also helped the poor. One day an angel appeared to him and told him to send for Simon Peter, who was in Joppa.

When Peter arrived at the house of Cornelius, it was filled with Gentiles. So Peter began to tell them the Good News about Jesus.

While Peter was still speaking,
the Holy Spirit came down on all those
who were listening to his message.

The Jewish believers
who had come to Joppa with Peter
were amazed that God had poured out
his gift of the Holy Spirit on the Gentiles also.

For they heard them speaking in strange
tongues and praising God's greatness.
Peter spoke up:

"These people have received the Holy Spirit,
just as we also did.
Can anyone, then, stop them
from being baptized with water?"
So he ordered them to be baptized
in the name of Jesus Christ.
ACTS 10:44–48

The important thing to note here is this: The Holy Spirit, which was poured out on the Jews in Jerusalem (Acts 2:4) and on the half-Jews in Samaria (Acts 8:17), is now poured out on the Gentiles in Caesarea. Progressively, the young Church reaches out to all peoples. Significantly, each "Pentecost" is presided over by Peter.

When Peter returned to Jerusalem, some Jewish Christians criticized him for going into the home of a Gentile. But Peter pointed out that the Holy Spirit went into the same Gentile house. "When they heard this, they stopped their criticism and praised God, saying, 'Then God has given to the Gentiles also the opportunity to repent and live!' " (*Acts 11:18*).

Later on, the question of the Gentiles surfaced again. This time, certain Jewish Christians insisted that Gentiles be circumcised before they became Christians. To settle the question, the Apostles called the first Church Council in history. After prayerful deliberation, they decided against it (Acts 15:22–29). A line from the letter informing Gentiles of this decision reads:

> *The Holy Spirit and we have agreed*
> *not to put any other burden on you.*

This sentence is a beautiful expression of the early Church's faith that the Holy Spirit was in their midst, guiding them when they deliberated as a Council.

Peter's Departure

> *About this time King Herod . . . had James,*
> *the brother of John, put to death by the sword.*
> *When he saw that this pleased the Jews,*
> *he went ahead and had Peter arrested.*
> ACTS 12:1–3

After his arrest Peter was placed in chains in prison. Then one night an amazing thing happened. A great light shone in the prison. The chains fell off Peter, and he walked out unnoticed by the guards. Going to the home of John Mark, Peter found many Christians praying for him. Peter told them everything that had happened. He also added that they should tell James (a different James from the one above). Then he "left and went somewhere else" (*Acts 12:17*).

Two points are important here. The first is Peter's instruction to tell James. This James became the leader of the Church in Jerusalem after Peter left.

The second point is the statement that Peter "went somewhere else." With these words, Peter is never heard from again, except for the brief meeting of the Church Council mentioned earlier. Presumably, the price on his head and the danger that his presence created for the Christian community were too great. A fourth-century church historian, Eusebius, says Peter went to Rome. There he was martyred twenty years later.

Roman Centurions

The Gospels mention centurions frequently, always with great respect (Luke 7:5, Mark 15:39). Centurions commanded one hundred soldiers.

Cornelius was not only a centurion but also a "religious man" (Acts 10:2). The Greek expression this phrase translates is a technical one. It means "a God-fearer," a Gentile attracted to Judaism.

In Cornelius' day, many Gentiles had grown weary of the various gods and widespread superstitions. They gravitated toward Judaism with its high moral code and noble worship style. Some of them eventually converted to Judaism. Jews called them proselytes. More often, however, a "God-fearer" merely attended synagogue services with some degree of regularity. Cornelius fell into this category, as did the Ethiopian official mentioned earlier.

Archaeological evidence relating to Roman soldiers, like Cornelius, has survived the centuries. The memorial stone, shown here, preserves the memory of a Roman soldier who died while serving in Judea.

Understanding Local Witness

Review

1. Who was Gamaliel, and what advice did he give the Jewish Council about dealing with Jesus' followers?

2. When Jesus' followers stopped going to the Temple, where did they gather to worship? When and by whom was the Temple destroyed?

3. Who was the first Christian martyr? What was a positive result of his martyrdom and the persecution triggered by it?

4. Where did Philip preach and with what success? What happened when Peter and John joined Philip and laid hands on the new converts?

5. What is meant by the "Gentile Pentecost," and in whose home did it take place? List the three progressive steps by which the early Church reached out to all peoples. Who presided over each step?

6. What procedure did the early Christians use to come to a decision about whether or not Gentiles had to be circumcised before becoming Christians?

7. What attitude toward Roman centurions is found in the Gospels? What is meant by a God-fearer? A proselyte?

8. What eventually happened to Peter, and who took his place as leader of the Church in Jerusalem?

Discuss

1. The Jewish Council followed Gamaliel's advice about how to deal with Jesus' followers. Two thousand years later, a non-Christian historian nominated Jesus as history's greatest person. He did so on the basis of Christianity's impact on history, saying, "The historian's test of an individual's greatness is 'What did he leave to grow?' Did he start men thinking along fresh lines with a vigor that persisted after him? By this test Jesus stands first."

Would you say history has "judged" that the Christian movement is from God? Explain.

2. Dr. Martin Luther King wrote a famous letter from a jail cell in Birmingham. Referring to the early Christians, he said, "In those days the Church was not merely a thermometer that recorded the ideas and principles of popular opinion; it was a thermostat that . . . brought an end to such ancient evils as infanticide and gladiatorial contests."

Explain King's distinction between the Church as a thermometer and the Church as a thermostat.

3. In his letter from the Birmingham jail, Dr. King also said, "If the Church today does not recapture the sacrificial spirit of the early Church, it will . . . be dismissed as an irrelevant fan club."

What does King mean by "recapture the spirit of the early Church"? Imagine that the bishop asked for suggestions to make the Church more relevant today. What would you tell him? Explain.

Activities

1. Stephen and Philip were both deacons.

Read Acts 6:1–6 and report briefly on why and how the early Church ordained deacons.

2. Find out the name of a deacon in your parish and contact him. Do a brief report on when and how he felt "called," what he does, and what he likes most/least about his ministry.

3. *Cornelius* is a book of cartoon strips based on the biblical centurion Cornelius. In one strip, Cornelius says, "A lot of folks don't believe in organized religion. But that only leaves one alternative: disorganized religion."

Interview a person who doesn't go to church regularly. Report briefly on who you interviewed, how old the person is, what his or her reaction was to your questions, how he or she answered, and why you think he or she did/did not answer sincerely.

4. Early Christians were jailed, whipped, beheaded, and stoned for following Jesus.

Describe a time when you suffered because you follow Jesus. What teaching of Jesus do you find most difficult? Explain.

Bible Reading

Pick a passage. After reading it, (1) summarize its main point, (2) tell how it relates to the chapter, and (3) list one or two thoughts that entered your mind as you read it.

1. The warning	Acts 4:1–21
2. The lie	Acts 5:1–11
3. Miracles and wonders	Acts 5:12–16
4. A quarrel	Acts 6:1–7
5. Simon the magician	Acts 8:4–25

Prayer Journal

The sudden death of Stephen makes us painfully aware that death is never far from any of us. Imagine you found out that you had only one more day to live.

What regrets, fears, thoughts would go through your mind? How would you spend that last day? With family? With friends? Alone? Write your answers to these questions.

Here is a college student's answer to the question, How would you spend your last day?

I would immediately contact all the people I had ever really loved, and I'd make sure they knew I had really loved them. Then I would play all the records that meant most to me, and I would sing all my favorite songs. . . . I would look at the blue skies and feel my warm sunshine. I would tell the moon and the stars how lovely and beautiful they are. I would say "goodbye" to all the little things I own, my clothes, my books and my "stuff." Then I would thank God for the great gift of life and die in his arms.

JOHN POWELL, *The Secret of Staying in Love*

16 World Witness

British newspaperman Douglas Hyde could not stomach Christianity. That is why he was reading Avro Manhattan's *The Catholic Church against the Twentieth Century*. He was preparing an article against the Church. Yet, in a matter of months, Hyde became Catholic himself. "Instead of gaining ammunition against the Church from Manhattan's book," he said, "I learned, despite tendentious writing, something of the Church's social teaching. It was written to make me anti-Catholic. It helped to make me 'pro' instead."

In the stormy days after Jesus' crucifixion, another man became a Christian in a strange way. He, too, had been an active opponent of Christ. In fact, he had accepted a commission to hunt down Christians and bring them in for public interrogation.

Paul Is Converted

One day this man and some of his friends were going to Damascus to bring in some Christians. Suddenly a light flashed, and the man fell to the ground. A voice called out:

"Saul, Saul! Why do you persecute me?"
"Who are you, Lord?" he asked.
"I am Jesus, whom you persecute,"
the voice said.
"But get up and go into the city,
where you will be told what you must do."
ACTS 9:4–6

Paul stumbled to his feet, unable to see a thing. His friends took him by the hand and led him into the city. There, a Christian named Ananias laid hands on him and healed him. Paul believed and was baptized.

Then Paul went "to the synagogues and began to preach that Jesus was the Son of God" (*Acts 9:20*). His preaching was so powerful that the Jewish leaders planned to kill him. But Paul fled the city, eventually ending up in Jerusalem.

There, too, serious trouble awaited him. The Christians could not believe that he had actually become one of them. Once again, the Jewish leaders plotted to kill him. And once again, Paul fled for his life. This time he went to Tarsus, his birthplace. There he remained for an extended period of time.

Old Roman gate outside Tarsus, Paul's birthplace.

Paul Makes His First Trip

Meanwhile, Christians began preaching the Gospel as far north as Antioch. When news of this reached the church in Jerusalem, they sent Barnabas to Antioch. Upon arrival, Barnabas saw the opportunities it offered. Immediately he thought of Saul in Tarsus.

> *Barnabas went to Tarsus to look for Saul.*
> *When he found him, he took him to Antioch,*
> *and for a whole year*
> *the two met with the people of the church*
> *and taught a large group. It was at Antioch*
> *that the believers were first called Christians.*
> ACTS 11:25–26

It was at Antioch, also, that Saul was first called Paul. He dropped his Jewish name in favor of its Gentile form, perhaps as a sign of his calling to preach to the Gentiles. It was at Antioch, also, that Paul and Barnabas set out on an extended preaching tour in A.D. 45.

The first port of call was the island of Cyprus. There they preached in the synagogues and even before the governor of the island.

From Cyprus they went to Asia Minor, modern Turkey. There they visited several cities, including Iconium, where they ran into stiff opposition. They left there and went to Lystra, where a memorable episode took place. It involved a man who had been crippled from birth.

As Paul preached to the people, he saw that the man believed and could be healed. So he healed him.

> *When the crowds saw what Paul had done,*
> *they started shouting*
> *in their own Lycaonian language,*
> *"The gods have become like men*
> *and have come down to us!"*
> *They gave Barnabas the name Zeus,*
> *and Paul the name Hermes,*
> *because he was the chief speaker.*
> *The priest of the god Zeus,*

whose temple stood just outside the town,
brought bulls and flowers to the gate,
for he and the crowds
wanted to offer sacrifice to the apostles.
ACTS 14:11–13

Why this surprising reaction? A clue may be contained in the writings of Ovid.

This first-century poet describes a legendary visit of Zeus and Hermes to Lystra. The gods, who came in disguise, received a cold reception. No one welcomed them, except an old peasant couple. Before departing, the gods punished the townspeople and rewarded the couple. Perhaps the people of Lystra remembered this legend and did not want to make the same mistake twice.

The people of Lystra mistook Paul for Hermes,
shown here on this pillar and in close-up.

The preaching of Paul and Barnabas was cut short in Lystra by the arrival of some Jews from Iconium. When they found Paul and Barnabas still preaching in their region, they flew into a rage. They stoned Paul, dragged him out of town, and left him for dead. "But when the believers gathered around him, he got up and went back into the town" (*Acts 14:20*).

After Paul recovered, he and Barnabas continued their tour of Asian cities. Finally, it came time for them to return home. They had been on the road four years and were in need of a well-deserved rest. The date was A.D. 49.

Paul Makes His Second Trip

Never in history have so many soldiers returned to so many battlefields as the soldiers of World War II. They return to Europe and to the Pacific to get back in touch with the past. Why do they do this? One man who had returned to Corregidor four times says,

"Because this is where the most exciting events of my life took place. I never did anything later in life to equal it."

Some months after Paul returned home, he found himself hankering to go back to the towns where he had preached earlier. Taking a companion, named Silas (1 Thessalonians 1:1), he set out on his second great trip.

At Lystra, Paul met a young Christian named Timothy. All spoke well of him (Acts 16:2), so Paul invited Timothy to accompany them. He would become Paul's closest co-worker and the recipient of two of his letters.

And so the three men preached the Good News in town after town, eventually ending up in Troas. There Paul had a vision of "a Macedonian standing and begging him, 'Come over to Macedonia and help us!' " (*Acts 16:9*).

This vision moved Paul deeply. He revised his plans and headed for Macedonia, which is on the mainland of Europe. There they went to the city of Philippi, where a painful ordeal lay in store for them.

One day they saw a slave girl. She "had an evil spirit that enabled her to . . . [earn] a lot of money for her owners by telling fortunes" (*Acts 16:16*). Paul was moved to pity and drove the evil spirit from her. Her owners "seized Paul and Silas

The ruins of Philippi lie at the foot of this mountain.

Close-up of ruins.

and dragged them to the authorities" (*Acts 16:19*). Figuring they were troublemakers, the authorities punished them and jailed them. That night a violent earthquake rocked the city, severely damaging the jail. The jailor woke up and found the prison doors wide open. Thinking his prisoners had escaped, he drew his sword and prepared to kill himself.

> *But Paul shouted at the top of his voice,*
> *"Don't harm yourself! We are all here!"*
>
> *The jailer called for a light, rushed in,*
> *and fell trembling at the feet of Paul and Silas.*
> *Then he led them out and asked,*
> *"Sirs, what must I do to be saved?"*
>
> *They answered, "Believe in the Lord Jesus,*
> *and you will be saved—you and your family."*
> *Then they preached the word of the Lord*
> *to him and to all the others in the house.*
> ACTS 16:28–32

Paul and Silas left Philippi and went to Thessalonica. Once there, they followed the usual practice of going to the synagogue.

> *There during three Sabbaths*
> *[Paul] held discussions with the people,*
> *quoting and explaining the Scriptures,*

> *and proving from them that the Messiah*
> *had to suffer and rise from death.*
> *"This Jesus whom I announce to you,"*
> *Paul said, "is the Messiah."*
> ACTS 17:2–3

Paul's words convinced many. But others opposed him violently. The situation grew so ugly that Paul's new converts feared for his safety and urged him to leave. Paul fled under cover of darkness and eventually ended up in Athens.

Witness in Athens

When Paul arrived in Athens, he spent several days walking through the city, studying its people. He was deeply distressed to discover how full of idols the city was. Finally, he decided it was time to begin teaching the people about Jesus.

> *So he held discussions in the synagogue*
> *with the Jews*
> *and with the Gentiles who worshiped God,*
> *and also in the public square every day*
> *with the people who happened to come by.*
> *Certain Epicurean and Stoic teachers*
> *also debated with him.*
> ACTS 17:17–18

Then one day Paul got an invitation to speak at a special meeting of Athenians. He began:

> *"I see that in every way*
> *you Athenians are very religious.*
> *For as I walked through your city*
> *and looked at the places where you worship,*
> *I found an altar on which is written,*
> *'To an Unknown God.'*
> *That which you worship, then,*
> *even though you do not know it,*
> *is what I now proclaim to you."*
> ACTS 17:22–23

Paul went on to explain that the God he proclaims made the universe and holds it in existence. God also filled the world with clues by which everyone can find him. Finally, God invites all people to turn from their sins and serve him.

*"For he has fixed a day
in which he will judge the whole world
with justice by means of a man he has chosen.
He has given proof of this to everyone
by raising that man from death!"*
ACTS 17:31

Paul's approach to his Gentile audience in Athens stands in sharp contrast to Peter's approach to his Jewish audience in Jerusalem. Peter's point of focus was Jesus who—

died and rose	(Acts 3:15),
fulfilled the prophecies	(Acts 3:18, 21ff.),
is the promised Messiah	(Acts 3:18, 20),
calls us to repentance	(Acts 3:19),
will come again	(Acts 3:21).

Epicureans and Stoics

Plato and Aristotle used to sit in the shadow of the Parthenon, shown here, and discuss philosophy with their students. Athens was a hotbed of philosophical theories, and that is one of the reasons why Paul found it hard to preach in the city. Referring to this difficulty, Luke says, "Certain Epicurean and Stoic teachers also debated with [Paul]" (*Acts 17:18*).

Epicureans accepted the atom theory of the philosopher Democritus. He said that life was the result of a chance coming together of atoms. Death was simply the breakup of the atoms. There was no such thing as life after death.

Stoics held that life came from a "fiery" spirit. Living things are "sparks" from that spirit. Stoics reasoned that the fiery spirit had no feelings. Otherwise people could make it sad or glad and, for the moment, exercise control over it. Stoics believed the goal of life was to imitate the spirit and banish all feeling from life. People should accept gracefully whatever life brings. "If we don't get what we want, then we should learn to want what we get."

It is against this background that the problems Epicureans and Stoics had with Paul's teaching must be understood. Epicureans could not accept life after death. Stoics could not accept a loving God.

These ancient fragments mention Gallio by name and help date Paul's stay in Corinth.

In contrast, Paul's point of focus was God who—

made us	(Acts 17:24),
preserves us	(Acts 17:25),
leads us to seek him	(Acts 17:27),
invites us to serve him	(Acts 17:30),
will judge us	(Acts 17:31).

The Athenian response to Paul's words was typical of the response that people still make to the Good News: Some "made fun of Paul," some "joined him and believed," others dragged their feet, saying, "We want to hear you speak about this again" (*Acts 17:32–34*). Paul left Athens and went to Corinth.

Witness in Corinth

Corinth was a great commercial hub in Paul's time. But Corinth paid a high price for its popularity. Riffraff from all over the world crowded its streets: gamblers, prostitutes, and hardened criminals. It was to this city that Paul came to preach "Blessed are the clean of heart." What could he possibly hope to achieve in such an environment? Possibly just another failure like that in Athens! But Paul was determined to try.

According to his custom, Paul went to the synagogue to preach. At first, his word fell on deaf ears. But finally it bore fruit. "Crispus, who was the leader of the synagogue, believed in the Lord, together with all his family" (*Acts 18:8*). A sizable number of others followed him. For every believer in Corinth, however, there were hundreds who did not believe, especially among the Jewish population.

Paul's preaching to the Gentiles of Corinth fared a little better. When his Jewish opponents saw this, they plotted his downfall. One day they seized him and brought him before Gallio, the Roman governor. " 'This man,' they said, 'is trying to persuade people to worship God in a way that is against the law!' " (*Acts 18:13*). Gallio saw at once that it was a religious dispute and dismissed the case.

Paul continued his preaching in Corinth. Slowly, a sizable Christian community developed. The day finally came when Paul knew he must return to Antioch. He bid the Christians an affectionate farewell and boarded his boat. The time was autumn A.D. 54.

Paul Makes His Third Trip

In his book *Dreams,* Morton Kelsey tells about a missionary friend who preached the Gospel on the island of Bali. His friend said that the person who was the easiest to convert was the witch doctor, because he was already a spiritual person. This prompted Kelsey to recall an observation by Jean Williams:

She said that it was perfectly clear to her how Paul could go to a community for only six weeks and immediately leave behind a body of believers. All he had to do was change their allegiance to a different morality, not a different world view, because they already believed in a spiritual reality.

This was also true of the people in Ephesus, whom Paul visited around A.D. 55 on his third missionary trip. They were already a spiritual people, but their allegiance was not to God, but to Artemis.

Paul spent two years in Ephesus. His success took a toll on the city's silversmiths. Before Paul's arrival, they did a booming business selling miniatures of the temple of Artemis to pagan worshipers. When Paul's preaching cut into their business, Demetrius, a leader of the smiths, called the others together. He said to them:

Ancient stadium at Ephesus. The worshipers chanted in it for two hours. It holds 24,000 people.

"There is danger . . . that this business of ours
will get a bad name. Not only that,
but there is also the danger that the temple
of the great goddess Artemis
will come to mean nothing
and that her greatness will be destroyed."
ACTS 19:27

Soon, word buzzed throughout the city that serious trouble was brewing between Christians and worshipers of Artemis. Within minutes the streets swarmed with people heading for the amphitheater—the meeting place at times like this.

Once there, the worshipers of Artemis began to chant, "Great is Artemis of Ephesus!" (*Acts 19:34*). For two hours they chanted. Finally, city officials brought the situation under control. "After the uproar died down, Paul called together the believers and with words of encouragement said good-bye to them" (*Acts 20:1*). He realized that his presence was becoming a liability to them. So he departed before he caused more trouble.

Paul left for Macedonia, eventually ending up in the port city of Troas.

This 2,000-year-old coin shows the head of Artemis. The reverse side shows a stag and a bee, symbols of the goddess.

Witness in Troas

Paul met Luke in Troas. Together they visited the Christian community that was thriving there. The most memorable moment of the visit came on Saturday night. Luke describes what happened.

On Saturday evening
we gathered together for the fellowship meal.
Paul spoke to the people
and kept on speaking until midnight,
since he was going to leave the next day.
Many lamps were burning in the upstairs room
where we were meeting.

A young man named Eutychus
was sitting in the window,
and as Paul kept on talking,
Eutychus got sleepier and sleepier,
until he finally went sound asleep
and fell from the third story to the ground.
When they picked him up, he was dead.
But Paul went down

and threw himself on him. . . .
"Don't worry," he said, "he is still alive!"

Then he went back upstairs,
broke bread, and ate.
After talking with them for a long time,
even until sunrise, Paul left.
They took the young man home alive
and were greatly comforted.
ACTS 20:7–12

Luke preserves for us not only a charming story but also a valuable record of how early Christians celebrated the Eucharist. They celebrated it after a "fellowship meal" on the Lord's Day in the house of a member of the Christian community. Paul makes a similar reference to this practice in chapter 11 of his First Letter to the Corinthians.

After their visit with the Christians in Troas, Paul and Luke began their long journey back to Jerusalem. The time was about A.D. 58.

Understanding World Witness

Review

1. Who was Saul, and where and how did his conversion take place?

2. In what city were Jesus' followers first called Christians?

3. Why did Saul probably change his name to Paul? How are the two names related?

4. What legend could explain why the townspeople of Lystra treated Paul and Barnabas as gods?

5. How long did the first missionary trip last, and when did it end?

6. Where did Paul meet Timothy, and what role did Timothy play in Paul's future ministry?

7. What happened at Troas to make Paul revise his plans and begin preaching in Europe?

8. How did Paul's preaching to the Gentiles in Athens differ from Peter's preaching to the Jews in Jerusalem?

9. Who were the Stoics, and what problem did they have with the Good News? Who were the Epicureans, and what problem did they have with it?

10. Why was Corinth an unlikely city for Paul to try to win converts to Christianity?

11. When did Paul begin his second missionary trip? His third?

12. How long did Paul preach in Ephesus, and why did he decide to leave at the end of that time?

13. Explain when, where, and how early Christians celebrated the Eucharist.

Discuss

1. In 1876, Western Union called the Bell Telephone patent useless, "except as a toy." In 1945, Admiral Leahy said the atom bomb would "never go off." The Apostle Paul also had to struggle against negative criticism.

Why are people—even experts—wrong so often about what is/isn't possible? What negative criticism are you currently battling in your life?

2. Paul had a physical handicap, which he doesn't describe. He only says, "Three times I prayed to the Lord . . . to take it away. But his answer was: 'My grace is all you need, for my power is greatest when you are weak' " (*2 Corinthians 12:8–9*).

Explain God's answer to Paul: "My power is greatest when you are weak."

3. Some of our great athletes were handicapped. Olympic decathlon champ Rafer Johnson lost the bottom of his left foot in a childhood accident. Triple gold medalist Wilma Rudolph couldn't walk without help until she was nine. Major league outfielder Pete Gray lost his right arm when he was six.

Why is a handicap a stumbling block for some and a stepping-stone for others? Do you know of any other famous people who overcame handicaps?

Activities

1. Imagine that television existed in Paul's time. Station SUN-TV Damascus sends you to interview Paul as he enters the city totally blind (Acts 9:1–9).

Report on the answers Paul might give to these four questions: What did the voice say, and what do you think it means? What makes you so sure you didn't imagine the voice? Do you think your punishment is a punishment from God? What are your plans now?

2. Team up with three friends. Using the information in this chapter on Paul's preaching and the philosophies of the Stoics and Epicureans, hold a panel discussion similar to the one Paul and these philosophers must have had in Athens (Acts 17:18). Have one person be Paul; another, a Stoic; a third, an Epicurean; and a fourth, the moderator. Prepare together ahead of time before presenting your panel discussion.

3. Apollos "was an eloquent speaker" (*Acts 18:24*).

Which priest/deacon in your parish gives the best homilies? List three things you like about them. Call him and read your responses to him. Describe his reaction to your call and your responses.

Bible Reading

Pick a passage. After reading it, (1) summarize its main point, (2) tell how it relates to the chapter, and (3) list one or two thoughts that entered your mind as you read it.

1. A dead woman lives   Acts 9:32–43
2. Strange vision   Acts 11:1–10
3. Elymas the magician   Acts 13:1–12
4. The decision   Acts 15:1–35
5. The riot   Acts 19:23–41

Prayer Journal

Paul had a lot of time to think as he walked along from city to city. Much of this time he spent in prayer. Prayer can take three forms: exploring something about God (meditation), enjoying God's presence (contempla-tion), expressing one's self to God (conversation). All three forms occur in this prayer experience that a high school boy had one day in a park.

> After our basketball game, I got a drink of water at a fountain. The water tasted good, and I felt refreshment enter my body. Then I lay down on the rocks by the lake and closed my eyes. Suddenly, I began to think: "We need water to live. But where does it come from? Clouds!" I thought. This think-ing went on until I got no answer. Or rather, I was left with only one answer: God! For the next few minutes I just lay there marveling at what God must be like. Then I made a short prayer to God and went home.

Pick out the three forms of prayer from the boy's prayer experience. Write out an imaginary or a real prayer experience that includes all three forms of prayer.

17 Unfinished Story

Twenty political prisoners stood in the public square of Saint Petersburg, Russia. The first three were led before the firing squad and prepared for execution. Just as the commanding officer was about to give the order to fire, a messenger rode up on a horse. The Russian emperor, Nicholas I, had just changed the sentences of the prisoners from death to hard labor.

One of the prisoners saved by the change was the Russian novelist Feodor Dostoevski. He went on to write some of the world's most influential literature.

Paul, too, had several similar narrow escapes from death. He, too, went on to write some of the world's most influential literature: his letters. One of Paul's escapes came upon his return to Jerusalem after his third preaching trip.

Paul Is Arrested

One day Paul went to the Temple to worship. Some of his opponents spotted him. When they did, they went completely wild. Pointing their fingers at him, they began to shout.

JEWS
Men of Israel! Help!
This is the man
who goes everywhere
teaching everyone
against the people of Israel,
the Law of Moses,
and this Temple.
And now he has even brought
some Gentiles into the Temple
and defiled this holy place!

NARRATOR
They said this
because they had seen
Trophimus from Ephesus
with Paul in the city,
and they thought that Paul
had taken him into the Temple. . . .

The people all ran together,
grabbed Paul, and dragged him
out of the Temple. . . .
The mob was trying to kill Paul,
when a report was sent up
to the commander
of the Roman troops. . . .

At once the commander
took some officers and soldiers
and rushed down to the crowd.
When the people saw him

*Roman soldiers in Paul's time were probably
attired much as those shown in this ancient sculpture.*

with the soldiers,
they stopped beating Paul.

The commander went over to Paul,
arrested him, and ordered him
to be bound with two chains.
ACTS 21:28–33

Then the commander tried to find out what the ruckus was about. But the mob only got more and more out of control. To keep a full-blown riot from starting, the commander took Paul off to jail. Meanwhile, he set up a meeting with the Jewish Council for the next day. He wanted to get to the bottom of the matter.

The next day Paul was marched before the Jewish Council and ordered to give an account of his actions. No sooner had Paul begun to talk when the Council began to contradict him.

The argument became so violent
that the commander was afraid
that Paul would be torn to pieces.
So he ordered his soldiers to go down
into the group, get Paul away from them,
and take him into the fort.
ACTS 23:10

When night fell, Paul found himself back in Roman custody. Then something strange happened. Paul experienced the Lord's assurance: "Don't be afraid! You have given your witness for me here in Jerusalem, and you must also do the same in Rome" (*Acts 23:11*). That night Paul slept soundly.

But while Paul slept, his enemies burned midnight oil. About forty of them got together and took an oath not to eat or drink until they had killed Paul. "But the son of Paul's sister heard about the plot; so he went to the fort and told Paul" (*Acts 23:16*). Paul alerted the commander, who did not waste a minute. He organized an armed guard and moved Paul to a safer jail in Caesarea.

Imprisonment in Caesarea

When Paul's opponents learned what happened, they were angry. Hastily, they organized a delegation to go to Caesarea and meet with the Roman governor, Felix. After the meeting, Felix called Paul and arranged an immediate hearing.

The delegation began by accusing Paul of stirring up the people and not respecting the Temple. After they finished making their charges, Felix asked Paul to respond. Paul denied the charges.

"The Jews did not find me
arguing with anyone in the Temple,
nor did they find me stirring up the people,
either in the synagogues or anywhere else. . . .
I do admit this to you:
I worship the God of our ancestors
by following that Way [Christianity]
which they say is false."
ACTS 24:12, 14

After Felix heard both sides, he promised to look into the matter more closely. He thanked the delegation and dismissed them.

After the hearing, Felix began to keep in closer touch with Paul. Why this sudden attention? Luke says Felix was looking for a payoff (Acts 24:26). Luke's remark agrees with ancient reports about Felix. They call him a bad governor, whose hand was always open for a bribe.

But Paul refused to play Felix's game. As a result, his stay in jail stretched into two long years.

Paul's hope for release soared temporarily when Festus succeeded Felix as governor. But his hope soon crashed. Shortly after taking office, Festus visited Paul's opponents, who were waiting for the new governor.

They begged Festus to do them the favor
of having Paul come to Jerusalem,
for they had made a plot
to kill him on the way.
Festus answered,
"Paul is being kept a prisoner in Caesarea,
and I myself will be going back there soon.
Let your leaders go to Caesarea with me
and accuse the man
if he has done anything wrong."
ACTS 25:2–5

Remains of a Roman aqueduct outside modern Caesarea.

Two weeks later, Paul's opponents arrived in Caesarea. The hearing was almost a replay of the one held two years earlier.

> *But Festus wanted to gain favor*
> *with the Jews, so he asked Paul,*
> *"Would you be willing to go to Jerusalem*
> *and be tried on these charges?"*
> ACTS 25:9

Paul saw the danger immediately. He would never get a fair trial in Jerusalem. So he did the only thing possible. He asked to be tried in Rome. Every Roman citizen living outside Rome had a right to ask to be tried in Rome if he feared he would not get justice in a local court. This was what Paul, a Roman citizen, now did.

Paul Witnesses in Rome

In 1912, five British explorers froze to death during an expedition to the South Pole. A passage from the journal of one of the explorers, Edward Wilson, sounds like something Paul might have written as he set out for Rome.

> *So I live, knowing that I am in God's hands,*
> *to be used to bring others to him . . .*
> *or to die tomorrow if he so wills. . . .*
> *We must do what we can*
> *and leave the rest to him. . . .*
> *My trust is in God so that it matters not*
> *what I do or where I go.*

Paul's Personality

This painting by El Greco makes us wonder about Paul's appearance and personality. What did he look like? What kind of speaker was he? How was he able to move so many people?

Strangely enough, there are clues in Paul's letters that suggest he was neither an impressive-looking person nor a dynamic speaker. For example, Paul writes to the Christians in Corinth:

> *I, Paul, make a personal appeal to you—*
> *I who am said to be meek and mild*
> *when I am with you,*
> *but harsh with you when I am away.*
> *By the gentleness and kindness of Christ*
> *I beg you not to force me to be harsh*
> *when I come.*
> 2 CORINTHIANS 10:1-2

Further on in the same letter, Paul writes:

> *Someone will say,*
> *"Paul's letters are severe and strong,*
> *but when he is with us in person,*
> *he is weak, and his words are nothing!"*
> 2 CORINTHIANS 10:10

Both of these statements suggest that Paul was unimpressive both as a person and as a speaker. How, then, do we account for his impact on people? Why did his opponents fear him so much? Again, Paul suggests the answer himself. In another letter to the Corinthians, he writes:

> *My teaching and message were not delivered*
> *with skillful words of human wisdom,*
> *but with convincing proof of the power*
> *of God's Spirit. Your faith, then, does not rest*
> *on human wisdom but on God's power.*
> 1 CORINTHIANS 2:4-5

The key to Paul's power over people was not his own power, but the power of the Holy Spirit working through him.

Just as Wilson kept a journal of his polar expedition, so Luke kept a journal of Paul's voyage to Rome. His description of the trip, written in the first person, is remarkably detailed. Paul was just one of many other prisoners being taken to Rome under military guard. The other prisoners were probably already condemned to death and scheduled to die in the arena to amuse Roman audiences.

Luke and Aristarchus (Acts 19:29) probably signed on as Paul's personal servants. An ancient letter of Pliny notes that Roman citizens had the right to servants, even in custody.

Roman Colosseum where thousands died to entertain Roman crowds.

Storm at Sea

The voyage to Rome had hardly reached its halfway point when a great storm blew up. It got so violent that the captain ordered some of the cargo thrown overboard. "For many days," Luke writes, "we could not see the sun or the stars, and the wind kept on blowing very hard" (*Acts 27:20*).

Then one night the ship was blown into dangerous waters. The situation looked bad.

Shipwrecked crew went ashore here.

*Just before dawn . . . Paul took some bread,
gave thanks to God before them all,
broke it, and began to eat. They took courage,
and every one of them also ate some food. . . .*

*After everyone had eaten enough,
they lightened the ship by throwing
all the wheat [cargo] into the sea.*

*When day came, the sailors did not recognize
the coast, but they noticed a bay with a beach
and decided that, if possible,
they would run the ship aground there. . . .*

*But the ship hit a sandbank . . .
the back part was being broken to pieces
by the violence of the waves. . . .
[An officer] ordered all the men
who could swim to jump overboard first
and swim ashore; the rest were to follow,
holding on to the planks
or to some broken pieces of the ship.*

And this was how we all got safely to shore.
ACTS 27:33–44

The shipwrecked crew was fortunate to land on friendly Malta. There were other shores where they would have been killed.

Eventually, the crew and passengers resumed their voyage to Rome on a ship called "The Twin Gods." It sailed to a port on the Italian coast. From there, soldiers marched the prisoners to Rome on foot. Luke writes of the march:

*The believers in Rome heard about us
and came as far as the towns of
Market of Appius and Three Inns
to meet us. When Paul saw them,
he thanked God and was greatly encouraged.
When we arrived in Rome,
Paul was allowed to live by himself
with a soldier guarding him.*
ACTS 28:15–16

In other words, Paul was put under a form of house arrest.

Paul's Preaching

Once Paul got situated, around A.D. 61, he called local Jewish leaders to a meeting. They were eager to talk with him, saying:

*"We have not received any letters from Judea
about you, nor have any of our people
come from there with any news
or anything bad to say about you.
But we would like to hear your ideas,
because we know
that everywhere people speak
against this party to which you belong."*
ACTS 28:21–22

Paul was delighted to have the opportunity to talk with the Jewish leaders.

*From morning till night
he explained to them his message
about the Kingdom of God,
and he tried to convince them about Jesus
by quoting from the Law of Moses
and the writings of the prophets.
Some of them were convinced by his words,
but others would not believe. . . .*

*For two years
Paul lived in a place he rented for himself,
and there he welcomed all who came to see him.
He preached about the Kingdom of God
and taught about the Lord Jesus Christ,
speaking with all boldness and freedom.*
ACTS 28:23–24, 30–31

With this final paragraph the Acts of the Apostles ends. It never does tell what happened to Paul. One of Paul's own letters suggests that he was freed after a first trial (2 Timothy 4:16–17). Possibly he then went to Spain (Romans 15:24), Asia Minor (Titus 3:12), Macedonia (1 Timothy 1:3), and Crete (Titus 1:5).

Once back in Rome, Paul was brought to trial a second time and convicted (2 Timothy 4:6). Finally, he was beheaded in Rome, around A.D. 67.

One last question remains. Why did Luke leave the Acts of the Apostles unfinished?

Of all the theories, perhaps the most satisfying is this: Luke left it unfinished because its story is still unfinished. The preaching of the Good News goes on—and must go on—until the world has been re-created and Jesus returns in final glory.

Paul's Rome

Ancient Rome was magnificent. It was ruled by Nero, pictured on the coin shown here. He became emperor in A.D. 54, six years before Paul's arrival, and ruled until A.D. 68, a year after Paul's execution.

A great fire swept Rome in A.D. 64. Nero falsely accused Christians of setting it and persecuted them mercilessly. Some were set ablaze on crosses in the arena; others were dressed in animal skins and torn apart by mad dogs.

It was for these suffering Christians, primarily, that Mark wrote his Gospel.

Although ancient Rome had its beautiful side, it also had its ugly side. For example, there was a total lack of sanitation in areas where the average citizen lived. Dung heaps and cesspools lay at intervals, and human refuse was carried to them. Unfortunately, many people simply dumped it into the street.

The noise was deafening. One ancient writer called it "unbearable." By day, pagan priests roamed the streets chanting prayers to the crash of cymbals. At night, wagons clanked over the cobblestones, waking everyone within earshot.

It was to this city that Paul brought the Gospel and began witnessing with all his heart.

Understanding Unfinished Story

Review

1. Why did the crowd at the Temple attack Paul?

2. What news caused the Roman commander to transfer Paul to a prison in Caesarea?

3. Why did Felix befriend Paul yet keep him locked up for two years without deciding his case?

4. What question raised by Festus led Paul to request trial in Rome? What gave Paul the right to make this request?

5. What evidence in the New Testament suggests that Paul was a weak speaker and an unimpressive-looking person? How do we account for his power to convert people to Christianity?

6. What gave Paul the right to request that Luke accompany him to Rome on the prison ship?

7. What did Paul do that restored courage to the ship's crew when they were all in grave danger?

8. Where and how did the ship eventually break up and sink?

9. In what year did Paul get settled in Rome? Who was emperor then? Why did that emperor persecute Christians a few years later? What evangelist wrote his Gospel primarily for these suffering Christians?

10. With what information about Paul does the Acts of the Apostles end?

11. When and how did Paul probably die?

Discuss

1. Paul spent two long years in prison in Caesarea.

What do you think Paul did in prison? For clues see Colossians 4:15–18; 2 Timothy 4:13; Acts 16:25, 28:23. What was the longest time you ever spent alone? How did you pass the time?

2. Millions of Christians have been jailed for their faith. *Time* magazine reported on a modern prisoner in Romania. He was kept in total darkness in a basement next to a foul-smelling pit into which toilets flushed. His bed was a plank on a damp floor. Rats bothered him constantly. He drew strength from meditating on Jesus' crucifixion. Commenting on these meditations, he said, "Believe me, all of you who are outside . . . there is a face on the cross which cannot be apprehended save by those who lie in jail. . . . God's happiness rests longer upon those who have not light's distraction."

What is the prisoner's point? What part of his confinement would you find the hardest to endure? Explain.

3. Fred Morris spent many gruesome hours in the Brazilian torture chamber. He drew great strength from prayers he knew by heart, like Psalm 23 ("The Lord is my shepherd").

On the chalkboard list the prayers the members of your group know by heart. Why do you think prisoners find memorized prayers more helpful in prison than prayers they make up themselves?

Activities

1. The ship's officer "ordered all the men who could swim to jump overboard . . . ; the rest were to follow, holding on to . . . broken pieces of the ship" (*Acts 27:43–44*).

Describe an accident or near accident you have had. What thoughts went through your mind during or after it? Or if you prefer, interview and report on someone who survived a serious accident.

2. Polar explorer Edward Wilson wrote in his journal, shortly before freezing to death, "I live knowing that I am in God's hands. . . . We must do what we can and leave the rest to him. . . . My trust is in God." Paul felt this way often in his danger-filled life.

Describe a time when you felt helpless and placed yourself completely in God's hands. Why do you think God answers some people's prayers and not others'?

3. Trace a map of the Mediterranean Sea and, using chapter 28 of Acts as a guide, chart Paul's course from Caesarea to Rome.

Bible Reading

Pick a passage. After reading it, (1) summarize its main point, (2) tell how it relates to the chapter, and (3) list one or two thoughts that entered your mind as you read it.

1. Paul's story   Acts 22
2. Plot to kill Paul   Acts 23:12–22
3. Take me to Rome!   Acts 25:1–12
4. The shipwreck   Acts 27:18–44
5. The snakebite   Acts 28:1–15

Prayer Journal

Journalist George Cornell reports that almost all U.S. prisoners in Vietnam said "that faith and the power of prayer sustained them" in their prison ordeals. Faith and prayer also sustained Paul in prison in Caesarea. One form of prayer Paul undoubtedly used was contemplation: marveling at some facet of God or creation. An example of contemplation is this excerpt from Psalm 139:

LORD, you have examined me and you know me.
You know everything I do;
from far away you understand all my thoughts.
You see me, whether I am working or resting;
you know all my actions.
Even before I speak,
you already know what I will say. . . .
Your knowledge of me is too deep;
it is beyond my understanding.
PSALM 139:1–4, 6

Select one of the photos in this textbook and contemplate it. Don't say anything; just gaze at it. When you finish, write down the page number of the photo you contemplated and record some of the thoughts that went through your mind during your contemplation.

18 Paul's Letters

Egyptian tombs and ruins have yielded up hundreds of ancient writings. Some of these writings are personal letters. One letter is from a runaway boy to his mother. It reads:

I write to you that I am naked.
I plead with you, mother, to forgive me.
I know I've brought this on myself....
I know that I've sinned.

Then the letter begins to trail off, too blurred and too frayed to read.

Few forms of writing can match letters. They are windows into the human spirit. The letters of Paul are no exception. They give us a glimpse into Paul's mind, heart, and soul.

Tradition says Paul wrote thirteen letters. They may be grouped as follows:

Early Letters: 1–2 Thessalonians;
Great Letters: 1–2 Corinthians,
                   Galatians, Romans;
Prison Letters: Philippians, Colossians,
                   Philemon, Ephesians;
Pastoral Letters: 1–2 Timothy, Titus.

Paul Writes His Early Letters

In the summer of A.D. 50, on his second missionary trip, Paul visited the city of Thessalonica. Later, in A.D. 52, while in Corinth, he received news that the Church there was having problems. This was not surprising because Paul had to leave the city before completing his instructions to the Christians there.

Many Thessalonians had the impression that Jesus was going to return any day. They also had the impression that *all* the believers would be alive when he returned. Therefore, when some of their members died, they were thrown into confusion.

Paul sat down immediately and wrote them a letter to clarify this matter.

1–2 Thessalonians

From Paul, Silas, and Timothy—
To the people of the Church in Thessalonica,
who belong to God the Father
and the Lord Jesus Christ:
May grace and peace be yours.

We always thank God for you all. . . .
Even though you suffered much . . .
you became an example to all believers
in Macedonia and Achaia. . . .

Our brothers, we want you to know the truth
about those who have died,
so that you will not be sad. . . .
Jesus died and rose again,
and so we believe
that God will take back with Jesus
those who have died believing in him. . . .

There is no need to write you . . .
about the times and occasions. . . .
For you yourselves know very well
that the Day of the Lord will come
as a thief comes at night. . . .

Be joyful always, pray at all times,
be thankful in all circumstances. . . .
Read this letter to all the believers.

The grace of our Lord Jesus Christ be with you.
1 THESSALONIANS 1:1–2, 6–7; 4:13–14; 5:1–2, 16–18, 27–28

Paul's first letter, apparently, brought the Thessalonians great joy. It clarified the matter about those who had died. But his letter failed to dispel the notion that Jesus' return was just around the corner. In fact, it seems to have fueled expectations about this. Some members even quit their jobs. This created a flurry of new problems. And so Paul wrote a second letter a few months later.

From Paul, Silas, and Timothy—
To the people of the church in Thessalonica,
who belong to God our Father
and the Lord Jesus Christ:
May God our Father and the Lord Jesus Christ
give you grace and peace. . . .

We must thank God at all times for you. . . .
We boast about the way you continue
to endure and believe. . . .

Concerning the coming of our Lord. . . .
Do not let anyone deceive you. . . .
For the Day will not come
until the final Rebellion takes place
and the Wicked One appears. . . .
Don't you remember?
I told you all this while I was with you.

Yet there is something
that keeps this from happening now,
and you know what it is. . . .

So then . . . hold on to those truths
which we taught you,
both in our preaching and in our letter. . . .

With my own hand I write this:
Greetings from Paul.
This is the way I sign every letter;
this is how I write.
May the grace of our Lord Jesus Christ
be with you all.
2 THESSALONIANS 1:1–4; 2:1–6, 15; 3:17–18

Paul's letter evidently produced the desired effect. For we hear of no further problems. Paul's reply boils down to this: Certain events must first take place before Jesus' Second Coming. One is a great clash between the forces of good and evil. Paul's letter is vague about these events, because he presumes his readers are familiar with the teaching he gave to them orally at an earlier date.

Paul's two letters illustrate the general format he used in most of his letters:

an opening salutation,
a thanksgiving,
the body of the letter,
conclusion and final greeting.

The opening *salutation* consists of the sender's name, the receiver's name, and a greeting.

The *thanksgiving* acts as a bridge to the *body* and the theme of the letter.

The *conclusion and final greeting* bring the letter to a close, frequently with some personal news and a blessing.

We might make one concluding observation. Paul's final greeting in his second letter reads as follows:

With my own hand I write this:
Greetings from Paul.
This is the way I sign every letter;
this is the way I write.

Paul's words make it clear that he did not write this letter with his own hand. He had a professional scribe do the actual writing for him. This was a common practice in the ancient world. Several of Paul's other letters indicate he used scribes to write them also (Romans 16:22, 1 Corinthians 16:21, Galatians 6:11, Philemon 19).

Paul's handwriting probably contrasted sharply with the scribe's neat handwriting, just as the author's handwriting (bottom) does with the scribe's (top) in this first-century letter.

Paul Writes His Great Letters

Sydney Piddington was nineteen when he was captured in World War II. He was imprisoned in Changeli in Singapore, with other Australian POWs. One thing that helped him survive the long hours was Lin Yutang's book *The Importance of Living*. It is the kind of book that you do not just read; you meditate on what it says.

The same kind of provocative reading Piddington found in Lin Yutang's book is also found in Paul's "great letters": Galatians, 1–2 Corinthians, Romans. These letters are called "great" because of their profound ideas and teaching.

Galatians

Probably written from Ephesus about A.D. 54, this letter was triggered by *Judaizers*—conservative Jewish Christians who followed Paul into his new Christian communities and told his converts that they must be circumcised. They also accused Paul of preaching a Gospel that was at odds to the one preached by Peter, James, and John.

When Paul heard that Judaizers were trying to impose Jewish laws on Galatian Christians, he fired off an emotion-packed letter to them. He explained the relationship between the Mosaic Law and Christianity. His point came down to this: The Mosaic Law is like a scaffolding of a building. Its purpose is to get the building in place. Once this is done, its purpose is achieved. You do not keep a scaffolding up after the building is in place.

As for being at odds with Peter, James, and John, Paul says they were the ones who commissioned him to preach to the Gentiles.

[They] shook hands with Barnabas and me, as a sign that we were all partners. We agreed that Barnabas and I would work among the Gentiles and they among the Jews.
GALATIANS 2:9

Paul concludes by returning to the matter of circumcision, saying, "It does not matter at all whether or not one is circumcised; what does matter is being a new creature" (*Galatians 6:15*). This echoes a passage Paul penned earlier in the same letter. It is a favorite among Christians.

> *I have been put to death*
> *with Christ on his cross,*
> *so that it is no longer I who live,*
> *but it is Christ who lives in me.*
> *This life that I live now,*
> *I live by faith in the Son of God,*
> *who loved me and gave his life for me.*
> GALATIANS 2:19–20

1–2 Corinthians

Ancient Greek plays portray Corinthians as drunks, perverts, and rowdies. Judging from Paul's letters, some of his converts fitted that stereotype. Thus, writing to them from Ephesus, probably around A.D. 57, Paul says:

> *Few of you were wise or powerful*
> *or of high social standing.*
> *God purposely chose*
> *what the world considers nonsense*
> *in order to shame the wise,*
> *and he chose what the world considers weak*
> *in order to shame the powerful.*
> 1 CORINTHIANS 1:26–27

It is understandable that some of Paul's converts slipped back into their old ways. Paul writes:

> *Now, it is actually being said*
> *that there is sexual immorality among you*
> *so terrible that not even the heathen*
> *would be guilty of it. . . .*
>
> *Don't you know*
> *that your body is a temple of the Holy Spirit,*
> *who lives in you*
> *and who was given to you by God?*
> *You do not belong to yourselves but to God;*
> *he bought you for a price.*
> *So use your bodies for God's glory.*
> 1 CORINTHIANS 5:1; 6:19–20

Another problem in Corinth was division within the congregation. Paul uses this striking image to illustrate the unity that should exist among Christians.

> *Christ is like a single body,*
> *which has many parts; it is still one body,*
> *even though it is made up of different parts.*
> *In the same way, all of us,*
> *whether Jews or Gentiles,*
> *whether slaves or free,*
> *have been baptized into the one body*
> *by the same Spirit. . . .*
>
> *All of you are Christ's body,*
> *and each one is a part of it.*
> 1 CORINTHIANS 12:12–13, 27

Paul concludes with a plea for unity, stressing the importance of love. He writes:

> *I may have all the faith needed*
> *to move mountains—*
> *but if I have no love, I am nothing. . . .*
> *Love is patient and kind;*
> *it is not jealous or conceited or proud . . .*
> *love does not keep a record of wrongs;*
> *love is not happy with evil,*
> *but is happy with the truth.*
> *Love never gives up. . . . Love is eternal!*
> 1 CORINTHIANS 13:2, 4–8

Fragment of a synagogue sign found at Corinth. The poor carving accords with the poor congregation Paul describes in 1 Corinthians 1:26.

Paul's Second Letter to the Corinthians was probably written some months after the first one, possibly from Macedonia. It addresses several issues. One is a challenge to Paul's authority and leadership. For example, some people accused him of—

being a poor speaker,
not being a true Apostle, and
being brave in letters, but weak in person.

Responding to these charges, Paul says, "Perhaps I am an amateur in speaking, but certainly not in knowledge" (*2 Corinthians 11:6*). Then, turning to the second point he cites the many "miracles and wonders" he worked among them as signs confirming his apostolic qualifications (*2 Corinthians 12:12*). Finally, he challenges his accusers to find any "difference between what we write . . . and what we will do when we are with you" (*2 Corinthians 10:11*).

Paul concludes his letter affectionately, saying, "Greet one another with a brotherly kiss." He then imparts his blessing:

> *The grace of the Lord Jesus Christ,*
> *the love of God,*
> *and the fellowship of the Holy Spirit*
> *be with you all.*
> 2 CORINTHIANS 13:13

Romans

The Guinness Book of World Records says the longest letter ever written was two-thirds of a mile in length. It was written on adding machine rolls in June 1969 by a girl in Hampshire, England, to her boyfriend at Goodfellow Air Base in Texas.

The longest letter Paul ever wrote was to the Romans. To set the stage for this letter, we should envision Paul in Corinth in A.D. 58. He often walked down to the waterfront to look at ships in the harbor. Whenever Paul spotted a ship from Rome, his thoughts flew westward to Rome— even to Spain (Romans 15:28). But visiting Rome was out of the question. So Paul did the next best thing. He wrote a letter to the Christians there. It contains one of the best statements of Christianity found in his writings. The letter follows this general format:

the world before Christ	(1:18–3:20),
the world after Christ	(3:21–5:21),
new life in Christ	(6:1–8:39),
God's plan for Israel	(9:1–11:36),
Christian witness	(12:1–15:13).

Paul begins his letter with a profession of faith in Christ: He is the fulfillment of the prophecies,

the son of David, and the Son of God (Romans 1:2–4).

Paul then turns to the Christian. By baptism Christians share in Christ's risen life. Thus, they should have nothing to do with their sinful ways (Romans 6). This does not mean that they will not feel attracted to sin. Paul himself felt this attraction (Romans 7:15–24). Rather, it means that Christ's risen life, which Christians receive in baptism, gives them power to overcome sin.

Paul's letter is also filled with some of the most uplifting passages he ever wrote. Consider the following:

> *What we suffer at this present time*
> *cannot be compared at all with the glory*
> *that is going to be revealed to us.*
> ROMANS 8:18

> *In all things God works for good*
> *with those who love him.*
> ROMANS 8:28

> *There is nothing in all creation that will ever*
> *be able to separate us from the love of God*
> *which is ours through Christ Jesus our Lord.*
> ROMANS 8:39

Paul Writes His Prison Letters

On the ground filth lies an inch thick. . . . We are packed like sardines in a barrel. . . . All the prisoners stink like pigs." This is how one Russian described conditions during his four-year confinement as a political prisoner in Siberia.

Paul, too, was familiar with prisons. He was confined in them on several occasions. He used this time not only to preach to fellow prisoners but also to write letters to recent converts. Paul's prison letters include Philippians (1:7), Colossians (4:10), Philemon (23), and Ephesians (6:20). Let us now take a look at each of these letters.

Ancient Writing

The two Egyptians shown here are gathering and splitting papyrus stalks. The split pieces were then pieced together to form a writing surface. The papyrus fragment behind the two Egyptians shows what the finished surface looked like. The writing on the fragment is Greek. This was the language the evangelists and Paul used in their writings.

Papyrus sheets could be cut to any desired size. They could be stacked one on top of the other to form a codex ("book"). Or sheets could be glued or sewed together and rolled into a scroll. A tiny dried reed, whose point was shredded, was used as a pen. Writing was done without sentence breaks, punctuation, or chapter divisions. These features were added much later by scholars to facilitate reading and studying the works.

Philippians

Written in Rome around A.D. 61, this letter contains a beautiful meditation on Jesus. It flows so rhythmically in the original Greek that some think it is a poetic hymn that Paul quotes. In any event, it is a summary of the Good News: Jesus, the eternal Son of the eternal Father, took flesh, suffered, died, rose, ascended, and now reigns over all creation.

> *[Jesus] always had the nature of God, but . . .*
> *of his own free will he gave up all he had,*
> *and took the nature of a servant.*
> *He became like man . . .*
> *and walked the path of obedience*
> *all the way to death—his death on the cross.*
>
> *For this reason God raised him*
> *to the highest place above*
> *and gave him a name*
> *that is greater than any other name.*
> *And so, in honor of the name of Jesus*
> *all beings in heaven,*
> *on earth, and in the world below*
> *will fall on their knees,*
> *and all will openly proclaim*
> *that Jesus Christ is Lord,*
> *to the glory of God the Father.*
> PHILIPPIANS 2:6–11

Whether Paul composed this beautiful meditation or merely cited it, he used it as the guiding star of his life.

> *All I want is to know Christ*
> *and to experience the power of his resurrection,*
> *to share in his sufferings*
> *and become like him in his death,*
> *in the hope that I myself will be raised*
> *from death to life.*
> PHILIPPIANS 3:10–11

Colossians

Paul probably wrote this letter from Rome around A.D. 62. He did not preach in Colossae. His letter was prompted by questions from church leaders about gnosticism (Greek word for "knowledge"). Apparently, Gnostics were upsetting Christian converts in Colossae.

One of the questions forwarded to Paul dealt with the claim that certain powerful spirits controlled human affairs. Paul responded not by entering into a useless debate about such spiritual rulers but by merely saying that Christ is "supreme over every other spiritual ruler."

> *Christ is*
> *the visible likeness of the invisible God.*
> *He is the first-born Son,*
> *superior to all created things. . . .*
> *Christ existed before all things,*
> *and in union with him*
> *all things have their proper place.*
> *He is the head of his body, the church;*
> *he is the source of the body's life.*
> *He is the first-born Son,*
> *who was raised from death, in order that*
> *he alone might have the first place in all things.*
> COLOSSIANS 1:15, 17–18

The second question dealt with the claim that people should perform certain external practices to win the favor of the ruling spirits.

Again, Paul avoided useless debate. He simply told the Colossians, "You have died with Christ and are set free from the ruling spirits of the universe" (*Colossians 2:20*).

In brief, Paul tells the Colossians to forget about any "spirits" and to keep their eyes and hearts fixed on Christ, the Son of the invisible God. It is he who freed them and whose life they share.

Slaves used to wear these around their necks.
The inscription reads: "I have escaped. Hold
me . . . you will receive a solidum *[gold coin]."*

Philemon

Onesimus was a runaway slave. Paul instructed and baptized him in Rome, probably around A.D. 62. Onesimus belonged to Philemon, a new Christian in Colossae. Paul asks Philemon to forgive Onesimus and welcome him back.

> *Now he is not just a slave,*
> *but much more than a slave:*
> *he is a dear brother in Christ.*
> *How much he means to me!*
> *And how much more he will mean to you. . . .*
> *So, if you think of me as your partner,*
> *welcome him back*
> *just as you would welcome me.*
> *If he has done you any wrong*
> *or owes you anything, charge it to my account.*
> *Here, I will write this with my own hand:*
> *I, Paul, will pay you back.*
> PHILEMON 16–19

This is Paul's shortest letter. It is also his warmest letter. It witnesses to the unity and love that should exist between baptized Christians.

> *You were baptized into union with Christ. . . .*
> *So there is no difference . . .*
> *between slaves and free men. . . .*
> *So then, as often as we have the chance,*
> *we should do good to everyone, and especially*
> *to those who belong to our family in the faith.*
> GALATIANS 3:27–28, 6:10

Ephesians

Thirty years after World War II, a Japanese soldier surrendered on a jungle island. The soldier, Hiroo Onoda, did not know the war was over.

Thirty years after Jesus' resurrection, there were people in Paul's world who did not know that a "new creation" had begun. To these people, Paul said, "Wake up, sleeper, and rise from death, and Christ will shine on you" (*Ephesians 5:14*).

Paul's Letter to the Ephesians was probably written from Rome about A.D. 62. It treats God's plan "to bring all creation together . . . with Christ as head" (*Ephesians 1:10*).

Ruins of ancient Ephesus. Paul walked down this same street.

Paul begins by noting that we were all once spiritually dead. But Christ has raised us by his death and resurrection.

> *God has made us what we are,*
> *and in our union with Christ Jesus*
> *he has created us for a life of good deeds. . . .*
> *He appointed some to be apostles,*
> *others to be prophets, others to be evangelists,*
> *others to be pastors and teachers.*
> *He did this to prepare all God's people*
> *for the work of Christian service,*
> *in order to build up the body of Christ.*
> EPHESIANS 3:10, 4:11–12

In brief, says Paul, we all share in the work of re-creation. What Christ began in his lifetime, we must complete in our lifetimes. As members of Christ's body, the Church, we share in the work of Christ our head. We are his hands, his feet, his voice. We must complete the work he began.

Paul Writes His Pastoral Letters

An artist's paintings often reflect stages in artistic growth. The letters of Paul do the same. The growth is so evident in the pastoral letters that some people think they were written by a disciple of Paul, after Paul's death. Others say they merely reflect Paul's own growth and the growth of the Church, and were probably written from Rome shortly before his death in A.D. 67. There are three pastoral letters: 1–2 Timothy and Titus.

1–2 Timothy

Paul and Timothy were close to each other. Paul mentions him in most of his letters. Timothy was young. He was also fragile in health (1 Timothy 5:23). These things handicapped him somewhat in his work (1 Timothy 4:12).

Paul's first letter opens with thanksgiving for his own conversion, proof that Jesus came to save sinners, not condemn them (1 Timothy 1:12–17). Next, Paul discusses the subject of community worship, especially prayer and conduct in church. Finally, he lists the qualities that church leaders and helpers should have (1 Timothy 3:1–13).

Paul ends his letter by encouraging Timothy: "Run your best in the race of faith, and win eternal life for yourself" (*1 Timothy 6:12*).

Paul's second letter instructs Timothy on how to hand on God's word, saying:

*Take the teachings
that you heard me proclaim . . .
and entrust them to reliable people,
who will be able to teach others also.*
2 TIMOTHY 2:2

Later on, Paul says:

*All Scripture is inspired by God
and is useful for teaching the truth,*

*rebuking error, correcting faults,
and giving instruction for right living.*
2 TIMOTHY 3:16

Finally, Paul warns Timothy that handing on of God's word will not be easy.

*The time will come when people
will not listen to sound doctrine,
but will follow . . . teachers who will tell them
what they are itching to hear.*
2 TIMOTHY 4:3

Titus

Titus, like Timothy, was a partner of Paul (2 Corinthians 7:6, 8:23). Paul begins his letter by recalling how he left Titus in Crete to "put in order the things that still needed doing and appoint church elders in every town" (*Titus 1:5*)

Paul continues his letter by listing the qualifications for a church elder. He must be a person who is "self-controlled, upright, holy, and disciplined" (*Titus 1:8*). Paul ends by telling Titus:

*In all things you yourself must be
an example of good behavior. . . .
Remind your people . . . to show
a gentle attitude toward everyone.
For we ourselves were once . . .
slaves to passions and pleasures
of all kinds. . . . God's grace be with you all.*
TITUS 2:7; 3:1–3, 15

As we look back over the letters of Paul, we see in them not only the thoughts of Paul but also Paul himself. He calls out to us across the centuries in words like this:

*I am not a book. I am a person, like you.
I laughed and I cried, just as you do.
I struggled to serve the Lord, just as you do.
So don't read my letters
just to learn about the early Church.
Read them to learn about me, also.
Discover that I had to labor to follow Jesus,
just as you do.*

Understanding Paul's Letters

Review

1. List the four groups into which Paul's letters fall. List the letters that fall under each group.

2. In what year and city did Paul probably write his two letters to the Thessalonians? What general topic did they treat?

3. What fourfold format did Paul follow in most of his letters?

4. In what year and city did Paul probably write his First Letter to the Corinthians? How does it reflect the type (stereotype) of person ancients associated with Corinth?

5. Who were the Judaizers, and in what twofold way did they try to upset Paul's converts in Galatia? How did Paul respond to each of their points?

6. List the fivefold outline that Paul follows in his Letter to the Romans.

7. What ancient language did Paul and the gospel writers use to record their works?

8. Did Paul write all of his own letters? Explain.

9. What was unusual about the sentence breaks, punctuation, and chapter divisions in ancient writings, like Paul's letters?

10. Why do some people think the "meditation on Jesus" in Paul's Letter to the Philippians may have been a poetic hymn that Paul quoted?

11. Did Paul preach in person in Colossae? Why were the Colossians upset? What does Paul say to them?

12. What is Paul's shortest and warmest letter? Why did he write it?

13. What does Paul say in his Letter to the Ephesians about the different roles Christians have in God's plan?

14. Who were Titus and Timothy? Which of these two young men appears to have had the closest relationship with Paul? Explain.

15. Why do some people suggest a later disciple of Paul wrote the pastoral letters? How do other people respond to this suggestion?

Discuss

1. Imagine you have been accused of being a Christian (a crime against the state). Your attorney knows you well and says, "Don't worry! Just answer my questions truthfully before the judge and I'll get you off." Here is what happened in court.

ATTORNEY   *[After reading a list of names] Do you know any of these people?*

YOU   *Yes. They're students in my school.*

ATTORNEY   *Tell me something about them.*

YOU   *They're students I don't particularly care for.*

ATTORNEY   *Ever hurt any of them?*

YOU   *Not really, but I do make fun of them occasionally.*

ATTORNEY   *Have you ever helped any of them?*

YOU   *No, not that I can recall.*

ATTORNEY   *Do you ever help people you dislike?*

YOU   *No, but I do help my friends.*

ATTORNEY   *[To judge] Your honor, let me read from the constitution of Christianity, the Sermon on the Mount:*

"Love your enemies. . . . Why should God reward you if you love only the people who love you?"

Your honor, I submit that I find no evidence to support the charge against my client. He's done no more than you or I have done: put up with people he doesn't like, treated them with the token respect that good breeding demands. He's as un-Christian as you and I are. I move the charges be dismissed.

If you were the judge, would you dismiss the charges? Explain.

2. Paul writes, "God loves the one who gives gladly" (*2 Corinthians 9:7*). Discuss the meaning of each of the following observations about giving.

    a. "What you give in health is gold; what you give in sickness is silver; what you give in death is lead." Jewish proverb

    b. "A candle loses nothing by lighting another candle." Author unknown

    c. "The fragrance always stays in the hand that gives the rose." Heda Bejar

    d. "Real charity doesn't care if it's tax deductible." Dan Bennett

    e. "Even a beggar who lives on alms should himself give alms." Talmud

Activities

1. Dr. Lloyd Judd, a doctor in a poor rural area, was the first to diagnose his own illness as cancer. Before he died, he made a series of tapes to be played by his two small children when they were old enough to appreciate them. A passage from one tape reads:

> *Are you willing to get out of a warm bed in the middle of the night when you desperately need rest, drive twenty miles—knowing you will not be paid—to see someone you know can wait until morning? . . . If you can answer yes to this, feel you are qualified to start the study of medicine.*

Before he died, Paul gave similar challenging advice to Timothy, his spiritual son (1 Timothy 6:11-21).

What was Dr. Judd's point? Describe a sacrifice you made recently to help someone in need.

2. Paul penned his Letter to the Philippians in a prison cell. Yet, it is positive and upbeat. Words like *joy, glad,* or *happy* occur at least fourteen times.

Locate as many of these words as you can, giving the chapter and verse in which each appears.

Describe one of the happiest moments in your life.

3. "Do not get drunk" (*Ephesians 5:18*). Paul's words are more relevant today than when he wrote them. With a view to combating drunk driving, the *Reader's Digest* challenged the nation's advertising agencies to produce a series of posters for display in high schools. The winning poster showed Stevie Wonder. The caption read, "Before I'll ride with a drunk, I'll drive myself." Another poster showed an empty wheelchair. Its caption read, "If you think fourth hour English seems endless, try sitting here for fifty years."

Design a poster similar to these.

Bible Reading

Pick a passage. After reading it, (1) summarize its main point, (2) tell how it relates to the chapter, and (3) list one or two thoughts that entered your mind as you read it.

1. Chosen by God	Ephesians 1:1–4
2. Victory in Christ	Romans 8:22-39
3. Body of Christ	1 Corinthians 12:12–31
4. Life in Christ	Romans 12:4–21
5. Be like Christ	Philippians 2:1–11

Prayer Journal

Paul's letters contain frequent meditations on life. Here is just one of many examples:

> *If God is for us, who can be against us? . . .*
> *Who, then, can separate us*
> *from the love of Christ?*
> *Can trouble do it, or hardship or persecution . . . ?*
> *There is nothing in all creation*
> *that will ever be able to separate us*
> *from the love of God.*
> ROMANS 8:31, 35, 39

An excellent way to meditate on the everyday episodes of life is to follow these three steps: *replay* an episode, *reflect* on it, *pray* to Jesus about it. Write out a meditation using these three steps. Here is one student's meditation:

> Replay. *Every day I hitchhike home from school. And every day I meet the same kind of driver. He motions he can't give me a ride because he's turning at the next street. Then he keeps going in the same direction anyway.*

> Reflect. *Why do people lie when they don't want to do you a favor? Why don't they tell the truth? Why do they have to mask their actions with excuses?*

> Pray. *Lord, give me the courage to be truthful in all my dealings, especially those with my own parents.*

19 *Other Letters*

A plane carrying thirty thousand letters to U.S. soldiers in Europe crashed off the coast of Newfoundland. At great expense, divers searched the sea bottom to find the plane and recover the canvas mailbags. For experience shows that soldiers can cope with food shortages much better than they can with mail shortages.

The leaders of the early Church knew the importance of letters, too. Thus, besides the thirteen letters attributed to Paul, the New Testament contains eight other letters from other church leaders.

These letters fall into two categories. The first category contains just one letter: Hebrews. The second category contains seven letters:

> James
> 1–2 Peter
> 1–2–3 John
> Jude

These seven letters are often called the Catholic ("Universal") letters, because they are not addressed to a specific audience, but to a more general audience.

A Leader Writes to Jewish Christians

In his youth, seaman-novelist Joseph Conrad went to sea. One day he was learning to steer a ship. Suddenly a storm blew up. The ship's skipper kept Conrad at the wheel, shouting instructions to him over the roar of the storm: "Keep her facing the wind, boy! Keep her facing the wind!"

This is pretty much the advice an unknown church leader gives in the Letter to the Hebrews. The Hebrews had run into a "storm" of opposition. The church leader encourages them to stand fast and "face the wind."

Hebrews

Probably written around A.D. 80, the Letter to the Hebrews is a "call to trust." It is not known who the "Hebrews" were. But they seem to have been suffering because of their faith. The church leader

217

encourages them to stand fast and imitate the faith of their ancestors.

> *It was faith*
> *that made Abraham able to become a father,*
> *even though he was too old. . . .*
>
> *It was faith that made Abraham*
> *offer his son Isaac as a sacrifice. . . .*
>
> *It was faith that made Moses . . .*
> *suffer with God's people.*
> HEBREWS 11:11, 17, 24–25

The suffering of the Hebrews recalls Jesus' words that a slave is no better than his master. "If they persecuted me," said Jesus, "they will persecute you too" (*John 15:20*).

The church leader tells the Hebrews to draw courage from Jesus, saying:

> *Think of what he went through; how he*
> *put up with so much hatred from sinners!*
>
> *So do not let yourselves become discouraged*
> *and give up.*
> HEBREWS 12:3

He assures the Hebrews that Jesus sympathizes with their weaknesses and their temptations. In a striking passage, he writes:

> *Our High Priest*
> *is not one who cannot feel sympathy*
> *for our weaknesses.*
>
> *On the contrary, we have a High Priest*
> *who was tempted in every way that we are,*
> *but did not sin.*
> HEBREWS 4:15

The letter ends as it began, with a "call to faith": "Remember your former leaders, who spoke God's message to you . . . and imitate their faith" (*Hebrews 13:7*).

Ancient Letters

Some fourteen thousand letters have come down from ancient times. Many are penned on papyrus. These letters range in length from 18 words to 4,134 words. Like the Letter to the Hebrews, some do not bear the sender's name. We can only guess at who he or she was.

When it comes to the Letter to the Hebrews, there have been all kinds of guesses as to who the sender was. They range from Paul, to Apollos, to Barnabas.

Here we need to recall an important fact about New Testament authorship. Roderick MacKenzie puts it this way in his *Introduction to the New Testament*:

> *An apostle's name attached to a book*
> *may indicate no more*
> *than that he gave it his approval,*
> *or simply that it is the written form*
> *of his personal teaching.*

A modern example illustrates. The president of the United States rarely writes his own official documents. He merely approves what someone else has written under his direction.

This leads us to a final point about ancient letters. John L. McKenzie refers to it in his *Dictionary of the Bible*:

> *The letter was almost always dictated to a scribe.*
> *It appears that word-for-word dictation*
> *was extremely rare; the scribe was given*
> *instructions and perhaps an outline.*
> *The part of the scribe in the composition . . .*
> *was thus considerable.*

The Egyptian sculpture shown here (missing the vital pen hand) illustrates the posture ancient scribes used when writing.

Leaders Write to Other Christians

The last seven letters of the New Testament include three attributed to John, two to Peter, one to James, and one to Jude. Unlike Paul's letters, which are addressed to persons or congregations, these seven letters are addressed to a wider audience. Thus the Letter of James bears this address: "to all God's people scattered over the whole world."

James

This letter contains a series of practical guidelines for Christian living. Written around A.D. 55, it treats such matters as—

persevering under trial	(1:2–18),
avoiding social discrimination	(2:1–13),
helping the poor	(5:1–6),
practicing patience and prayer	(5:7–20).

The letter contains a number of sayings that recall the Sermon on the Mount. For example, James writes:

Happy is the person
who remains faithful under trials . . .
he will receive as his reward
the life which God has promised.
JAMES 1:12

Jesus says in the Sermon on the Mount:

"Happy are you
when people . . . persecute you . . .
because you are my followers. . . .
A great reward is kept for you in heaven."
MATTHEW 5:11–12

Again, James writes:

God will not show mercy
when he judges the person
who has not been merciful.
JAMES 2:13

Jesus says in the Sermon on the Mount:

"Happy are those who are merciful to others;
God will be merciful to them!"
MATTHEW 5:7

One section of the letter, especially, needs careful reading. It discusses the relationship between faith and action.

What good is it for someone to say
that he has faith if his actions do not prove it?
Can that faith save him?
Suppose there are brothers or sisters
who need clothes and don't have enough to eat.
What good is there in your saying to them,
"God bless you! Keep warm and eat well!"—
if you don't give them the necessities of life?
So it is with faith; if it is alone and
includes no actions, then it is dead.
JAMES 2:14–17

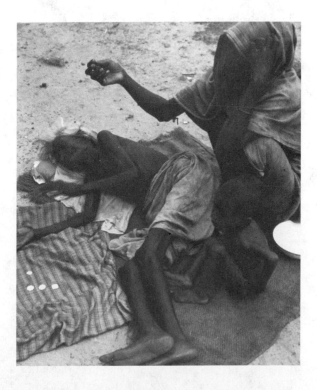

1–2 Peter

During World War II, a priest from Holland, named Titus Brandsma, died in a Nazi concentration camp. Among his possessions was a tattered prayerbook. The Nazis failed to notice that between the lines of print he had written reflections on his prison sufferings. Kilian Healy quotes one of them in his book *Walking with God.*

No grief shall fall my way, but I
*   Shall see Thy grief-filled eyes;*
The lonely way that Thou once walked
*   Has made me sorrow-wise. . . .*

Stay with me, Jesus, only stay;
*   I shall not fear*
If, reaching out my hand,
*   I feel Thee near.*

Peter's first letter is addressed to Christians who, like Father Brandsma, were suffering for their faith. Probably written around A.D. 64, the letter seeks to bolster their sagging spirits the way the old priest bolstered his, by recalling Christ's suffering.

Christ himself suffered for you
and left you an example,
so that you would follow in his steps.
1 PETER 2:21

The cause of the suffering is not stated, but it can be guessed at from what Peter says elsewhere in the letter.

The heathen are surprised
when you do not join them
in the same wild and reckless living,
and so they insult you. . . .
Happy are you if you are insulted
because you are Christ's followers.
1 PETER 4:4, 14

To appreciate Peter's second letter, it helps to keep in mind that time colors events. Whether it be the Vietnam War or the civil rights movement, time tends to generate its own slants and theories.

Something like this happened in biblical times. Some people began changing or slanting things that Jesus had said or done. Commenting on these people, Peter laments that they have strayed from the flock and have become lost. He concludes:

It would have been much better for them
never to have known the way of righteousness
than to know it and then turn away
from the sacred command that was given them.
2 PETER 2:21

One area on which some Christians were casting doubts was Jesus' Second Coming. They expected Jesus to come quickly. But when Jesus was slow in returning, they became even slower in believing that Jesus would ever come. Addressing himself to Jesus' "slowness," Peter reminds his readers that in God's sight there is no difference "between one day and a thousand years; to him the two are the same" (*2 Peter 3:8*).

Reassuring those who may have been shaken by the doubters or their false teaching, Peter writes:

We have not depended on made-up stories
in making known to you
the mighty coming of our Lord Jesus Christ.
With our own eyes we saw his greatness.
We were there when he was given
honor and glory by God the Father,
when the voice came to him
from the Supreme Glory, saying,
"This is my own dear Son,
with whom I am pleased!"
We ourselves heard this voice coming
from heaven, when we were with him
on the holy mountain.
2 PETER 1:16–18

Peter concludes his letter by encouraging his readers to do their best "to be pure and faultless in God's sight and to be at peace with him" (*2 Peter 3:14*).

1–2–3 John

Few letters in the New Testament can match the lyrical beginning of John's first letter.

We write to you about the Word of life,
which has existed from the very beginning.

We have heard it,
and we have seen it with our eyes;
yes, we have seen it,
and our hands have touched it.
When this life became visible, we saw it;
so we speak of it
and tell you about the eternal life
which was with the Father
and was made known to us.
1 JOHN 1:1–2

Written before A.D. 90, this letter indicates that false teachers had infiltrated some Christian communities. John identifies these false teachers, collectively, as the "Enemy of Christ"—or, as some Bibles translate it, "Antichrist" (John 2:18, 22; 4:3). This expression means "one who opposes Christ" or "one who replaces Christ" (Matthew 24:24, 2 Thessalonians 2:3–8).

These false teachers deny that Jesus is the Messiah (1 John 2:22), the Son of God (1 John 2:23), a human being (1 John 4:2). They also claim a special knowledge from God (1 John 4:1–6).

Commenting on these teachers, John warns his readers to be extremely cautious, saying:

Do not believe
all who claim to have the Spirit,
but test them to find out
if the spirit they have comes from God.
1 JOHN 4:1

And so the First Letter of John has a special value for two reasons. First, it affirms the humanity and the divinity of Jesus. Second, it stresses the close link between Christian morality and Christian doctrine. John says:

If someone says he loves God,
but hates his brother, he is a liar.
For he cannot love God, whom he has not seen,
if he does not love his brother,
whom he has seen.
The command that Christ has given us is this:
whoever loves God must love his brother also.
1 JOHN 4:20–21

John's final two letters are little more than notes. One is addressed to "the dear Lady and to her children," probably a church in Asia Minor; the other, to Gaius. The first appeals to church members to continue to love one another and to look out for false teachers. The second praises Gaius and warns him against a wayward church leader.

Jude

This last of the "other" letters was probably written before A.D. 90. As we read it, it helps to keep in mind a parable Jesus told about a farmer who planted a field. At night, an enemy oversowed it with weeds. Later on, when the servants saw the weeds growing with the grain, they asked the farmer if they should uproot them.

" 'No,' he answered,
'because as you gather the weeds
you might pull up some of the wheat. . . .
Let the wheat and the weeds
both grow together until harvest.
Then I will tell the harvest workers
to pull up the weeds first,
tie them in bundles and burn them,
and then to gather the wheat
and put it in my barn.' "
MATTHEW 13:29–30

Jude's letter concerns a situation like the one in the parable. Some "godless people" are distorting "the message about the grace of our God in order to excuse their immoral ways" (*Jude 4*).

Jude's observation is a good one. Psychologists say that when people's behavior contradicts their belief, they can split down the middle, believing one way and behaving another. Since living in this way is uncomfortable, people try to resolve their conflict. First, they try to change their behavior to fit their belief. If they cannot do this, they change their belief to fit their behavior.

The "godless people" picked the latter path. Jude says of them:

They are like wild waves of the sea,
with their shameful deeds showing up
like foam.
They are like wandering stars,
for whom
God has reserved a place forever
in the deepest darkness.
JUDE 13

Understanding Other Letters

Review

1. Besides the thirteen letters of Paul, how many other letters are there in the New Testament? List these letters. Which of them are sometimes called the "Catholic" letters? Why?

2. Does the fact that an Apostle's name is attached to a writing mean, necessarily, that he wrote it? Explain.

3. What role did a scribe play in writing letters in ancient times?

4. Briefly describe the situation of the people to whom the Letter to the Hebrews was addressed. What approach did the author use in dealing with them?

5. What does the Letter to the Hebrews say concerning Jesus, "our High Priest," and our weaknesses and temptations?

6. When was the Letter from James written, and what are some of the topics it treats? What does it say about the relationship between faith and action?

7. When and to whom was the First Letter from Peter written? What is one of the big problems it deals with? What solution does the author propose?

8. What letter talks about the Antichrist? Who is the Antichrist?

9. How does Jesus' parable of the weeds and wheat apply to the people to whom Jude wrote his letter?

Discuss

1. Years ago, Coach Don Shula of the Miami Dolphins was vacationing in a small town in Maine. One rainy afternoon, he took his family to the town's only theater. When the seven Shulas walked in, the handful of people in the theater stood and applauded. As Don sat down, a man ran up and shook his hand. "How did you recognize me?" Don asked the man. "Mister," said the man, "I don't know who you are. All I know is that just before your family came in the manager said that unless five more people showed up, there wouldn't be a movie today."

Describe the most embarrassing or humbling moment in your life. Read what 1 Peter 5:5–6 says about humility. How would you define *humility*?

2. The Letter to the Hebrews parades before its readers the heroic example of their ancestors. The American poet Longfellow does the same thing in his poem "A Psalm of Life." He writes:

> *Lives of great men all remind us*
> *We can make our lives sublime,*
> *And, departing, leave behind us*
> *Footprints on the sands of time.*

Explain Longfellow's point. Of the people living today, which one do you admire the most and why? Which do you admire the least and why?

3. The play *The Teahouse of the August Moon* opens with Sakini, an interpreter for the American army on the island of Okinawa, walking to the front of the stage. He bows and introduces himself to the audience. After describing Okinawa's bloody history, Sakini says this has helped to educate his people: "Not easy to learn. Sometimes painful. But pain makes man think. Thought makes man wise. Wisdom makes life endurable."

Explain Sakini's statement. Where is the same philosophical approach to suffering and trials discussed in the Letter from James? Describe some suffering that made you wiser.

Activities

1. Paul's letters contain several references to sports, especially track (1 Timothy 6:12; 2 Timothy 2:5, 4:7; 1 Corinthians 9:25; and Philippians 3:14).

Copy two or three sports quotes from Paul's letters. Illustrate them with photos from *Sports Illustrated, Track and Field, Runner,* or some other magazine.

2. The Letter from James says: "Is there anyone who is sick? He should send for the church elders, who will pray for him and rub olive oil on him" (5:14).

Find someone who has received the sacrament of the "Anointing of the Sick." Ask the person these four questions: Who suggested that you be anointed? How did you feel about the idea of being anointed? What impressed you most during the anointing? What effect did the anointing have on you psychologically and spiritually? Record the person's answers and comment on the interview.

Bible Reading

Pick a passage. After reading it, (1) summarize its main point, (2) tell how it relates to the chapter, and (3) list one or two thoughts that entered your mind as you read it.

1. Remember these things   Hebrews 13:1–8
2. Faith's twin sister   James 2:14–26
3. The tongue   James 3:1–12
4. All about love   1 John 4:7–21
5. God's people   1 Peter 2:1–10

Prayer Journal

The Letter from James tries to apply the Gospel to daily life. This brings us to another way to meditate on the Gospel.

1. Pick a gospel story. Read it slowly, imagining you are present.

2. Ponder the passage prayerfully. Ask yourself what the point of the story is and how it applies to you.

3. Talk to Jesus about the passage. How does he see it applying to your life—right now?

4. Listen to Jesus. What response might he make to you?

Use these four steps to meditate on the storm at sea. Write out your answers to the questions in steps 2, 3, and 4. Here is the story of the storm at sea, as described in Matthew 8:24–27:

*Suddenly a fierce storm hit the lake,
and the boat was in danger of sinking.
But Jesus was asleep.
The disciples went to him and woke him up.
"Save us, Lord!" they said. "We are about to die!"*

*"Why are you so frightened?" Jesus answered.
"What little faith you have!"
Then he got up
and ordered the winds and the waves to stop,
and there was a great calm.*

*Everyone was amazed.
"What kind of man is this?" they said.
"Even the winds and the waves obey him."*

20 Revelation

The immediate audience of the Book of Revelation is Christians who were being persecuted for their faith toward the end of the first century. The book contains a series of visions, given to John. Many people think this is John the Apostle. Others are not so sure. John begins this way:

> This book is the record of events
> that Jesus Christ revealed. . . .
> This is his report
> concerning the message from God
> and the truth revealed by Jesus Christ.
> Happy is the one who reads . . .
> and obey[s] what is written in this book!
> REVELATION 1:1–3

John Has a Vision of Christ

John's first vision came one day when he heard a voice speaking behind him. Sounding "like a trumpet," the voice told him to write down what he sees and send it to seven churches, which will be named.

Turning around, John saw a figure standing amid seven lampstands, symbolizing the seven churches. The figure's face was "bright as the midday sun." In his right hand the figure held seven stars, symbolizing the angels of the seven churches. Then he said to John, "Don't be afraid! . . . I was dead, but now I am alive forever and ever" (*Revelation 1:17–18*).

The figure then dictated seven letters, one to each of the seven churches. The message of each letter followed a similar format. It rebuked the church for present failures and exhorted it to change. Typical is the letter to the church of Ephesus.

> "I know how hard you have worked. . . .
> You are patient,
> and you have suffered for my sake. . . .
> But this is what I have against you:
> you do not love me now
> as you did at first. . . .
> Turn from your sins
> and do what you did at first."
> REVELATION 2:1–5

John ends the section on the letters with the figure saying, "If you have ears, then, listen to what the Spirit says to the churches!" (*Revelation 3:22*).

225

"Surrounding the throne . . . were four living creatures. . . . The first one looked like a lion; the second looked like a bull; the third had a face like a man's face; the fourth looked like an eagle in flight." Revelation 4:6–7

John Has Other Visions

Following his first vision, John had another. He saw an open door in heaven. Then, suddenly, he found himself in heaven. There he saw a figure with a shining face seated on a large throne. On each side of the throne were "living creatures covered with eyes." The first creature looked like a lion, the second looked like a bull, the third had the face of a man, the fourth resembled an eagle in flight. The creatures sang, "Holy, holy, holy, is the Lord God Almighty, who was, who is, and who is to come" (*Revelation 4:8*). Finally, around the throne were twenty-four smaller thrones on which sat twenty-four elders wearing twenty-four gold crowns.

Next, a Lamb, which seems to have been killed, appeared at the main throne. The Lamb had seven horns and seven eyes. It was given a scroll by the figure seated on the throne. At this point, singing broke out. John says:

I heard . . . all living beings in the universe—
and they were singing:
"To him who sits on the throne and to the Lamb,
be praise and honor, glory and might,
for ever and ever!"
The four living creatures answered, "Amen!"
And the elders fell down and worshiped.
REVELATION 5:13–14

The "Lamb" recalls the words of John the Baptist as he pointed to Jesus: "There is the Lamb of God" (*John 1:29*). It also recalls the words of Isaiah: "Like a lamb about to be slaughtered . . . he never said a word" (*Isaiah 53:7*). Jesus, the Lamb of God, shares his Father's kingship and glory forever.

Seven Seals

The scroll that the Lamb was given had seven seals. John watched as the Lamb broke the first four seals. After each seal was broken, a horse and rider appeared.

The first horse was white, and its rider carried a bow; the second was red, and its rider carried a sword; the third rider was black, and its rider carried a small weighing scale; the fourth rider was pale-colored, and its rider bore the name "Death."

Now was the time to break the fifth seal. As it was broken, John saw a huge crowd of martyrs. Each was given a white robe and told to wait patiently, for more martyrs would soon join them.

Then came the sixth seal. As it was broken, the earth quaked, the sun stopped shining, stars fell, people called out to the mountains, "Fall on us and hide us from the eyes of the one who sits on the throne and from the anger of the Lamb!" (*Revelation 6:16*). As this was going on, an angel went about marking the 144,000 people on earth who were to be saved from the catastrophe that was to follow.

Next, John saw countless people standing before the Lamb's throne. Each wore a white robe and held a palm branch. John was told that these were all the victorious martyrs.

It was now time to break the seventh seal. As it was broken, a great "silence" fell upon heaven.

This last sentence brings to an abrupt end the vision of the seven seals. The vision's overall meaning seems to be contained in the single word *silence*. Old Testament prophets used it as a code word to indicate that the time of judgment was near. Thus, Zechariah says, "Be silent, everyone, in the presence of the LORD, for he is coming" (*Zechariah 2:13*). And Zephaniah says, "The day when the LORD will sit in judgment is near; so be silent in his presence" (*Zephaniah 1:7*).

Seven Trumpets

The vision of the seven seals is followed by the vision of seven angels blowing seven trumpets. The first trumpet touched off a fire that destroyed a third of the earth. The second trumpet turned a third of the sea to blood. The third trumpet polluted a third of the earth's waters. The fourth trumpet caused heavenly bodies to lose a third of their brightness. The fifth trumpet unleashed a plague of locusts. The sixth trumpet caused fire, smoke, and sulphur to kill a third of the world's population. Finally, the seventh trumpet caused a cheer to go up in heaven: "The power to rule over the world now belongs to our Lord and his Messiah" (*Revelation 11:15*).

The catastrophes recall the ten plagues in Old Testament times. Just as the plagues signaled the end of Pharaoh's power over the Hebrews, so the catastrophes signal the end of evil's hold over God's people.

The Woman and the Dragon

Next, John looked to the sky. There he saw a woman dressed in the sun. The moon was beneath her feet, and she was wearing a crown of twelve stars. The woman was about to give birth.

A dragon with seven heads and a crown on each head tried to destroy the newborn baby. But the child was snatched to safety, and the woman escaped into a desert.

Then a great battle took place between the dragon "with his angels" and "Michael and his angels" (*Revelation 12:7*). The dragon's forces were defeated and cast down to earth. They pursued the woman, unsuccessfully, into the desert.

The identity of the woman is debated. Some think she symbolizes Mary, reasoning this way. Just as the dragon tried to destroy the woman's baby, so Herod tried to destroy Mary's baby (Matthew 2:13–15). And just as the dragon sought to destroy the woman's descendants (Revelation 12:17), so the Roman emperor sought to destroy Mary's descendants (her son's followers, the infant Church).

God's in Control

The Book of Revelation is hard to understand. One of the things that complicates it are the many visions it contains. These visions are filled with symbols that range from eyes (standing for knowledge) to the color white (standing for victory). The visions are also filled with pictorial images, not unlike the image being drawn on the sidewalk by this London artist. Sometimes the images in the Book of Revelation are bizarre, like those found in dreams. Bible readers hoping to find clear meanings to all of these symbols and images are in for a big disappointment. Even scholars cannot figure some of them out.

The name given to the style of writing found in the Book of Revelation is *apocalyptic* ("veiled") writing, that is, writing that hides its meaning from the ordinary person. This style of writing is also found in the last half of the Book of Daniel. Occasionally it is found in the Gospels (Matthew 24:29-31).

Apocalyptic writing was influenced by *prophetic* writing, which also uses a lot of symbols and images. But the purpose of these two kinds of writing is totally different. Prophetic writing tries to get people to act. Its big message is "Do something!" Apocalyptic writing tries to get people to be patient. Its big message is "Trust God!" The apocalyptic writer tells his readers, "Don't panic! Hold on! God's in control. When the right time comes, he will act in a way that will exceed your wildest dream!"

And so, even though the meaning of every symbol and image in the Book of Revelation is not known, its main message is known. And that's what is important. The message of the Book of Revelation is one of hope. It is God reassuring his persecuted children that he is soon going to act in their behalf in the near future—in a marvelous way.

Two Beasts

Yet another vision followed. It concerned two beasts. The first beast emerged from the sea and waged a terrible war against God's people. Then the beast died.

Soon, however, a second beast emerged, this time, from the earth. This beast breathed life back into the first one. And it killed all who refused to worship it. The beast had a number—666. That number has been identified with Nero Caesar (A.D. 54-68). He was the first emperor to persecute the Christians. He "came back to life again" in Domitian (A.D. 81-96), the second emperor to persecute Christians.

Seven Bowls

John's next vision centered around seven angels in heaven, who were given seven golden bowls of misery to pour out on the earth. It paralleled the vision of the seven trumpets. Finally, it was time for God to act in a decisive way.

End of Satan

John says:

> *After this [the vision of the bowls] I saw*
> *another angel coming down out of heaven. . . .*
> *He cried out in a loud voice: "She has fallen!*
> *Great Babylon [Rome] has fallen!"*
>
> REVELATION 18:1–2

The heaven opened and revealed a rider on a white horse. He bore the name "King of kings and Lord of lords." John says, "Then I saw the beast and the kings of the earth and their armies gathered to fight against the one who was riding the horse" (*Revelation 19:19*).

But the battle ended quickly. The beast, the kings, and their armies were no match for the rider on the white horse.

Next, an angel came down from heaven, seized the dragon, and confined him for a "thousand years." Then the just souls rose from the dead and ruled with Christ for a "thousand years." John comments, "This is the first raising of the dead. . . . The second death has no power over them" (*Revelation 20:5–6*). When the thousand-year period ended, Satan went about on earth again and assembled a vast army of nations, "that is, Gog and Magog," to war against God's people (*Revelation 20:8*).

The meaning of the "first raising of the dead" is debated. Inspired by Ezekiel 37:1–14 and Isaiah 26:19, some interpret it to symbolize the recovery of the Church after the Roman persecution. The "thousand years," then, symbolizes the reign of Jesus' Church on earth from the end of the Roman persecution to the final judgment (Revelation 20:11–15). The "first death" is the loss of earthly life; the "second death" is the loss of eternal life.

The reference to "Gog and Magog" echoes Ezekiel 38–39, where a mysterious leader of the future, Gog of Magog (unidentified region on earth), will subject God's people to a final ordeal. Here they symbolize the godless nations arrayed against the Church in the end times. "But fire came down from heaven and destroyed them. Then the Devil . . . was thrown into the lake of fire . . . forever and ever" (*Revelation 20:9–10*).

John concludes:

> *Then I saw a great white throne*
> *and the one who sits on it.*
> *Earth and heaven fled from his presence*
> *and were no more.*
> *And I saw the dead, great and small alike,*
> *standing before the throne. . . .*
> *And all were judged*
> *according to what they had done.*
> *Then death and the world of the dead*
> *were thrown into the lake of fire.*
> *(This lake of fire is the second death.)*
> *Whoever did not have his name*
> *written in the book of the living*
> *was thrown into the lake of fire.*
>
> REVELATION 20:11–15

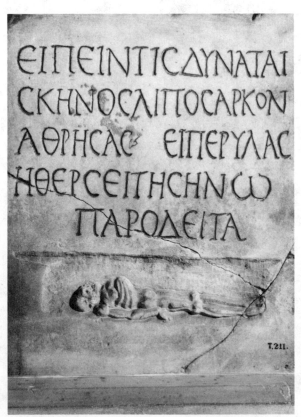

This tomb inscription dates from about the time of the Book of Revelation. It reads: "Looking at the fleshless corpse, who can say, passerby, whether it is a Hylas [beautiful youth] or a Therseites [ugly old man]."

John Has a Vision of the New Jerusalem

In his book *God of the Oppressed,* James Cone describes what life was like for black people in early America. One scene from the book describes how blacks used to come together once a week to worship.

On Sunday morning,
after spending six days of struggling
to create meaning out of life,
the people of Bearden would go to church,
because they believed that
Jesus was going to be there. . . .
Sister Ora Wallace would line
a familiar hymn. . . .

Immediately, the entire congregation
would join her in the singing of this hymn,
because they felt the presence of Jesus. . . .
When the pastor would say,
"I know the Lord is in this place!
Can I get a witness?" the people responded
with shouts of praise saying
"Amen" and "Hallelujah."

Through song, prayer, and sermon
the community affirmed Jesus' presence
and their willingness to try to make it through
their troubled situation.
Some would smile and others would cry.
Another person,
depending upon the Spirit's effect on him,
would clap his hands and tap his feet. . . .
All of these expressions were nothing
but black people bearing witness
to Jesus' presence among them.
He was the divine power in their lives. . . .

How could black slaves
know that they were human beings
when they were treated like cattle?
How could they know
that they were somebody
when everything in their environment
said that they were nobody?
How could they know that they had a value
that could not be defined by dollars and cents,
when the symbol of the auction block
was an ever-present reality?

Only because they knew that Christ
was present with them and that his presence
included the divine promise to come again
and to take them to the "New Jerusalem."

This is exactly how the Book of Revelation ends: with all eyes focused on the "New Jerusalem" and on Jesus' promise to take believers there.

Then I saw a new heaven and a new earth.
The first heaven and the first earth
disappeared, and the sea vanished.
And I saw the Holy City, the new Jerusalem,
coming down out of heaven from God,
prepared and ready,
like a bride dressed to meet her husband.

I heard a loud voice speaking from the throne:
"Now God's home is with mankind!
He will live with them . . .
and he will be their God.
He will wipe away all tears from their eyes.
There will be no more death, no more grief
or crying or pain.
The old things have disappeared." . . .

The Spirit took control of me,
and the angel carried me
to the top of a very high mountain.
He showed me Jerusalem, the Holy City,

*coming down out of heaven from God
and shining with the glory of God. . . .*

*I did not see a temple in the city,
because its temple is the Lord God Almighty
and the Lamb.
The city has no need
of the sun or the moon to shine on it,
because the glory of God shines on it,
and the Lamb is its lamp.*

REVELATION 21:1–4, 10–11, 22–23

Then John hears the voice of Jesus:

*"Listen!" says Jesus, "I am coming soon!
I will bring my rewards with me,
to give to each one
according to what he has done.
I am the first and the last,
the beginning and the end."*

REVELATION 22:12–13

John answers, "Come, Lord Jesus!" (22:20).

The re-creation of the world, begun in Abraham, advanced in Moses, David, and the prophets, now reaches completion in Jesus.

Interpreting Revelation

Three different interpretations of the Book of Revelation have emerged over the centuries. They may be summarized as the *early history* approach, the *sweep-of-history* approach, and the *end-of-history* approach.

The early history approach holds that the book's primary audience is the persecuted Christians of first-century Rome. To these Christians it says, "Hold fast in your time of suffering. Christ has conquered; so will you."

The sweep-of-history approach holds that the book's primary audience is Christians of all time. To these Christians it says, "There will be times of testing and suffering, but in the end, the re-creation of the world will take place according to God's plan."

The end-of-history approach holds that the book's primary audience is the Christians who will be living in the last days. Describing the end of the world, it says to those Christians who will be living at that time, "When you see these things happening, hold your heads high. The hour of final glory is at hand."

Each approach has its own value. The first makes the book a guide to Christians of early times. The second makes the book a guide to Christians of all times. The third makes the book a guide to Christians of the final times. Perhaps the best approach is to realize that the book was intended to speak—in its own special way—to each of these audiences.

Understanding Revelation

Review

1. Who is the immediate audience to whom the Book of Revelation addresses itself?

2. Who wrote the Book of Revelation? Who revealed it to him? How?

3. What similar format do the seven letters to the seven churches follow?

4. Who is the "Lamb" in the first vision in heaven? What does the vision tell about the Lamb?

5. What happened when the Lamb broke the seventh seal? How might its meaning be interpreted?

6. What ancient catastrophe does the vision of the seven trumpets recall? What meaning may be attached to this vision?

7. Explain how some see the woman, in the vision of the woman and the dragon, as symbolizing Mary. What meaning may be attached to this vision?

8. Who do the two beasts stand for in the vision of the beasts? Explain.

9. Why is the writing style of the Book of Revelation called "apocalyptic"? In what two other places in Scripture is this style of writing found?

10. How is apocalyptic writing similar to prophetic writing? How is it different? Explain.

11. What is the overall message of the Book of Revelation?

12. In the vision of the defeat of Satan, how may the following be interpreted: the first raising of the dead, the thousand years, the first death, the second death, Gog and Magog?

13. How does the Book of Revelation end?

14. Who addresses the author of the book in the end? What does he say?

15. Explain the three different approaches people use to interpret the Book of Revelation. What is, perhaps, the best approach?

Discuss

1. "Listen, I stand at the door and knock; if anyone hears my voice and opens the door, I will come into his house and eat with him, and he will eat with me" (*Revelation 3:20*). A real example of this passage occurs in *Surprised by Joy* by C. S. Lewis. Before his conversion, Lewis was riding on a bus in London. Suddenly he got the feeling that he was keeping a door shut on something in his life. He writes: "I felt myself being, there and then, given a free choice. I could open the door or keep it shut. . . . Neither choice was presented as a duty; no threat or promise was attached to either, though I knew that to open the

door . . . meant the incalculable. . . . I chose to open." That decision changed Lewis's life forever. It was a decision he never regretted.

How does Lewis's experience illustrate Revelation 3:20? Explain his statement that neither choice was presented as a duty, threat, or promise. What does he mean when he says "to open the door . . . meant the incalculable"? What was one of the hardest, but best, decisions you ever made in your life?

2. Recall the three approaches to interpreting the Book of Revelation. The first holds that it is a guide to Christians of early times; the second, that it is a guide to Christians of all time; the third, that it is a guide to Christians of the final times.

Granted that all three approaches should be considered, which one would you tend to stress most and why?

Activities

1. Read the letter "to the angel of the church in Ephesus" (Revelation 2:1–7).

What compliments and what criticisms are given the people? What warning and what promise are given? Imagine your pastor asks you to write a similar letter to the people of your parish for publication in the Sunday bulletin. Compose that letter.

2. John describes his vision of heaven in Revelation 4:1–11. Reread it, paying special attention to the symbols.

Describe your own imaginary vision of heaven. End with an explanation of the symbols you use. If you can, make a diagram of your view of heaven.

3. In his book *Sense and Incense,* Thomas Blackburn has several people say what they were doing when the world came to an end. For example, a housewife says, "I had just put the coffee on to boil when I felt the whole house start to shake. Then there was this terrific flash of lightning and the whole sky lit up. And I thought, my heavens! The children are going to get soaking wet!" A sailor in a New York bar says, "I was in a booth drinking beer with this blonde. . . . Things were just getting interesting when all of a sudden the whole joint started coming apart at the seams. There was a real weird light in the sky."

Read Luke 21:25–28. Using it as your guide, pick two people and have them say what they were doing when the world came to an end.

4. Draw a picture of the four "living creatures" as described in Revelation 4.

Bible Reading

Pick a passage. After reading it, (1) summarize its main point, (2) tell how it relates to the chapter, and (3) list one or two thoughts that entered your mind as you read it.

1. John's vision	Revelation 1:1–8
2. The enormous crowd	Revelation 7:9–17
3. Seventh trumpet	Revelation 11:15–19
4. New creation	Revelation 21:1–8
5. Come, Lord Jesus!	Revelation 22:8–21

Prayer Journal

The Book of Revelation contains a number of prayers. One appears in chapter 15, verses 3–4:

"Lord God Almighty,
how great and wonderful are your deeds!
King of the nations,
how right and true are your ways!
Who will not stand in awe of you, Lord?
Who will refuse to declare your greatness?
You alone are holy.
All nations will come and worship you,
because your just actions are seen by all."

Compose your own prayer to God. Let it come from your heart and express how you honestly feel about God. Here is one person's prayer.

Lord God Almighty,
we ask you for a rose;
you give us a rose garden.
We ask you for a drop of water;
you give us an ocean.
We ask you for a grain of sand;
you give us a beach.
We ask you for a blade of grass;
you give us a lawn.
We ask you for something to eat;
you give us the body and blood
of your only Son, Jesus.

INDEX
Selective Listing
of Persons and Places

Acknowledgments

Scripture text, unless otherwise noted, is from the *Good News Bible*, the Bible in Today's English Version. Copyright © American Bible Society 1966, 1971, 1976. Used by permission of the American Bible Society and the British and Foreign Bible Society.

Specified excerpt from pages 123 and 130 in GOD OF THE OPPRESSED by James H. Cone (see page 230). Copyright © 1975 by The Seabury Press, Inc. Reprinted by permission of Harper & Row, Publishers, Inc.

Excerpt from *Everyday Life in Bible Times* by the National Geographic Society. Copyright © 1967. Reprinted by permission of the National Geographic Society.

Excerpts from *The Source* by James Michener. Copyright © 1965 by Marjay Productions, Inc. Reprinted by permission of Random House, Inc.

The poem "Noah Built the Ark" from *God's Trombones* by James Weldon Johnson. Copyright 1927 by The Viking Press, Inc. Copyright renewed 1955 by Grace Nail Johnson. Reprinted by permission of Viking Penguin Inc.

Photo Credits

H. Abernathy/H. Armstrong Roberts 96

Corinth Excavations, American School of Classical Studies, Athens 208

Bill Aron 204

The Bettmann Archive 188B

Biblical Archaeology Review 54TR and 54BR (from March 1976 issue), 56 (from June 1975 issue) Subscriptions can be obtained by writing to 3000 Connecticut Avenue NW, Suite 300, Washington, D.C. 20008.

Reproduced by courtesy of the Trustees of the British Museum 13, 31T, 50, 54L, 68, 76, 78, 81, 84, 185T, 229

Syndics of Cambridge University Library 207

The Trustees of the Chester Beatty Library, Dublin 210T

David Daniels 169

Fred Dole/Freelance Photographers Guild 57L

Don Doll 64, 129

Ecole Française d'Archeologie 189

Dennis Full 16, 17, 27L, 38, 92, 131, 145T, 173, 192

Georg Gerster 57R

Fred Hartray 160

Courtesy of The Harvard University Art Museums (Arthur M. Sackler Museum) 191

Michael Hayman/Corn's Photo Service 21

Scott Hewitt 145B

Holy Shroud Guild 156

Weems Hutto 151

By courtesy of the Israel Department of Antiquities and Museums 77, 122, 150R, 154, 157, 176

Israel Government Tourist Office 35, 48, 90, 91

Israel Museum 14, 74, 80

Algimantas Kezys 18, 23, 166

Ken Lambert/Freelance Photographers Guild 60

Jean-Claude Lejeune 28, 117

Archie Lieberman 47

Mark Link 4, 5, 8, 15, 24, 26, 27R, 33, 36, 39, 40 (2), 51, 59R, 70, 93, 95, 103, 104, 106, 110B, 111, 113, 115, 118, 130, 134, 138, 139, 142, 143, 146, 148, 149, 155, 162, 163 (2), 164, 172, 174, 177, 179, 181, 182, 193, 194, 198, 203, 212, 216, 222, 223R, 224, 226, 228, 230, 231, 233, back cover (5)

R. Llewellyn/Freelance Photographers Guild 141

R. McCahill, M.M./Maryknoll Missioners 219

Lisa Means 63, 83, 105, 119, 202, 215, 223L, 232

The Metropolitan Museum of Art 210B

Garo Nalbandian 102, 109, 110T, 112, 116, 124, 125, 126, 132, 136, 140, 150L, 152, 153, 158, 161, 178

NASA 10

National Museum of Rome 211

Richard Nowitz front cover, 52, 72, 120, 127

Oriental Institute 22, 31B, 67

Photo Network 25, 37, 43

John Rylands Library 98

Raymond V. Schoder 3, 6, 12 (Courtesy of Oriental Institute), 41, 46, 59L, 79, 87, 171, 184, 185B, 186, 187, 188T, 190, 196, 199 (2), 200, 201, 218

Bernard Surtz 100

Steve Thompson/Corn's Photo Service 170

James Vorwaldt 88